GW00792939

This text provides a very useful addition to the te[...] leadership and management training and it is also a[...] relevance as a tool for self development.

The work has both intellectual depth and breadth. Its [...]........pment provides a useful accumulative progression whereby successive chapters build on each other. There is the sense that it is necessary to read the whole book to capture what is not just a series of facts but something of a personal journey. Yet this is not the case and having grasped the essential content and recognised its considerable scope, it is perfectly possible to alight on individual themes as a source of personal introspection and development.

The material is organised in a most user friendly way. Its text is neatly punctuated along its course by useful boxes in the text containing learning points that reinforce its principal messages. It is conceptually comprehensive and its diagrams are illuminating, plentiful and serve as valuable metaphors for what the author is advocating.

Its application is practical and the exemplars bring this out with clarity. But it is its underlying philosophical tenets that mark it out as something different. It is therefore, something of interest to both the aspiring professional and to the highly experienced who will also be made to think seriously about what the work proposes. As someone involved in teaching managers who are parodied for their macho approach to management, I see this as a breath of fresh air that I would commend to all of them most strongly. This text is not just a read, it is an experience!

Professor Peter L. Bradshaw: Professor in Health Care Policy [University of Huddersfield] and External Examiner for the NHS National Management Training Scheme.

I enjoyed reading this book. It challenges and inspires us to make a profound journey of self-discovery and clarifies our understanding of the human condition. It gives us the tools to facilitate problem-solving and personal development, and provides us with the personal power to see those dreams fulfilled. The author is eager for his readers to find their true potential fully satisfied, and he provides an impressively detailed and comprehensive analysis of how this can be done. His enthusiasm for his subject is infectious.

The author's use of language and illustration is engaging and interesting, and he avoids much of the jargonese that often seems to accompany books on self-help and self-actualisation. Embedded in the text are frequent boxed summary statements which are helpful, and the numerous illustrative diagrams and tables are useful. He highlights the importance of asking powerful questions, and there are appropriate exercises for the reader to complete that accompany each section. These make the keeping of a journal advisable. The book concludes with explanatory notes, a list of quoted sources, and a bibliography.

This 'Coaching Framework' uses as a model the 5 external, physical senses that steer all of us through our physical environment, and makes them metaphors for the 5 senses of the inner self: namely, the sense of where we belong, the sense of the primary values we choose to live by, the sense of where we are, where we are aiming and why, the sense of what we are capable of, and the sense of our ability to make powerful decisions, and achievements. After an inspiring opening, this analogy is explained and followed through clearly and meticulously to the end. Careful study will amply reward the reader."

Mr Michael Flowers MBE FRCS. Retired Consultant in Accident and Emergency Medicine.

Many of us live lives that are hindered by limitations that we impose upon our selves. It may be our past failings, or our difficulty in seeing ourselves as we really are, or simply an unrealistic view of what we might achieve. In this text Richard outlines key aspects of powerful living. Knowing where I fit into life, how it should be lived, what my purpose may be, what I could become and being motivated to turn decision into action are critical stages in the process.

This book offers inspiration to find personal transformation though the application of right thinking. Through helpful diagrams and many examples, Richard shows how we do not need to remain fixed in our present state. Winston Churchill said "Success is not final, failure is not fatal: it is the courage to continue that counts." In other words, we are all at a stage that can be developed. Richard articulates means by which these wished-for keys can become reality.

Mr John Sloan BM. BS. FRCS. FCEM. Consultant in Emergency Medicine. Countess of Chester Hospital.

The 5 Senses of Self is a clear and engaging self help and training manual of techniques for discovering and using human potential in personal, work and social life. Richard provides a collection of useful exercises set within the context of his coherent model of self development. Psychotherapists who want to extend their clinical toolbox, particularly within the positive psychology framework, will find this a useful addition.

Barbara Clarkson BSc, MA, PTSTA, Psychotherapist, Trainer and Supervisor

---

Training Packages
Companies, organisations, or individuals wishing to find out the range of available training packages, and to employ a licensed trainer, or to explore coaching options, should contact the author via info@thecoachingdynamic.com and at www.thecoachingdynamic.com

Training Licences
Licences for training, based on the original models and framework of *The 5 Senses of Self: A Coaching Framework for Personal and Team Development* may be made available only at the discretion of the author, and any training presentations or use of the contents and materials in this book to third parties will be restricted solely to licensed trainers, who have received formal training from, and entered into an agreement with, the author for designated uses of this material.

Updated material will be made available to all current licence holders.

THE 5 SENSES OF SELF

A Coaching Framework for Personal and Team Development

Richard A. Burwell

AuthorHouse™ UK Ltd.
500 Avebury Boulevard
Central Milton Keynes, MK9 2BE
www.authorhouse.co.uk
Phone: 08001974150

First published by AuthorHouse 3/25/2010

ISBN: 978-1-4490-7821-8 (sc)

Library of Congress Control Number: 2010901949

Printed in the United States of America
Bloomington, Indiana

Contents

DEDICATION

For Mum and Dad – thank you for always believing in me.
Here is the fruit of your faith.

For Cathy, my wonderful wife – you have supported me from
the beginning; I couldn't have done this without you.

For Hollie and Judah, my fabulous children, may you grow
into the fullness of all your potential.

I love you

INTRODUCTION

FINDING YOUR WINGS

There is something in the human soul which calls us to greatness. We yearn for a quality of life which calls us up beyond our current experience, and which stretches us to reach further, to aspire higher, to see more clearly, to feel more fully, to serve more effectively, and to live in a way which fulfils us, sustained by the knowledge that our lives have made a lasting difference.

We celebrate the heroes of history because they have answered the call to greatness and through their story we are inspired. As we read of their courage, their compassion and their perseverance, we find hope that our lives too can count for something. We are pulled along in the exhilarating water-wake of their single minded passion and purpose. Men and women like Churchill, Lincoln, Mandela, Nightingale, Secole, Flemming and Earhart. They are men and women who according to their ability and determination found their wings and flew.

Amelia Earhart found her wings when she received her pilot's licence from the Federation Aeronatique Internationale. Among her many accomplishments, she set a women's altitude record of 14,000 feet in an open cockpit single engine biplane at the age of 25. In 1932, she flew solo across the Atlantic, the first woman to do so. Her flight lasted 15 hours, and despite a broken altimeter, gasoline in the cockpit, flames in the exhaust manifold, and a sudden drop of 3000 feet in a spin, she finally landed safely on the coast of Ireland.[1] Aside from the factual bravery of her life, we can see in her accomplishments a metaphor for finding our own wings in life.

More recently we have heard of Mike Perham who, at the age of 14 in 2007, became the youngest person to sail solo across the Atlantic; and in August 2009, at the age of 17, became the youngest sailor to circumnavigate the globe, travelling 28,000 miles in just 9 months.

> Whether it's an evolutionary principle or a spiritual instinct, the internal desire to be more than we currently are is natural. It is part of our glory as human beings that we are endowed with the consciousness to reflect on where we have come from, where we are now and where we want to be; and also, that we have the capacity to grow, to change and to develop. This capacity for self development enables us to respond to life well and also, to influence our environment by *making* opportunities in addition to responding to the opportunities which come our way.

Though we cannot always determine what life brings to us, we *can* determine the way we will respond to our experiences, and indeed, the way we respond to our experiences determines to a large degree the future experiences that we will have. A negative response to a negative experience only reinforces the discouragement we feel, predisposing us to focus on further discouragements and causing us to miss the new opportunities before us. In contrast, a positive response to a negative experience causes us to learn necessary lessons, adjust our perspective and maintain a hopeful outlook which helps us to see the way forward.

When we hear stories of great courage and compassion, we are often inspired to believe that we too can achieve great things; and yet sometimes we are discouraged or disappointed with what we have achieved in the face of other people's success. We desire more, but may feel unable to attain it. How we respond to these moments of disappointment is more important than how we respond to our moments of success, because disappointment is the axis on which we turn – face downward towards resignation, or face upwards with renewed determination.

> Every disappointment leaves us with a key choice in life - to resign from the resources available to us, or to re-appropriate our resources towards our future fulfilment.

At the point of disappointment, what will we choose?

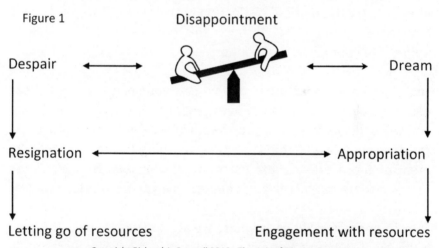

Figure 1

Copyright Richard A. Burwell 2010: The Axis of Disappointment

Disappointments seem to confirm to us the apparent inaccessibility of our hopes and dreams. Our temptation is to let the disappointments of the life we now live, define the future we have yet to live; but as soon as we abandon our dreams of the future to the disappointments of today, we begin to lose sight of the opportunities of tomorrow.

Throughout this book, I will make the assumption that you want to live a life of distinction, and that your heart aspires to the thought that it is possible. I will make the assumption that even in the face of your greatest challenges the desire to rise above them remains, motivated by the hope of a more fulfilled way of living. The life you have lived may not yet have met your expectations, but you refuse to remain where you are.

I will also make the assumption that you have already lived well in many key areas of your life, which you may fail to recognise as a success, but which others who know you and appreciate you would say are your great qualities. You may have already loved your children well, served others to the detriment of your own opportunity, worked faithfully, loved sacrificially, kept going in the face of ill health, been inventive, creative, artistic or courageously entrepreneurial. If these and other qualities are true for you, you already carry the mark of distinction in the eyes of those you have influenced. I hope that through this book, you will be able to appreciate yourself in like manner.

The chances are that other people see your achievements more easily than you do, but fail to name them for you. My hope is that you will begin to recognise your own achievements and name them for yourself, while at the same time reaching further for the fulfilment of those dreams and personal qualities which have, as yet, remained elusive. Past failure does not bar you from future success.

The disconnection between where we are and where we want to be is universal. It expresses itself at one level, in the desire for material gratification – we want to *have* more things. It also expresses itself at a deeper level in the qualities of our soul – we want to *become* more courageous, more loving, more faithful, more compassionate, more inspiring and more creative.

This paradox between the reality of our current experience and the anticipation of our hopes and dreams is something we all share.

Many fight this disconnection for a while, but eventually give in to the struggle, accepting a poorer definition of themselves and finally making friends with a lesser dream. That you have picked up this book and read these pages indicates that the will to develop, to dream and to do still lives within you.

How we handle this disconnection in the journey between where we are now and where we want to be, ultimately lies in the quality of the questions that we ask of ourselves. These questions and the answers we provide will define the quality of our journey through life.

The Questions which Define Your Journey

Life will influence you, life will inform you, but life does not need to form you or to frame you. Your experiences may delight you, or they may cause you to despair, but they do not need to define you. It is within your gift and responsibility to define your own life by the questions you ask and by the decisions you make in response to the experiences life gives to you.

> The answers you look for in life are only as good as the questions you ask. You need courage to ask great questions if your life is to be a great quest. If you are content with your current condition you won't ask questions which compel you to change.

In the realm of the soul, your appetite determines the size of your plate and the food it contains. 'Please, sir, can I have some more?'[2] is not the question of a pauper; it is the question of a king in the making. They are the words of a man or woman asking more of life and eventually getting it.

In order to take the right action, or make the right change, you need to ask the right question. Asking the right question at the right time is what coaching is all about. The question leads you to the insight which leads you to the pot of gold. Without the right, or the best question, you are unlikely to get to the right, or the best result.

The *type* of question you ask yourself is critical. A negatively framed question will lead to a negative conclusion. A positively framed question on the other hand, helps you to see the answer, because the question causes you to look for it. A positive question begins to determine a positive outcome. A 'What's going wrong?' question causes you to look at the thing that's wrong; a 'How can I do better?' question causes you to look for the better route to the better result. If you want a grade 'A' result, begin by asking a grade 'A' question.

Grade 'A' or Grade 'D' Questions – You Choose

Here are some examples with negative counterparts.   Figure 2

Grade 'A' Questions	Grade 'D' Questions
Action Questions	Debilitating Questions
What do I need to learn/do? What are my options	When am I ever going to get it right? What can I do?
Accountability Questions	Drifting Questions
When do I need to do this by? Who do I need to involve?	How long have I got? (ie how long can I get away with it?)
Affirmation Questions	Denigrating Questions
What are the areas I'm doing well in? What's working?	What's wrong with me?
Awareness/Insight Questions	Despairing Questions
What am I not seeing that I need to see? What can I learn?	What have I done wrong now? When will I learn?
Aspiration Questions	Demotivating Questions
What am I dreaming for? What do I hope to achieve? What is the purpose?	When will it ever change? Why does it never work? What's the point?

Copyright Richard A. Burwell. 2010: Grade A or Grade D Questions

The questions you ask define the quality of the life you live. Grade 'A' questions lead to action, accountability, affirmation, awareness, and aspiration. Grade 'D' questions on the other hand, lead only to debilitation, drift, self denigration, despair and demotivation. A good question challenges the status quo, leading you on a journey of discovery which requires courage, commitment and change.

Cinderella's Issues

Behind every problem which resists us there is a question of identity, meaning and fulfilment. This is illustrated graphically in the fairy tale of Cinderella, which can be seen as a metaphor of self definition and aspiration in a struggle with external difficulties and inner conflict pictured in the form of Cinderella's step mother and her two step sisters (self doubt and despair).

Cinderella knew that she was made for more, but her step mother and sisters each resisted her aspiration for a better life. They tried to beat her down and limit her expectation, but Cinderella allowed her dream to live in the form of the fairy Godmother who said, "You shall go to the ball!" But a dream can only live for a brief spell of time before it fades into half forgotten memories or is transformed into the substance of life. Soon the carriage turned into a pumpkin and the conflicts of life again asserted their dominance over Cinderella's dream of a better future. There needed to be a strong voice of declaration and affirmation if Cinderella's dream was to become a reality. This came to Cinderella in the form of the Prince, who said, "You are the person you dream of becoming- the shoe of royalty is yours!"

Glass Slipper Questions

Like Cinderella's step mother and sisters, life difficulties and inner conflicts accuse us, by saying in effect, "You are not who you think you can be, don't rise above your station." Problems in life will inevitably stand in our way causing us to see our limitation, but we must take the role of the Prince and affirm ourselves with the question that we already know the answer to: "Does this slipper belong to you?" We already know that it does. We are royalty in the making. The key questions we must ask in the face of any problem which resists us, is not simply, "Who or what is resisting us?" but also, "Who are we being resisted from becoming?" "What are we being resisted from expressing?" and, "What type of person do we need to become in order to handle this resistance wisely?"

The great issue at stake is not the nature of the problem which resists us, but the nature of the person who is being resisted. For despite the obvious limitations of human nature, our capacity to rise to great heights of achievement and expressions of benevolent character is undeniable. We all share the same basic DNA – we all share a potential for creativity, courage, compassion and commitment to excellence in any field of human endeavour.

Just as the right slipper for Cinderella reveals the princess, so the right questions and affirmations reveal the hidden dimensions of who *we* are. We are more than is currently seen, our capacity has not yet been fully explored, there is still more meaning and fulfilment yet to be found.

A Strong Sense of Self

The capacity we have as human beings is the capacity for personal growth and transformation which moves us beyond a parochial concern with ourselves into an altruistic focus on other people. It is the greatness of how we live, how we love and how we serve which ultimately defines us, and which determines the impact we have while we live, and the legacy we hope to leave.

But the position we live from, love from and serve from is of critical importance. When we live from the mindset of Cinderella we live in oppressive servitude because we *have* to, but when we live from the mindset of a prince or princess, we can live as benevolent kings and queens - making a positive difference because we choose to. The difference is in the definition. The difference is in our identity.

The root of our difficulty in living to our fullest capacity lies in having a poor sense of who we are and what we are capable of, and in a lack of power to make decisions which truly represent the heart of who we are and who we want to be. Answering the question of identity and gaining a stronger sense of self is vitally important in the path to more purposeful and powerful living.

Our first route to a stronger sense of self awareness and self definition is found in the way we connect with the world using our five physical senses. Through these senses we gain awareness of ourselves and begin to define ourselves in relation to what we see, hear, smell, taste and touch. These external senses also empower us to know what we want and to make decisions which fulfil us.

A great deal has already been written by others on the subject of the five physical senses. However, there is also a more internal dimension to self awareness which is where the real power for transformation lies. I call this internal dimension to self awareness – the internal senses of self.

The Five Internal Senses of Self

The *internal senses of self* greatly empower our ability to express ourselves and make decisions which fulfil us at the deepest level. In this regard, Steven Covey writes:

> "People can't live with change if there's not a changeless core inside them. The key to the ability to change is a changeless sense of who you are, what you are about and what you value...Whatever is at the centre of our life will be the source of our security, guidance, wisdom and power." [3]

Knowing who we are, and what we are about, is essential if we are to manage change in our lives. Facing negative change positively and facilitating positive change courageously both require a strong sense of self, and coaching helps to secure this.

> Just as our five physical senses contribute toward our self awareness and power for living, we also have *internal senses* of awareness which relate to the <u>places</u>, or contexts we belong; the <u>purposes</u> we assign to our life; the <u>potential</u> we believe we possess; the <u>principles</u> and values we choose to live by; and the sense of <u>personal power</u> we feel. Our internal senses of self contribute towards our *exercise* of personal power in every opportunity we encounter and in every trial we face.

This framework and the exercises which follow throughout this book can be applied in any context of life – be it family, work, faith community, house or home. The framework will help you to recognise the reality of what is occurring for you, and help you to address the changes which need to be made, in order for you to gain a stronger sense of self, and ultimately, to grow in the appropriate exercise of your personal power in making decisions which will benefit both you, and all those who you seek to serve.

The 5 Senses of Self

Figure 3

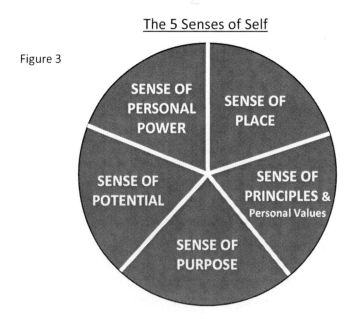

Copyright Richard A. Burwell 2010: The 5 Senses of Self

Place: The sense of <u>where</u> I belong. My sense of belonging measures how strongly I feel I have a place, how strongly I feel 'at home', how strongly I feel accepted and how strongly I feel I have a contribution which is received. The places or contexts of belonging are varied, for example – house, home, family, work place, team relationships, local community, faith community, office space and so on. A key question for self development is 'how can I enhance and improve my sense of connection to the places I occupy?'

Principles and Values: The sense of <u>how</u> to live. My sense of the primary values I choose to live by measures how strongly I know which values are important to me, and how much my values are in alignment with the values of those around me. My sense of the primary values I hold, determines how congruent I can be with myself and how much in alignment I am with others. A key question is 'how can I enhance and improve my connection to the values which are important to me?'

Purpose: The sense of <u>why</u> I am here. My sense of purpose measures how strongly I know my reason for being in any particular setting of life. What are the purposes I assign to my life and how strong are they? My sense of purpose addresses what I do and why, touching on my motivations and the meaning I gain from what I do. A key question is 'how can I enhance and improve my senses of purpose?'

Potential: The sense of <u>what</u> I believe I am capable of. My sense of potential measures the potential I believe I possess to grow, develop and improve in different areas of life - including my character, my abilities and my skills. My sense of potential affects every other dimension of self. If I feel that I have no potential, then I will believe I have no possibility for growth or development in any area. A key question is 'how can I enhance and improve my sense of potential in any area of life which requires it?'

Power: The sense of <u>will</u> or power of decision and consequent action.

My sense of personal power measures the sense of enablement
I have in any particular area of life. My sense of personal power is
the power and authority I have to turn a decision into action. My
sense of personal power is affected by my internal self beliefs and
by external factors of permission and opportunity. A key question
is 'how can I enhance and improve my sense of personal power in
any area of my life which requires it?'

Each of these senses of self contributes to our exercise of powerful
decision making and purposeful living. 'The 5 Senses of Self' offers
a map or description of how we are living in each arena of our lives.
'The 5 Senses of Self' are an ideal way to map who we are and who
we wish to become. Each sense of self is distinct yet also connected
to the other senses. The health of one sense of self enhances the
health of the others.

A strong sense of personal power affects the degree to which I can
carry out my purpose. A sense of purpose energises me, and also
contributes to my sense of personal power.

A strong sense of place offers a foundation from which I can launch
out and fulfil my purpose. Purpose helps to determine the degree
to which I have a sense of place.

A strong sense of place enhances my sense of potential, the
strength of my self-belief. A strong sense of potential enhances my
ability to find a place and to be received within it.

A strong sense of my personal power enhances my ability to live out
my principles and values, rather than allowing them to be overrun.
These primary values help to inform the way in which I release my
personal power in any environment.

Each of these areas in life affects our power to live to our fullest
capacity. A deficiency in any one area becomes a fundamental
yearning of the soul, and is expressed in the context of our homes,

our relationships, our communities and in our places of work.

'The 5 Senses of Self' coaching model seeks to address these common yearnings of the soul – for a sense of place, a sense of purpose, a sense of potential, a sense of our principles and personal values and for a sense of personal power which energises us to live the life we want to live.

Perhaps we feel disconnected from the contexts, places and people who surround us, or who we wish to be surrounded by. Perhaps we lack a sense of place – whether at home, at work, or with God and a faith community.

Perhaps we strive for fulfilment in a fog. Perhaps we are unclear about why we do the things we do and the way we do them, or why we make certain decisions, or why some things inspire us and other things disturb us. Perhaps we lack a clear sense of the principles and values which motivate us.

Perhaps we live by habit and routine rather than by wholehearted commitment to a cause which would sustain and fulfil us in the service of others. Perhaps we lack a sense of meaning or purpose.

Perhaps we have set a ceiling on our ability to learn, to develop, to grow and improve; this ceiling becomes something we are constrained by, rather than something we reach out for. Perhaps we lack a sense of self belief and personal potential.

Perhaps we know what we want to do, or what we need to do, but we seem to lack the fortitude to carry our knowledge or desire through into action. Perhaps our place of work or the community we associate with prevents us from doing what we want to do. Perhaps we lack the sense of personal power we need to convert our desires into deeds. Or perhaps we lack the self discipline to hold back our power and wait for the best time to act.

In the same way that the 5 physical senses (see appendix 2) of sight, touch, taste, hearing and smell work in harmony with each other, enhancing their respective contributions to self awareness, so the 5 internal senses of self operate within the dynamic system of the whole. No one sense stands alone, each sense influences and enhances the other senses.

HOW TO APPLY THE 5 SENSES OF SELF

'The 5 Senses of Self' can be applied systemically, both to:

· a community/organisation within its own system of relationships
· a participant within the system of the community or organisation
· an individual person open to the world with all its systems

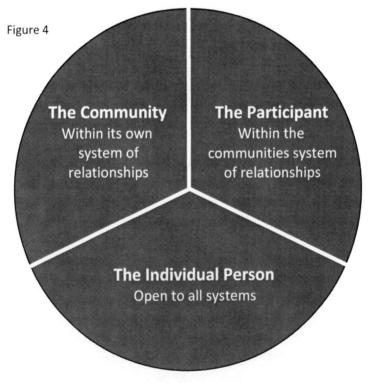

Figure 4

The Community
Within its own
system of
relationships

The Participant
Within the
communities system
of relationships

The Individual Person
Open to all systems

Copyright Richard A. Burwell 2010: Applying the 5 Senses of Self Systemically

www.thecoachingdynamic.com   Richard A. Burwell

The Community

The community could be the community of family, business, school, faith community, hospital or sports club. A small business for example, is a community of relationships, but this community of relationships also has a network of other relationships that it is part of. It interacts with its customers, its suppliers and its competitors and has a sense of itself in relation both to itself and these wider networks of relationships. The business can seek to enhance its sense of place, principles, purpose, potential and power as it fulfils its mission in relation to itself and these other relationships.

The Participant

The participant is the worker or member as he or she operates within the relationships of family, business, school, or community. The participant will have a sense of his place within his community. He will have a sense of his principles, personal needs and preferences of self expression there; he will have a sense of his purpose there, and a sense of his potential to fulfil his purpose; he will have a sense of the power he possesses to be fulfilled and to fulfil his purpose.

The participant may be a teacher in a school for example, who defines herself as an educator, but who still may have a weak sense of her place, or a weak sense of her power within the school. The teacher will be empowered to operate more effectively, as all her senses of self within that community are strengthened.

The Individual Person

The 5 Senses model can be applied more personally for ourselves as an individual in our own right, by considering our place on the planet. 'What is my core sense of self in life?' Used on the personal level, we can gain a clearer picture of our *core* sense of place in the big picture of our lives and of our *core* sense of purpose for being here. We can gain a clearer picture of our potential for growth and development in the *grand scheme* of our whole life span, and of the

Page 21

core values which guide our decision making and of the personal power we possess and whether there is a power beyond us to whom we may be responsible, and from whom we may be further empowered. These are the spiritual questions of *where* we are, *who* we are, *who* we will *become*, of *why* we are, and *how* we are to live. These big picture perspectives can help to inform the way we live in all the other places of family, work and community.

The Sense of Self Framework

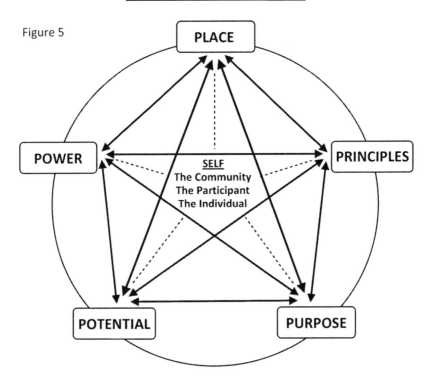

Copyright Richard A. Burwell 2010: The Sense of Self Framework

The remainder of the book is a detailed and practical reflection on who you are and how you define yourself in the different areas of your life, and how you then express the power of decision in living a life which is worthy of the gift. Using coaching principles you are helped to embed these discoveries in the way you live, so that the way you live reflects the potential living within you.

At the beginning of your exploration, as you read this book and apply its teaching, I encourage you to <u>celebrate</u> and improve the positive aspects of your life and seek to <u>change</u> and transform those aspects which are not as you dream they can be. This process will require you to be THIRSTY:

T   <u>Thankful</u> for the good of what is
H   <u>Hungry</u> for the good of what has yet to be
I   <u>Inquisitive</u> and courageous to know the reason why
R   <u>Restful</u> in the process of change, learning to live gracefully in the tension of what is now and what has yet to come.
S   <u>Supple</u> to apply your values and dreams appropriate to each context you encounter.
T   <u>Tireless</u> for change and to not give in to a lesser dream.
Y   <u>You</u>. Be yourself. No one else can be, and everyone else needs you to be.

Three Approaches taken in this Book

Each chapter will move between three learning approaches. The book will offer you a <u>motivational challenge</u> for change; a <u>conceptual framework</u> supporting the change you determine to make; and a <u>practical toolkit</u> of exercises designed to help you see your life as it is, to picture how you want your life to be and what you need to do.

I encourage you to create a '*Transformational Journal*' for use with this book, as you work your way through the exercises in each chapter. This journal will act as a road map showing where you have come from and where you are going to, and how you will get to your desired destination. I trust that in the reading of these pages and in the exercises which follow, you will discover a stronger sense of self and ways in which you can more effectively express the uniqueness of who you are and who you will become.

Chapter 1

THE SENSE OF PLACE

Sometimes the best way to figure out who you are is to get to that place where you don't have to be anything else. Anon.

One of the signs of passing youth is the birth of a sense of fellowship with other human beings as we take our place among them.
Virginia Woolf.

The Power of Place

Every geographic space is a place for some*thing* or some*one*, but spaces which are simply occupied are quite different to places which are endowed with meaning and heart connection. Such a space becomes a place to be, to dwell and to thrive; then the space has been gifted with a sense of place. When we live our life moving from space to space only, we live in barren spaces of broken relationships, meaningless associations and unfulfilled purpose; but we are made to thrive in places where heart connections are formed, where meaning is found and purpose is pursued. This desire for a place to be, for a sense of place to find or recover, is almost edenic in nature. We are made to enjoy strong senses of place, to pursue them and when found, to open out that sense of place to others, so that they too can share our meaning with us.

A sense of place defines the extent to which you feel that you do or do not belong. A positive sense of place is a particular environment in a particular season of time when you've known that you seemed to fit - that you were connected in some way. The environment received you and you received the environment; it's a place where you felt accepted and you accepted others. It's a place where who you are and what you have to offer has been received and valued, even if it has also been critiqued.

The beautiful illustration of Canada geese flying in formation (first brought to the world by Dr Robert McNeish 1972) [4] offers a powerful picture of the benefit that a sense of place offers to us. When geese fly together in V formation, the flapping of each goose's wings creates 'uplift' for the birds that follow. So by flying together, the whole flock adds 71% greater flying range than if each bird flew alone. That's a tremendous picture for finding your place! By being 'in place' *we* are likely to increase our capacity, to increase our flying range. Here's another lesson from the geese:- whenever a goose drops out of formation, it feels air resistance pushing it back behind the flock; the goose has lost its place, it's lost the *power* of place. The goose soon seems to recognise the need to get back into formation and benefit from the lifting power that a sense of place provides. A sense of place is hugely empowering.

Migrating geese make loud honking noises, which are called 'contact calls' and these honks help them to stay in place in formation. In a similar way, when we make helpful 'contact calls' encouraging each other, we strengthen each other's sense of place. The power of this picture of geese doing what they do naturally, and providing a place for each other, is reinforced further by James Mitchener, in his novel 'Chesapeake'[5] where he describes what happens when a goose gets sick or wounded and drops out of formation. From observation, he describes how two other geese within the same family also drop out of formation in order to help it and protect it. Loyally, they stay with the injured goose until it recovers or dies. Then they join another formation or catch up with their own flock.

Notice how the geese have a shared sense of purpose, which gathers them together into a shared sense of place within the flock. Notice how the geese live out their strong sense of direction and purpose from the context of a strong sense of place. Place and purpose work hand in hand – or wing in wing! To see geese flying in formation is an incredible picture of the power of community. People who share a common sense of direction and a sense of place within the community can get farther and faster by travelling together on the uplift of each other's effort and encouragement.

A positive sense of place provides a safe centre from which we can go out and make a positive contribution. It offers a safe environment which helps us to be ourselves and to offer the gift of ourselves without undue fear of rejection. A positive sense of place also offers us the security of being able to receive well formed critique without feeling crushed. A strong sense of place provides a secure foundation out of which we may feel confident to explore new possibilities. A strong sense of place contributes towards a strong sense of self, a strong sense of who we are.

However, a sense of place may also become a straight jacket 'comfort zone' which we may be fearful of venturing beyond. It may become a 'feather bedded prison' where we feel so comfortable that we no longer feel the need to explore new possibilities in life. These comfort zone limitations on a sense of place can be overcome with a stronger sense of purpose which keeps us moving forward into our destiny. A genuine sense of place will offer us a genuine purpose to engage with, even if the purpose is to rest, until a new active purpose is discerned. Purpose enhances place and place offers purpose.   Place without purpose is pointless. Perhaps we could also say that place without purpose is not possible.

The power of place is immense. It's probably our most significant internal sense – the sense of where we are accepted and where we belong, for example, in God, in ourselves, and among other people - our family, our friends, our colleagues, and our community. Human beings are relational; we naturally look for connections and associations as a way of making sense of our surroundings and of our self, and as a way of feeling secure and grounded. We naturally seek to place our roots of belonging into a locality and we place our roots relationally into other people. Place and the people we find a place amongst are foundational to who we are.

> In a way, we could say that when we are found in a loving way by others, we then have a foundation, a sense of place. When we are found in a loving way by ourselves, we also have a centre.

The Dimensions of Place which Empower Us

There is always a place we come from, a place we are living in and a place we are going to; these are the three places of *past*, *present* and *future*. We also have a sense of place in the *relationships* we have with people, and a sense of place in the *locations* we occupy, where we find our heart at home, whether in the place of bricks and mortar, or the place of hills and fields. We can draw strength from all these senses of place right into the present moment of now. In what follows, we will first reflect on our sense of place in our relationships and locations, and then our sense of place in the past, present and future of our lives.

The Locational Sense of Place

The importance of a sense of place is evident everywhere. People need a *locational place* where rest can be enjoyed, purpose explored and boundaries maintained so our place can be protected. Another way of seeing this is to call it 'territory' or 'land'. The desire for place expresses itself on the macro scale of land wars and territorial disputes, but is also seen on the smaller scale of house boundaries, work roles and responsibilities, and even the chair we sit on and the desk we work at.

These very human and instinctive feelings begin early with the child who says to another "I was sat here first!" It continues into adulthood when we say, "You're in my parking place!" or, "Can daddy sit in his chair now please!" My 10 year old daughter illustrated the territorial sense of place for me recently when she explained how she gets frustrated with a boy at school, who lets all his paper work and pens spill over onto her side of the desk – into her place. We protect our space because we need to have a sense of place. When it's removed or changed, our sense of place - our sense of connection has also changed.

The new house owner has a sense of place in the security and safety she feels in her own plot of land; the solitary walker on his favourite walk also has his place. The driver's seat on the way to work and the canteen at coffee break, the cosy corner in the coffee shop with its distinctive aroma or the mountaintop view can all offer a sense of place. People will naturally return to the same seat in a conference the following day because a place offers familiarity, a sense of security, the space where we can feel 'at home' and be ourselves.

> A positive sense of place does much to engender and sustain a strong sense of self because it's 'in a place' that my sense of self expands and develops, or finds rest and restoration.

A sense of place can be found even on the superficial level of the clothes we wear. For example, do you feel at home, or at ease in this jacket or the other one, in this shirt or that one? Self esteem can receive a momentary boost, simply by changing the clothing you find a place within. It's perfectly legitimate for us to find a degree of self esteem and sense of self from these outward factors.

They can build upon a more fundamental and essential dimension of self. The problem occurs when we depend solely on the external factors of the house we live in, the clothing we wear or the car we drive, rather than building up our more fundamental self identity.

The Relational Sense of Place

We also need a *relational place* where we can connect meaningfully with each other. The phrase 'there's a place for you in my heart' illustrates this well. We need to feel that we belong. It's not enough to simply belong to a physical space; ultimately we want to know that we belong to each other in an equal and meaningful way— it's a mutual belonging.

We express this most deeply when we say to our child, "I'm glad you are mine", or to our partner, "I want you" or to our colleague "I appreciate you." The football fan walking with other fans on the way to the match has a sense of place; the regular at the local pub; the worker awarded for her achievements; the sportsman playing with his team; the soldier with his battalion - all have a sense of place.

The fireplace has long been a point of human connection, a place to gather around, to keep warm in body and soul as deep connections are made with others. Yet sadly, the fireplace has been replaced by the television as a thing, (not a place) to gather around. Where the hearth warmed the heart through meaningful conversation and soul connection, the television now freezes the heart through passive isolation; yet still people everywhere yearn for a place of intimacy, a place to connect relationally. The need for a place is paramount.

The Loss of Place

The *loss of place* is also something we can identify with. This is something Paul Tournier writes about at length in his wonderful book 'A Place for You'.[6] He writes of a couple at a restaurant looking hopefully to find a table, a place for them, but all the places are taken.   We could each find our own examples of the loss of place, like the couple who arrive at a hotel, having made an earlier booking, but who are told at the registration desk that there is no record of their booking, there is no place for them; or of the new employee who doesn't yet understand the jargon, or the pecking order hierarchy who feels out of place; or the business man who arrives at a meeting when everyone is talking to some-one else, he pauses for a moment and thinks 'will someone talk to me, welcome me, will I find a sense of place?'

When friends move away, when my office is moved, when redundancy hits, when a relationship breaks down, there is always a loss of place, both relationally *and* locationally. We know the power of place when we no longer feel it. The sense of place, or the lack of it is particularly powerful at work and at home.

We feel it at work when we dread Monday mornings; when we don't understand the ground rules; when we're not included in the 'in' jokes or when we become the butt of them; when we feel victimised by the boss; when our desk is moved; when our hard work is not praised; when we don't get that job and we are not told why.

We feel it at home when the neighbours are thoughtless or rude; when the music is too loud, too late; when they park in front of our house rather than theirs; when we are bored with the old decor; when our friends have moved; when the children have left home.

The desire to feel at home with others can also turn imperceptively into the formation of a clique. The problem with a clique is that it's a closed system where its purpose is turned in on itself; it's a relational territory with very strong boundaries; people cannot easily enter and people cannot easily leave. Eventually the sense of place becomes polluted. When a relational place has become a clique, a true sense of place has been lost.

> The desire for a place where we are 'at home', where we belong, where we are received and where we are connected with others may cause us to stay in a place too long, or leave a place too soon.

It's important that we understand the specific elements we are looking for in a strong sense of place, and that we work through the process of changing what we can about our environment and ourselves, in order to enhance our sense of place in the present, before we seek to move to another place. If we don't work through the process of change, we may find that we bring our problems with us.

The 6 Dimensions of Place

Though the reasons for a loss of place are many, and the pressure to escape the loneliness intense, there are ways we can increase our sense of place now, even before we consider changing our location.

Wherever we work, rest or play, we carry within us both positive and negative senses of place. Our sense of place is so defining that it's important we learn how to maximise its positive power. We can do this by:

1. Living from the good of past places
2. Living in the hope of future places
3. Improving our connection to present places

Our sense of place is multi-dimensional. We have the places of 'Past Locations', 'Past Relationships', 'Present Locations' and 'Present Relationships' and 'Future Locations' and 'Future Relationships'. Each place offers us a resource for living in the present moment of now.

The 6 Dimensions of Place

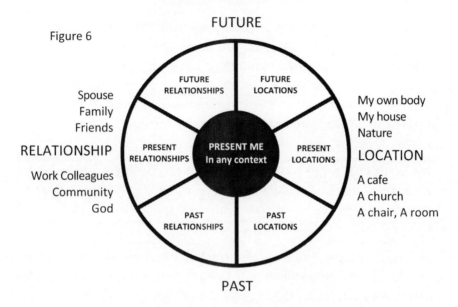

Figure 6

Individuals, families, tribes and nations throughout history have learnt the benefit of living from the good of the past and from their hope for the future. For example, the exiled Hebrew nation would retell the good of their collective past in the context of corporate song by referring to the successful reigns of King David and King Solomon and of their love for the City of Jerusalem and the Temple. They also anticipated the future freedom promised to them - when land – a sense of place would be restored. These moments of recollection and anticipation became a resource they lived *from* while living *in* the present moment.

Often the Israelites lived under a state of occupation – Egyptian, Babylonian, Assyrian, Greek or Roman. Being able to live from the resource of other locations and relationships in the past and from the future they hoped for, made the present easier to bear. African American slaves also recalled their place of home in Africa through songs, and also sang of their hope for freedom in the future – pictured in the language of heaven.

Living *from* the Past

By developing a memory of place, we train ourselves to see and hope from the perspective of the past. When we live from the wealth that past positive experiences of place have provided, we set up within ourselves a perpetual place of positive memories which help to shape our current perspectives and also shield us from the negative experiences we may be facing.

> We don't live in the past; we live from the positives of the past. Past experiences of place do not need to be 'dead' long forgotten experiences, they can still live within us today.

I remember playing table tennis, snooker and darts with my parents and sister as a young child in our living room, and Monopoly on the old green card table by the fireside. I can hear the laughter and feel the fun; I can see the smiling faces, I am right there, it was a 'place' which lives in me still. The intensified memory is a good place to be.

I remember Wednesday evenings at the Badminton club in the old church hall, the half time break with tea and biscuits and the sense of family camaraderie and competition. I can see it, I can feel the anticipation of competition, I recall the conversation - it's a positive memory of place. I breathe deeply, a feeling of satisfaction and rest comes over me. I am thankful for these memories and therefore I am resourced by them.

These memories provide a foundation of positive feelings in the present. These are positive experiences of place which are resource experiences to me now. I don't allow myself to be regretful that they have gone; I look for ways to build the quality of those times into my present. As I enjoy these moments of recollection, I notice that I want to build more family time playing games with my children now. I change the image, and place my children in the picture. I anticipate a future, just around the corner, where my family has a stronger sense of place together.

Using Memory to Enhance a Sense of Place

Some people remember easily, others find remembering a more difficult activity, but we can all sharpen our memory skill. In the west, we are not taught how to remember - it's an assumed skill that we suppose some people have and others don't. This is unfortunate because it's the personal long term memory of positive place experiences which helps to build a strong foundation of self, a sense of self rooted in locational and relational places.

Memory is a collection of thoughts, mental images, sounds, feelings, smells and tastes associated with specific places and people at specific times. Every memory is located and framed in a location. There are specific physical surroundings associated with the memory, and many memories are also framed in the context of relationships that we either felt 'at home' among, where we 'belonged' and 'had a sense of place' with, or where we felt that we didn't 'fit'.

> We 'burn' these locational and relational 'place' experiences into our memory using the reference points of the five physical senses - what we saw, what we heard, what we felt (physically and emotionally), what we smelt and what we tasted.

If memory is a collection of experiences gathered through our 5 physical senses, then remembering is a re–collection of those 5 senses experiences. By paying special attention to what Neuro Linguistic Programming (NLP) [7] calls the 'submodalities' of the 5 physical senses, we can enhance our memories and therefore enhance our sense of place rooted in the past. Submodalities are the finer distinctions of what we see, hear, feel, smell and taste; such as colour, brightness, location, distance, size, movement, pace, rhythm, tone, intensity of feeling, duration, texture, weight, degree of focus and so on.

Using these finer distinctions, I can recall the white radiator on the landing of my childhood home, the flower patterned carpet bathed in winter sunlight, the balcony in front of me, with birds playing in a puddle of water. I associate myself into the memory and rather than seeing a picture of myself separate, I am now right there, fully associated into the memory, sat against the radiator feeling its warmth against my back. I see the book I am reading, as I underline key passages. I pick up my coffee made with hot milk and I recall the moment of deep reflection and contemplation.

That radiator and floor was a 'place' for me. It became a sacred spot, a place of reflection where I explored the meaning of my life. Even now, when I sometimes sit on the floor, my back against a radiator, and pull out a book, I carry the memory and meaning of that first place with me, and I can still find a new sense of place against a radiator, even if there is no sunlight.

Living *from* the Future

By developing a *future* imagination of place, we can train ourselves to see and hope from the perspective of the future. By associating into the future we hope for, we gain strength in the present moment. This is different to living *in* the future. Associating into the future we hope for is not for the purpose of escaping, it's for the purpose of re-engaging with the present, with hope renewed. Having been envisioned, we are better able to indwell the present places we occupy, and transform them into the image we have seen in our imagination.

Living from the future place I envisage, I re-enter the present with the emotional resource and motivation to see the present transformed. The future positive I live from, energises me to re-engage with the present places in my life that need further attention.

Why is it that some people, who only have a very weak sense of place now, or a weak sense of place from the past, are still able to live with courage and purpose, pioneering new ideas, businesses, relationships, and new places to be? I believe it's because they still live from a positive sense of place – they live from that future place they envisage, the future they dream for, or the future that their faith calls them to.

This is why refugees and illegal immigrants are able to endure such hardship in their long journey to a more positive place. When people have no place in the present that they can root into, they will reach into the future and plant seeds of hope there, enduring incredible hardship for the dream their future sense of place offers to them.

Living *from* the future is not only true of people who are struggling with their present; it's also true of many successful people who step into the imagination of the future they are dreaming for, into a time when they have already achieved their goals. They allow themselves to *see* the success they desire, to *feel* what it will be like and to *hear* what they and others will be saying when it's all working well.

Not only does this exercise of the imagination give them a clear view of what they are aiming for, it is also energising and empowering. It doesn't matter that it may not work out exactly as they see it; at least they've been encouraged and motivated to try. The famous British entrepreneur Sir Richard Branson, best known for his Virgin brand of over 300 companies, is reputed to have said, "Fantasizing about the future is one of my favourite pastimes!"

Drawing Strength from Past and Future Places

Building a stronger sense of place at work, at home, or in our local community, requires us to be in a resourceful state of mind and heart. When we are in a resourceful state, we are empowered to persevere through the process of change, transforming our present places into more positive environments.

We can enter into a more resourceful state by recalling positive places from the past and by imagining what a more positive place in the future may be like. As we do this, a by-product is that we may notice transferrable elements that we will want to introduce into our present situation.

Though we live *in* the present, we can live *from* the resources of the past or the future, by drawing strength into the present from past and future places. When I recall these positive memories of good relationships and locations I have enjoyed, or when I initiate imaginations of future places I look forward to, I find resource feelings available now: rest, peace, joy, energy, hope, anything in fact, which the memory recalls to me or the future imagination fosters in me.

> By associating into these resource feelings, I bring the good of the past I have experienced, or the future I hope for, into the present place of now. These positive memories and imaginations strengthen me while I make adjustments to the present places I occupy. In this way, I am enabled to transform my sense of place in the present.

It seems easier for some of us to replay the negative memories and emotions of negative place experiences over and over in our minds, rather than feeding from positive times and places. Through a combination of mental imagery and emotional reconnection, we may be tempted to live in a regretful state of mind, or we can live in an anxious state of future worry. When we live and breathe these negative experiences and imaginations in a recurring manner, we feed off them in a perverse act of self sabotage.

Often when we do take a positive trip down memory lane, or allow our imagination to conjure up a wistful daydream of the future, we don't allow it be intense enough. So when the memory is finished, or the imagination ends, we leave the feelings behind us, rather than letting them linger with us in the present and into the future.

> The danger we must navigate, of course, is not continuing to live in the past or continuing to live in our imagination of the future. The past tends to hook us into regret and the future hooks us into unfounded fear or unproductive longing, neither of which are resourceful states to live in. Instead, the present moment needs to become a magnetic moment – drawing into itself the positive resources it needs. The present place is the powerful place to be, because you have access to both positive past experience *and* future hope.

By rehearsing the positive memory, or initiating the positive imagination, I cue the positive experience. Through practice, we can interrupt regretful memories or anxious worries, by replacing them with a positive memory of place or the imagination of a positive place in the future. Being thankful then helps to root these feelings into the present.

Thankful for the Past and the Possibility of the Future

Gratitude enables us to take the positive feelings associated with the past and the future, into the present, without having to live in the memory of the past or in the imagination of the future.

> Thankfulness which looks back enables us to _rest_ on the foundation that a previous sense of place has provided. Thankfulness which looks forward enables us to _trust_ in the anticipated provision that a future sense of place may offer.

Thankfulness makes both *rest* and *trust* possible while keeping us rooted in the present. Thankfulness then magnetises the resource of past and future places into our present experience, so that we are empowered to live transformationally now. Of course, we cannot guarantee our hopes for the future, but thankfulness for the future, rooted in an optimistic approach to life is simply a healthier mental attitude to cultivate, and it trains us to be open to provision and opportunity in all its forms.

In the Journal of Personality and Social Psychology, Dr Robert A. Emmons and Dr Michael E. McCullough [8] describe research they conducted over three separate studies, with three groups of people. The first study group were required to write down five things they were thankful for every week for 10 weeks. This group was called the *gratitude condition*. The second group were required to write down five things they were bothered by every week for 10 weeks. This group was called the *hassles condition*. The third group were required to write down any five things that had happened every week for ten weeks, but not to concentrate on either positive or negative experiences. This was called the *events or control condition*. Emmons and McCullough noted that,

"Participants in the gratitude condition felt better about their lives as a whole, and were more optimistic regarding their expectations for the upcoming week. They reported fewer physical complaints and reported spending significantly more time exercising." [9]

In a second study they found that people in the gratitude group,

"...reported significantly...more positive effect (*attentive, determined, energetic, enthusiastic, excited, interested, joyful, strong*) than did participants in the hassles group" [10]

"They were also more likely to report having helped someone with a personal problem or offered emotional support to another." [11]

In a third study they noted that the gratitude group,

> "...reported getting more hours of sleep each night than did participants in the control condition." [12]

They noted that the 'gratitude' and 'hassles' groups experienced almost equal and opposite effects. Emmons and McCullough concluded that,

> "to the extent that gratitude, like other positive emotions, broadens the scope of cognition and enables flexible and creative thinking, it also facilitates coping with stress and adversity... gratitude not only makes people feel good in the present, but it also increases the likelihood that people will function optimally and feel good in the future." [13]

Exercise – Resourcing Present Places:

With these studies in mind, the following exercise asks you to reflect on positive past places you have enjoyed and positive future places you anticipate.

As you engage with this exercise, I encourage you to notice which elements of your memories and imaginations hearten you; and then to be specifically thankful for them. Next, take note of what you were doing in these memories and imaginations, and of other elements in them which made the experience a success. These may be the transferrable qualities that you may wish to recreate in the current places you occupy.

Finally consider which goals you want to set for yourself in light of the positive things you have seen and wish to introduce into your life now. In a work context, you can't guarantee that everything you want to introduce will be possible, but you won't know unless you try. As a manager, if you can implement some of your teams requests, their sense of place will increase, and so too their motivation to perform their duties well. It may be as simple as introducing some plants, rearranging the desks, or providing fresh coffee; or as profound as clarifying the principles of operation in the team or developing their sense of personal power by finding ways to trust them more. Our sense of place is affected by our location and surroundings, by the quality of our relationships, by the values we share with others, by the potential we possess and by the power and permission given to us. As we reflect on the positive places we have enjoyed from the past and the future places we hope for, we can apply those positive elements into the present place we work in. It is the responsibility of managers and leaders to facilitate the development of a positive place at work if the team is to work at their optimal level of performance. It takes courage for the manager / leader to begin the process of listening, but the fact that the good manager listens proves him/her to be worthy of the role of leading.

The Process in Brief:

1. Think about a sense of place which needs to be strengthened in your life (home, work, local community etc), in terms of how you belong, how accepted you feel, how your contribution is received.

2. Choose a positive sense of place from the past that has elements you would like to recover or see implemented in the area you have chosen which is weak. Or let your imagination create a more fulfilling sense of place in the future that you can aspire to

a. What specifically, do you appreciate about this place?

b. Express gratitude for the past time and place or thankfulness for the possibility of the place you have just imagined.

c. What are the transferrable qualities that you might want to see recreated into your current setting?

d. What goals and actions do you need to set for yourself, in order to see these elements become a reality today?

See figure 7 on the next page...

For a detailed explanation of this process see Appendix 3

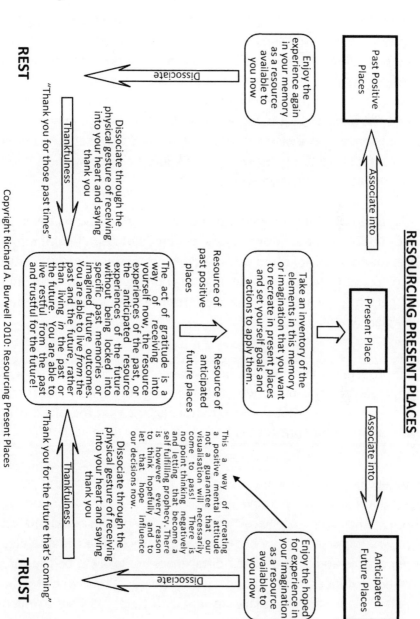

Figure 7

RESOURCING PRESENT PLACES

Copyright Richard A. Burwell 2010: Resourcing Present Places

The Process Matters - A Cautionary Note:

The *process* of perfecting the place you are in whether it's the physical environment surrounding you (locationally) or the people you interact with (relationally), is as much about the process of change in you, as it is the process of change in your outer circumstances and the other people involved. Transformation is as much about the process as it is the end result. If the change in our outer circumstances were instantaneous, there may then seem to be no need for change in us. However, we know only too well, that we carry <u>us</u> with us, wherever we go.

The *process* of change is an opportunity for inner growth as well as outer improvements in our places of home, work and community. Often our own actions and ways of seeing things weaken our sense of place, so unless we deal with our own behaviour and perspectives, we are likely to encounter the same problems in any new place we may settle.

> The *process* of transition and transformation is often as important as the place we are dreaming for, simply because the process is what it takes to mature us, so that the place we are in ourselves contributes to the place we share with others.

Finding a good fit between you and the other people around you is essential if you are to know you are in the right place. Working through the issues of shared values, shared purpose and shared style are important. Also, it's important to recognise the qualities other people add to you! Their differences are likely to be the very qualities you need for further growth. The questions which follow over the next few pages are designed to help you gain a much clearer picture on what is working and not working for you in your places of home, work, community and spirituality.

Wheel of Place I

For each area on the wheel, rate your sense of place out of ten, (10 is high) in terms of how strong your sense of place / belonging / connectedness is. The following questions may help. How strong is my sense of place here? How much do I feel I fit in? How at home do I feel here? How accepted do I feel? How connected do I feel? How strongly do I feel I belong? Which place do I feel tempted to exit, before I have really attempted to build a sense of place there which empowers?

The Wheel of Place I

Figure 8

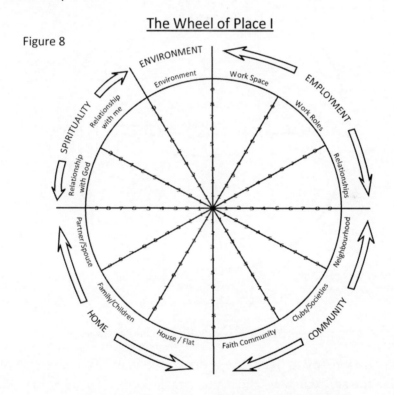

Copyright Richard A. Burwell 2010: The Wheel of Place I

Having taken an inventory of the many and various places in your life, choose the one you most wish to improve (it could also be for a specific task you have to perform), and work your way through the questions in the next section, Wheel of Place II.

Wheel of Place II

Take a look at figure 9 below and notice how your sense of place (any of the 12 segments from the wheel of place) is affected by the strength of your other senses of self.

The Wheel of Place II

Figure 9

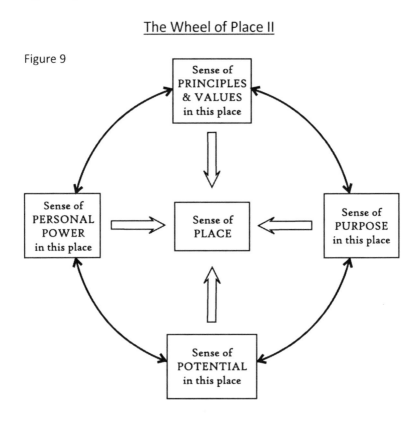

Copyright Richard A. Burwell 2010: The Wheel of Place II

You are now ready to begin the process of enhancing your sense of place in the area you have chosen to look at. I encourage you to work your way through these questions using your 'Transformational Journal' noting your answers for each sense of self in the place you have chosen to improve. As you work through the process of improving your current places, you will gain great insight into what is working, what could work better and what you need to do about it, for each of the 12 segments in the wheel of place.

Sense of principles and personal values
I know what my values are for this place/situation (out of 10)
What's important to me in this situation is...
For it to work well, I feel I need to have / I feel I need to be...
What is hindering me is...? What may hinder me is...?
My options for seeing my principles and values honoured are...
What I intend to do about it is...

Strength of purpose is... (rated out of 10)
I give it this rating because...
My purpose in this place is...
What I want is...
What is hindering me/ may hinder me from fulfilling my purpose is?
My options for improving my sense of purpose are...
What I intend to do about it is...

Sense of potential here is ...(rated out of 10)
I give it this rating because...
What I want is...what I want is to feel...what I want is to believe...
What is hindering me having a stronger sense of potential is...?
My options for seeing my sense of potential increase are?
What I intend to do about it is...

Sense of personal power to make decisions and take action is...
(rated out of 10)
I give it this rating because...
What I want is...
What is hindering me is...
My options for improving the situation are...
What I intend to do about it is...

Taking the other senses into account, how strong is my sense of
place here? (rated out of 10)
I give it this rating because...
My sense of place is improving (yes/no) getting worse (yes/no)
The sense of place I want is...
What is hindering me is...
My options for improving the situation are...
What I intend to do about it is...

If having worked through the issues fully, you establish that a current place is not the right soil for you to grow in, then you should make every effort to leave well, without recrimination. An old Viking proverb states, "Leave in such a way as you are able to return...." In addition, if you find that you have a very weak sense of place with your partner, I encourage you to seek out professional relationship support.

The following questions will help you to explore your sense of place in more detail by asking probing questions relating to each of your other senses of self in the place you have chosen to consider.

They have been based around your sense of place at work, but they can also be modified to help you gain a sense of your place in other areas of your life. *Give attention to those questions which resonate with you, and give most attention to the questions which challenge you or irritate you.*

> Managers also can ask themselves how much they contribute to helping their employees feel a strong sense of place by reflecting on these questions as they think about each employee.

General Sense of Place Choose an area, such as work, home, local community etc.

What do you appreciate about this place? What do you not appreciate about this place? What is working / not working for you here? How well received / accepted do you feel at work? How well do you feel able to be challenged to develop and improve your performance at work? How well are you able to be critiqued? How much do you feel you identify with the people you work with? How much do you feel you identify with the job you do? How connected do you feel to the people you work with? How connected do you feel to the environment you work in? How well are your colleagues getting to know you? Do you want to be known? How affirmed do you feel in the work you do?

How much do you accept the place and the people you work amongst? How strongly do you feel you belong at your place of work? What do you receive from being in this place? How much do you value your colleagues? How much in your place of work and the work that you do is familiar, or is it all change all the time? How much continuity is there to the change that occurs? How well are you getting to know your colleagues? How much do you take an interest in your colleagues? Do they want to be known?

What can you personally do to improve the situation?

What would you like to see change and improve? How could you imagine you having a stronger sense of place here? What can you do personally to help improve your sense of place? In which ways can you alter your perspective? How can you see things differently? What can you say or do to help? What changes do you need to make personally that you know will help, but you are afraid of making? What are you afraid of? What will you commit to do, to help improve your sense of place here? What else can you do to strengthen your sense of place here?

Sense of Potential In relation to your work place, home place, local community.

In which ways is your potential recognised and explored? In which ways do people express an interest in you? In which ways are you known or understood for what you can contribute? In which ways are you in the process of becoming known? How much do you feel valued here? In which ways are you exploring other people's potential and expressing an interest in them? What needs to be different for your sense of potential to be stronger here? How much do you feel your potential is recognised or realised at work?

Use the questions 'what can you do to improve the situation?' as above.

Sense of Purpose In relation to your work place, home place, local community.

What do you appreciate about your sense of purpose in this place? How can you describe your sense of purpose in this area or place in your life? In which ways do you feel excited about being here? In which ways does being here energise you, excite you and make you want to make a difference? If you have felt this once, but have now lost it, how can you recover this sense of energy and purpose? Are you on track or directionless? What needs to be different for your sense of purpose to be different in this place? How connected to a sense of purpose at work do you feel? What is your purpose at work? How much do you identify with it?

Use the questions 'what can you do to improve the situation?' as above.

Sense of Your Principles / Preferences / Personal Needs
In relation to your work place, home place, local community.

In which ways do you feel you fit? In which ways are your needs catered for? Describe the ways you are in harmony with the way other people see things and do things? What are the values and principles you share with others in this place? Do you feel your preferences of style are acceptable? Do you feel the confidence to be you? How can you share your needs and preferences more openly? In which ways are you exploring the principles, preferences and personal needs of others in this place? In which ways are you at ease in this place? What else can you do to improve your sense of shared values here? How much do you understand the principles and values which operate around your place of work? How much do you identify with them?

Use the questions 'what can you do to improve the situation?' as above.

Sense of Personal Power In relation to your work place, home place, local community.

Potential and power are similar, yet subtly different. Power is the expression of potential. Power is about decisions and results. Do you have a sense that you can make a difference, that your contribution will add something positive to this place? In which ways and areas do you feel you can influence things? In which ways are you given room to express your power of decision and contribution? What do you give? In which ways is your contribution welcomed or received?

In which ways is your contribution invited? How significant do you feel your contribution is? How much do you feel able to exercise your power, the fullness of who you are without fear of being misunderstood or rejected? What are the reasons you exercise your power, your contribution in this place? Are you able to withhold your power, your contribution as appropriate? Do you withhold your power, your contribution too much? If so what are the reasons for this? What else can you contribute?

How much do you affirm and encourage other colleagues in your place of work? How much do you feel able to sensitively challenge other colleagues and the status quo at work? How much freedom do you have to be yourself at work? How much ownership do you feel you have with the environment you work in (desk, canteen, equipment etc)? Do you feel empowered and facilitated or controlled and constrained? Do you feel owned or do you feel like a stakeholder? How much ownership do you feel you have with what you do?

Use the questions 'what can you do to improve the situation?' as above.

Questions for Managers and Team Leaders:

If you are a manager or team leader, you can use the questions above to reflect on how effective you are in helping your team to have a sense of significant place in the work that they do. You could devise your own questions based on the last 5 pages. Simply change the form of the questions in the following ways...

For example: In which ways do you express interest in your staff? In which ways do you encourage your staff? In which ways do you value your team? Have you communicated what the team values are adequately? Have you sought to understand the personal values of your team? In which ways do you invite contributions and provide new opportunities for your team to use their talents and explore new areas of potential? In which ways do you coach and facilitate, in contrast to lead and direct your team? In which ways have you communicated the purpose of the team? Is it clear the ways in which your team members can use their unique talents to contribute towards the overall purpose of the team? Do your team members understand their own role specific purpose? What can you do to enhance and improve the situation? In which ways do your team members express their personal power? Do they feel confident to make decisions within their orbit of responsibility, or do they look for reassurance or permission unnecessarily?

If you are planning to make a change of place (house, work etc)

Is the change in location you are looking to make congruent with who you are not just what you feel? Is it in harmony with your values? If you make this change of place, what will you have to give up? What would be difficult about this new place you are considering? Be honest! We tend to romanticise every new possibility in life, and it rarely fully meets our full expectations.

Imagine yourself there. What might not work for you in this new place/environment/job/community? What might be the difficulties for you to work through? What processes would you need to work through in this new place for it to become the ideal place? What changes would you need to make in yourself, to yourself?

Ultimately, 'a place' is unlikely to be a truly satisfying place to be, unless it includes an opportunity for contribution, where one's potential is exercised, where one's purpose is fulfilled, or at least recognised and valued, and where one's values are understood, honoured and indeed, where one's values find a shared home, and finally where one has a sense of personal power. A place, in fact, where you thrive, and your presence makes a difference. These will all become the themes of the following chapters, as we explore together the various senses of self and find greater empowerment in living life well.

Chapter 2

PRINCIPLES, PREFERENCES & PERSONAL NEEDS
(The values we live by)

Values provide perspective in the best of times and the worst
Charles Garfield

INTRODUCTION

On April 14, 1912, at 10.00pm, the Titanic crashed into an iceberg in the mid-Atlantic and four hours later sank. The hours surrounding the collision are an amazing lesson in values-based living.

Following the tragedy and once in safe harbour, the Titanic's Captain - Captain Smith - was accused of "gross carelessness" by Major A. H. Peuchen, one of the passengers. Peuchen wanted to know why Captain Smith had remained in the dining hall when he knew they were entering an ice field. Major Peuchen, we can surmise, would have exercised personal responsibility to oversee the safety of the ship in the face of such potential danger. Captain

Smith on the other hand was seemingly happy to leave the responsibility to the crew, and trust that the ship builders were correct in their assertion that the Titanic was 'unsinkable'. Values affect decisions.

Even the woefully few lifeboats that were supplied on the ship were not fitted with strong enough ropes to lower a full load of passengers to the sea in case of an emergency. A value-based decision no doubt – monetary cost over human life.

Once in a lifeboat, Major Peuchen asked helmsman Robert Hitchens to row back to the sinking ship and look for survivors. Hitchens is reputed to have replied by saying that his responsibility was to the living, not the crying and the dead. Again, values shine through – especially in times of crisis.

Newspapers also reported that Major Peuchen had left more than two hundred thousand dollars in money, jewellery, and securities in his cabin. As the evacuation began, he took a values-based decision, which may have saved his life. Arriving at his cabin he saw what his true values were, and rather than gathering his precious possessions, he turned away and grabbed some oranges instead. One hour before, he might have chosen the money over the fruit, but in the face of death, values were seen more clearly.

In the aftermath of the Titanic's sinking, there were reports that eleven millionaires had been among the hundreds who had died that day. Their combined wealth totalled nearly two hundred million dollars. Could it be that some of those millionaires may have gone back for their money and jewellery, so missing their chance of a place on a life boat? We will never know. [14]

Perhaps we can imagine ourselves in their shoes. What would we have done? Making our way back to our possessions in our cabin, we may have felt that we could not leave without them. But fighting our way through narrow cabin corridors already piled high with abandoned possessions and the ship tilting dangerously, perhaps we would make a different calculation - could we live *with* them?

Having a correct perspective on what was truly important to Major Peuchen meant that he was able to make a life-saving decision. This is what values do for us when they are at the forefront of our conscious thinking. They help us to make the best decisions based on what we believe will be our greatest good and the good of others.

Of course, life does not always help to define our values as clearly as occurred on the awful day of the Titanic's demise. When our values are not clear, we may make poor decisions based on a poor understanding of what's truly important to us. The immediate results of our decisions may not be as obvious as they were for Major Peuchen. But every decision has its consequence, and every decision has a value underlying it.

> The decisions of principle that we make and the preferences of style and activity we adopt, and the personal needs we seek to satisfy are all based on what we value for our personal fulfilment and the benefit of others.

It may not be a higher value which motivates a decision, but it will always be a value which guides us, whether consciously or not. Values are highly motivating. When you know what you value as important, you will go out of your way to fulfil it.

Sometimes, the desire for immediate gratification, preservation or adulation takes precedence over principled, value-based decisions. Sometimes, the pressure of a moment may elevate a lower level value to higher prominence, as may have initially occurred for Major Peuchen before he chose the oranges over the money, or for Robert Hitchens when he refused to go back for survivors.

For Hitchens, the value of self-preservation was clearly more important than selfless leadership. But Hitchens was not necessarily a bad man, and perhaps, despite his coldness of heart in the crisis, he may have been ridden with guilt afterwards. A lower level value or need of personal survival overwhelmed the higher value of protection, which is what his position of helmsman required of him. *Perhaps if he had done some values reflection earlier on, he would have been ready to make a decision which was more worthy of him*. When we are not aware of what's truly important to us, we may be tempted to make decisions based on convenience rather than principle.

What do we do, for example, when confronted with a scene of bullying on the high street, while we are driving home in our new and expensive car, late to our son's birthday party? The son whose party we missed the previous year. Perhaps the easy thing to do is nothing; just to keep on driving, motivated by the real but hidden values of 'personal safety' and 'honour of family'. Yet perhaps 'responsibility' and 'courage' are also values within us, and if we consciously acknowledged them, may motivate us to step in, fight for justice and protect the vulnerable. Clearly our values influence what we do, and why.

A stay-at-home mother, or a father who makes a values-based decision to work half time and share equally in the upbringing of his pre-school children, may both feel inadequate when chatting to a high flying business executive, unless they remember that the value which motivated their decision was to socialise their little children into becoming responsible, joyful and well equipped adults. The high flying executives may also feel inadequate when chatting to the hands-on parents, unless they remember that the value which motivated their decision to work so hard was to provide the best education they could afford for their children and an experience of world travel and culture.

This is why knowing our values, and the reason why we do things, empowers us in the decisions we make.

The Study of Value, Ethics, Morality and Virtue

With the introduction of the first moral codes in the ancient world, notably the law codes of Hammurabi (1750 BC) and the commandments given to Moses covering religious, social, legal and ethical instructions (1400 BC), humanity's concern for an ethical and values based way of living had begun. Around 1500 BC, the Indian *Vedas* were written and also included ethical instructions. Buddhist philosophy flourished in India between the Sixth and Fourth Century BC, while in China the two greatest moral philosophers were Lao-Tzu (Sixth Century BC) and Confucius (Fifth Century BC).

Western philosophical ethics as we know it today, found its birth-place in ancient Greek philosophy (Fifth to Third Centuries BC). The investigation into what has 'value' or 'worth' in life was called 'axiology' and it included the study of ethics and aesthetics. *Ethics* is the study of how we can live a good life, and of what constitutes good conduct. It is much broader than simply what is right and wrong. *Aesthetics* is the study of emotional value judgements on art, culture and nature. In relation to ethics, value describes the degree of importance that can be given to actions which have ethical significance.

For ancient classical Greek thinkers like Socrates, Plato and Aristotle, and the later Greek and early Roman thinkers such as the Stoics and Epicureans, a primary question was, "How can we live a life in which we and others thrive?" Their answer to this question was that we must live a virtuous life.

These ethical ideas were later dramatically influenced by the arrival of Jesus and the Christian theologians who followed Him. Jesus did not come specifically as an ethical teacher, but as saviour from man's inability to live the ethical life. His teaching was rooted in the Jewish ethic of obedience to God as the foundation for moral conduct, but His particular focus was on the kingdom of God, and the values of that kingdom, notably love and compassion as the motive for action, and also on the power of God's Spirit empowering people to live according to those values.

St Paul took up these themes when he taught that the 'letter of the law kills, but the Spirit in us gives life' and that, 'the fruit of the Spirit is love, joy, peace, patience, gentleness, kindness and self control'. Early Christian thinkers such as Ambrose, Augustine and Aquinas also embraced what were then seen as the classical Greek virtues of prudence, temperance, fortitude and justice, and added the specifically Christian virtues of faith, hope and love.

With the onset of the Renaissance in the 15th Century, there was a rebirth of interest in classical thought and culture, and man once again took centre stage in philosophical thought. Professor Peter Singer writes:

> "Its significance for ethics lies, rather, in a change of focus. For the first time since the conversion of the Roman Empire to Christianity, man, not God, became the chief object of philosophical interest, and the main theme of philosophical thinking was not religion but humanity - the powers, freedom and accomplishments of human beings." [15]

This trend was reinforced as Protestant Christians insisted that individuals could read and understand the Bible without papal interpretation. The invention of the printing press also enhanced everyone's access to theological and ethical philosophy.

Between the 18th and 19th Centuries, one of the main concerns of western ethical thinking was whether ethical value judgements were to be based on objective universal principles, or simply on the subjective moral sense of the individual who feels them.

In the 18th Century, beginning with the theories of Adam Smith, values also began to be thought of in terms of economic value (concerning the value of a product and people's choice). In the 19th Century, sociology became concerned with how personal values operate in community contexts and affect social behaviour. This was a response to the challenges of industrialisation and urbanisation.

In the 19th Century, Nietzsche wanted to re-evaluate ethical thinking as it had evolved since classical Greek times. He proposed that values were to be discovered, arising out of one's own individuality and to be freely chosen, rather than being based on philosophical or religious principles. He called for a 'transvaluation of values'.

John Heenan, in the online article 'Making Sense of Values', explains the evolution of the word:

> "With the growing use of the word values, the word virtues (those traits of character that aspire to moral excellence like honesty, compassion, courage and perseverance) fell into disuse. But contrary to Neitzsche's belief and hope, virtues did not die but became regarded as moral or objective core values... For this reason, today, any list of values is likely to include the old virtues." [16]

By the mid 19th Century, a new way of thinking about values had begun, rooted in the preferences, emotions and desires of the individual. This new way was not tied to the older framework of ethical principles or moral behaviour, but it was not divorced from it either. This new concept of values began to enter into early 20th Century psychological and social theory, and with it, an increasing individualisation of the word 'value' occurred.

Where once the word 'value' referred to 'what is valuable', now it refers more to what I personally value, appreciate or feel to be important. This is especially true for the Humanistic psychologists who, in the words of A.C. Tjeltveit,

> "...focussed on a person's freedom to choose values and on values as the products of one's true self or inner nature, on values as the products of Maslow's self actualising tendency, or of Roger's organismic valuing process." [17]

To summarise, in the western world, the investigation into what values are began with ancient Greek philosophy (axiology). It developed into moral theology up to the 15th Century, and began to branch into the values of ethical philosophy, economic value and sociological values between the 18th and 19th Centuries, and also into the psychological values of the individual during the 20th Century.

As we can see, there has been a long and varied history in the development of value theory, and this makes a universal definition almost impossible to find. But we can be clear that _a personal values_ profile will probably include a combination of

1. _universal principles_ (including virtues and aesthetic values),
2. _personal preferences_ of behaviour, and
3. _psychological needs, desires_ and motivations.

> These diverse elements of what has 'value' to an individual have now become absorbed into the post-modern definitions of what personal values are. Values, as they are now used, have come to represent a wide spectrum of meanings and words which carry personal meaning from value principles and virtues, to personal preferences to personal needs and desires.

How Do Values Develop Within Us?

Cultural framing

Cultural values are values which have been formed over a long period of time, and which are specific in time to a particular social, religious and historical context. Cultural values are norms of aesthetic appreciation and social and ethical behaviour that the culture as a whole tends to value. In urban societies, distinct cultural and religious groups with their own values exist within the wider cultural setting. There can also be shared cultural values within institutions, large organisations and smaller groups. Cultural values are the values we live amongst, they frame us and they influence us profoundly and imperceptibly.

Childhood nurturing and experience

In our formative years, as we are nurtured by parents, guardians, teachers and siblings, their values become the norm that we see, hear and experience. These important people exert a profound influence upon us either positively or negatively. We will either embrace (mostly subconsciously) the values we see 'lived out' around us, or we will react against those values, and develop alternative values in their place.

For example, perhaps 'fairness' seemed absent in our childhood, and now we value fairness very strongly. Perhaps feeling 'freedom' was a core value for our parents, and this expressed itself through keeping options open and being spontaneous, and we personally felt the benefit of this approach to life. Alternatively, perhaps spontaneity caused us to miss out on opportunities through a lack of planning, and now we value order, expressed through planning for things in advance. Perhaps we began to recognise that conversation over the meal table brought feelings of warmth and intimacy and we now value intimacy through meal time conversation. Perhaps we saw compassion or honesty lived out before us in a powerful and unforgettable way, and these moments have imprinted similar values on us now.

Choices - where we adopt some values in preference to others

During teenage years and into early adult life we begin to make value judgements about the lifestyle we wish to adopt. In adult life, our society, our friends, our colleagues, our heroes or the significant books we read can all have an influence upon our values. As long as a value and the expression of that value continues to work for us, we will consciously or subconsciously find ways to express it.

As we reflect on the way we live and on what works or doesn't work for us, we may begin to recognise that some values no longer serve us in the way they once did, or at least, that the way we express a value now needs to change in order for life to work more effectively.

For example, perhaps we valued autonomy, and expressed this through independence and being our own boss, but now feel that autonomy can still be valued in the context of interdependent relationships in partnerships with others. Sometimes, the time to choose new values or modify the expression of those values occurs after moments of life crisis, when we recognise that the way we have lived needs to be different.

Core Personal Values

A core value is based on deeply held subconscious beliefs about what is good and right and of benefit to us and others. It is something that we believe to be true for us and of great importance to us for personal well being and fulfilment. Ultimately, the power of a value is that we are motivated to honour it, because in honouring it we feel fulfilled. When we dishonour a value we feel incomplete, but may not know why.

Examples of values could be creativity, intimacy, order, freedom, achievement, honesty and integrity. Your values influence the way you live, the way you carry yourself - your values reveal your personal style. Your values add colour and fragrance to the way you live out your purpose.

Core life values are relevant to every aspect of life, whether at home, at work or at play; but the order they come in your hierarchy of importance may vary, depending on your context. For example, achievement at work may be high on your list, but low when at home; or intimacy and affection may be a high value for home, but a low value at work.

Some people may have values which are specific to work or specific to home. So, a value which may be true for you in the work environment such as 'control', may be expressed through leading and directing; but this value may not be relevant in the home setting, where the value of freedom is expressed through facilitating family members to become all they are capable of becoming.

> Values are motivating influences which guide our decisions
> great and small. They are an inner 'voice'; part of our internal
> guidance system inclining us to do those things which bring us
> fulfilment.

Hyrum Smith has written that:

> "Values are our blueprint for a fulfilled life. They are our
> internal compass and whether we are aware of it or not,
> they impact our behaviours, reactions to events and the
> decisions that we make." [18]

Core values are our internal and mostly intuitive reference point
which help us to clarify where we are in relation to other people
and which direction we should take. For example, we may apply
for a new job, and the job description may be very prescriptive,
defining exactly what should be done and when, leaving little
room for the imagination. If core values for us are personal
creativity and originality, we will probably have a conflict of values
if we take the job. Knowing our core values in this situation helps
us to know what to do.

Our Values Need to be Recognised and Discovered

Values influence us at the subconscious level, but when we fail to
give our values a necessary voice in the shaping of what we do,
and instead allow ourselves to be influenced by other peoples
values or agendas, we run the risk of living out of alignment with
our deepest core. This leads to stress (the conflict of values) and
the inability to set goals or make plans which fulfil us at the
deepest level.

The guidance which values bring is experienced as a nudge, a
whisper, an inexplicable reluctance or a release of energy and
enthusiasm. Things just feel right or wrong, sometimes strongly

sometimes weakly, but often, we don't really know why because we don't consciously know what our values are.

> Values are uniquely powerful, yet also, often strangely hidden. We have lived with them and they have lived within us from early days, and yet rarely do we know their name. The influence they have upon us comes unrequested, moving us to act in ways we may not understand.

Although our values are often hidden, we can begin to recognise them by noticing the ways we behave and the things we do in our attempts to express them. By asking good questions we can begin to understand the value influence behind the way we live; we can begin to see the hidden values which motivate our actions.

When we are able to put a name to our values and understand the meaning they hold for us, we are empowered to enhance their good effect, and find better ways to express the values we hold. When we consciously recognise our values, we are more likely to make better decisions which are in harmony with who we know ourselves to be. When brought into the conscious realm, values are powerful motivators for abundant living.

Whether our values include classical or religious virtues, ethical principles, aesthetic values or personal motivations and desires; and however they were formed within us, whether through cultural framing, childhood nurturing or specific choices; the fact is, that for personal values to be truly effective for us, they need to be recognised and discovered by us. In this respect, the humanistic psychologist Carl Rogers wrote that self actualised persons ..."live by values which they discover within." [19]

Not knowing our values is normal for most of us. We leave them at the intuitive and subconscious level of awareness, but there is a better way. By asking the right sort of questions, it's possible to ascertain the values which guide us and to bring them more into the conscious realm. Then we can more easily make decisions which fulfil us and be confident that we are on the right track for our lives because we know the direction our internal value compass is pointing in.

> When we understand our values consciously for the first time, it's like we have recognised our self, a sort of personal embrace, a moment where we welcome a part of ourselves which has in the past only partially been recognised. It's an act of kindness to oneself, it's worth the effort of exploration.

To List or Not to List

There are many lists of values which have been compiled by counsellors, coaches and business consultants over recent years. Most of these values lists include of a variety of principles, behaviours, needs, attitudes and virtues. A values list can be used as a starting point for discovering the values which are important to you. The idea is that you choose those 'value' words which you most resonate with; then you determine the meaning that they have for you and then you rank them in priority order, placing highest, those values which you feel to be most important to you.

These lists can be helpful in providing a starting point for a values enquiry, especially when you might not have a large repertoire of 'value' type words to choose from, from your own vocabulary, and when you don't have access to a personal coach who can take you through a 'values coaching session'. If you decide to use a values list, it's important to recognise that it's only the first stage in a personal values search. If you rely on a values list alone, you are likely to get only a surface level result, and with each new list you use, a different result will be found, based on the pre-determined words on the list. Also, once you've seen the list, it can be hard to see beyond the list to the hidden values which you really live by.

Another danger in providing a substantive list of values and using this alone to determine the values which are important to you, is that you might approach the list as a wish list, ticking those value words you would *like* to have, rather than those values which you recognise you *already* have. The list may also become prescriptive or suggestive of what 'should' be important to you. It may be hard to look at certain values like 'integrity', 'responsibility' or 'creativity' and not feel that they *ought* to be, or *should* be your values. Equally, you may look at other words like 'ambition' or 'control' and feel that they shouldn't be your values at all.

Does this mean that a values list is unhelpful? Not at all. It's simply the *start* of an important process of self discovery. A values search is a deep quest for meaning, identity and purpose which eludes easy definitions. One thing becomes very clear for all those who engage on the quest to discern their values – the main value of a values search is the value of the search! That is to say, the very process of thinking about these things is deeply rewarding.

> The point of a values enquiry is not to judge whether a value is a good one or a bad one, but to discern whether it is actually a value you are influenced by. Once you have discerned your values, you can then consider how well they serve you, and how helpful your current ways of expressing them actually are.

Digging Deeper for Core Personal Values

The list helps to kick start your thought process, and offers you a helpful basis from which you can begin your values search. The limitations of a values list are overcome when you are able to ask penetrating and searching questions about your life and work, and use your answers to discern the values which are already true for you. So, for example, if 'control' is on your list of personal values, it's worth asking what 'control' gives to you. It might be that a deeper, underlying value is security, but that might not be immediately apparent to you without some deeper digging.

So, let's use a values list as a starting point, but let's also move beyond the values list to a deeper values quest. Let's ask those searching questions which will elicit those values which actually do belong to us.

Discovering your core values is not an easy or quick process. This stands to reason of course, as it's already taken many years for those values to form within you, so it should at least take several hours, days, weeks or months to discover them. Finding a coach skilled in values elicitation is well worth the effort, because a coach is able to ask you questions about your life which help you to uncover the core values which deeply influence you. A coach is able to help you uncover the principles, the preferences and the personal needs which you deeply value, but which you hardly knew were there.

Exercise 1:
How to uncover your core values from a values list:
Please follow our website link www.thecoachingdynamic.com for a values list. Print off the page, then tick the 'value words' which resonate with you most strongly.

What does it do for you, what does it give to you?
A great way to find out what the core values are which motivate you, is to ask yourself ,"What does this 'value word' do for me, or give to me?" and to ask this question for each of the value words you have ticked from the list. For example, you may have ticked the word 'planning', and as you ask yourself "What does 'planning' do for me, or give to me?" you may find that you say , "It gives me 'structure'", and as you ask yourself, "What does 'having structure' do for me?", you may say, "It gives me a sense of order." You may then feel that you have found a core value for yourself, or you may wish to keep asking the question, and find that the root value is 'safety', or 'security', expressed by you through planning.

You may tick the word 'excellence', and as you ask, "What does this do for me, or give to me?" you may struggle to find other words, and it may become clear to you that actually, excellence *is* a core value which requires little further explanation. Or as you continue to ask the question, you may find that further words come to you, such as 'quality' and 'being my best'. The word quality may offer a richer meaning to the value of excellence for you, and the phrase 'being my best' suggests a preferred way of expressing this value. The answers will be different for everyone, because we all bring different nuances of definition and meaning to the words which resonate with us.

As you keep asking the question of the words that surface, you will the find the core underlying value which motivates you from the initial word which resonated with you, and you will be helped to reflect on your preferred ways of expressing those values.

Write a definition or description for each core value:
Write a supporting definition or description of the core values you have uncovered, explaining what the core value does for you or gives to you, using a list of words you have found to be connected to each other. By using several connected words to define the core value word, you get a richer fuller meaning for the core value word you have uncovered. For more in depth values coaching, I suggest working with a coach who can lead you through a values elicitation process. Once you have written a description for each value, continue with the following section, and then complete exercise 2 the 'Values Category' and 'Order of Importance' exercise on page 75.

Types of Values

An accurate elicitation of values can be gained when we recognise the different categories which personal values fall into. Personal values can be categorised under two main groups – principles and personal needs.

<u>Principle Values</u> are the principles of 'being' and 'beholding' which define what we believe to be true, moral or virtuous in life. They are the principles we live by, the natural laws we honour and the aesthetics we appreciate. We could call them values of 'being'.

<u>Personal need values</u> define what we believe we need for personal fulfilment. They are the emotional and psychological needs we value having fulfilled in our life beyond the needs of physical sustenance. We could call them values of 'having'.

'Principles', and 'Personal Need' values become visible in our preferences of behaviour and activity.

<u>Preferences</u> are our preference expressions of 'doing'. They are not strictly values, but are the visible expression of the way we seek to fulfil our values. The preferences of doing and activity which we find most enjoyable, energising and rewarding, are closely related to personal talents.

Marcus Buckingham and Donald O. Clifton define talents in their book *'Now Discover Your Strengths'* as...

> "...naturally recurring patterns of thought, feeling or behaviour." [20]

Behind any talent there will be a value which inspires it, and any true value will have a preference expression giving voice to it.

Figure 10

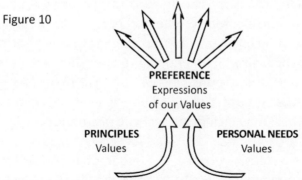

PREFERENCE
Expressions
of our Values

PRINCIPLES   **PERSONAL NEEDS**
Values   Values

Copyright Richard A. Burwell 2010: Principle, Preferences and Personal Needs

The principles we live by, the preferences of the way we do things and the personal needs we desire to have met, all find their place in the wider context of our purpose and the goals we set on the road to fulfilling our purpose and attaining our vision. Purpose sets the direction for our life and is the motivational engine which drives us on the road to achieving our goals which in turn fulfil our vision. Values are the way we drive and they also influence the way we act and what we do when we get there.

> Our *values of principle* are like the Highway Code, our *preferences* are like our personal style of driving within the code and our *personal need values* are like the things we take with us on the journey, making it more comfortable.

The more we are able to define our principles, preferences and personal needs, the more rewarding our journey is likely to be. We express these core values in various ways through our family, faith, work and community relationships. Our different life contexts affect the importance we attach to our values, and bring other values into play which may or may not be in evidence in other situations of life.

Principles (or Higher Values)

A principle is a fundamental truth or law. Principles operate in many areas of life, from scientific principles to principles of human conduct and relationship, to psychological processes. In the world of relationships, principles are obvious standards which form the foundation on which all well functioning relationships are built. In so far as we value these principles we can call them 'values of principle'. Another way of looking at principles is to see them as higher values which may include ethical and aesthetic principles.

Within our core values, we have a number of higher values or principles, which may be closer to an ethical code than things we simply value highly. It's probable that conscience is aligned to these principles or higher values. Some of these higher values such as respect, fairness and integrity, act as the building blocks of community cohesion.

Values of principle are relevant to all cultures because they relate to the human condition as a whole; and though cultural standards may change, the principles on which well functioning relationships are built do not change. For example, when relationships are not built on the principles of honesty, understanding, or responsibility, the relationship will not function well. In this regard, Steven Covey writes that principles are...

> "...guidelines for human conduct that are proven to have enduring permanent value...One way to quickly grasp the self evident nature of principles is to simply consider the absurdity of attempting to live an effective life based on their opposites," [21] Principles, "govern human growth and happiness." They are "natural laws that are woven into the fabric of every civilised society throughout history." [22]

When principles are honoured they create the space where life can flourish, needs can be fulfilled and personal preferences find their place.

A principle is a natural law which simply 'makes sense'. To do the opposite of a principle is to rupture a relationship, or to rob a relationship of the nutrients it needs to thrive, or to remove the boundaries of protection which help to contain the environment of growth.

But just because a principle is a good thing, doesn't mean that we all value them equally. This is why a principle may be a value low on my list and high on yours. Examples of principles might be respect, honesty, truth, fairness, mercy, forgiveness, integrity, service, excellence, potential, nurture, patience, encouragement, freedom, choice, responsibility, creativity, interdependence and understanding. We might all accept these as principles, but they might not all be on our personal top ten list.

Personal Needs

A 'Personal Need Value' (emotional / intellectual / relational / spiritual) is a need I must have met, or satisfied in my life for my personal well being. When my need is met I am strengthened. Personal need values are things we feel we need to have in order to function well. When a personal need is not met I am diminished or weaker in some way. A need is an *inner drive* <u>to have</u> the thing which brings me fulfilment. Needs are satisfied in the having. Personal needs are inwardly oriented and cause me to think about the fulfilment of those needs.

> By having my needs satisfied, I am empowered to fulfil my other values, and by honouring values of principle in my interaction with others, I am more likely to have my own needs met. This is a virtuous circle of value fulfilment.

Preferences of Doing and Action

Core values of principle and personal need are honoured and fulfilled when they are expressed in our own preferred ways of doing things. These preferred expressions can be seen as values, in as much as we do, in fact, value our preferred ways of doing things. Preferences of behaviour are expressions of the core values they are based upon. But a preference expression is more properly *an expression* of a core value, than a value in itself.

> Preference expressions are an *inner drive* <u>to do</u> something which brings me fulfilment because the action or expression fulfils a core value of mine.

A true value in itself is never wrong. By nature, it measures the good worth and importance of something in our lives; but it is the way we *express* that value which may not serve us or other people to our or their best advantage. It is the unrestrained or imbalanced expression of certain values which may lead to ill effect. For example, when freedom is expressed without responsibility, or when honesty is expressed without compassion. Another example could be someone who says that they 'value' violent video games. But is this a value, or an expression of a value? If we ask what the violent video game does for the person, the answer may be 'gives me excitement', or a 'sense of adventure'.

If beauty is a principle I honour, I may express this by seeking to be my best, or by beholding and appreciating beautiful things. Similarly, if hope is a principle I honour, I may express this principle value by thinking and speaking optimistically. If loyalty is a principle I value, I may express this by being faithful and dependable. In these examples, our values have a simple cause - effect relationship on how we live.

In other situations, the things we do and the way we do them are often the result of a complex interaction of several values working together, especially in team and community settings. For example, a manager has a meeting to consult with his team over an important course of action. The team have been part of the process, but the manager makes the decision. He sends out an email to confirm his decision, knowing that everyone has already been part of the process. However, new information comes to light later that week, suggesting there is a better course of action. There is little time to inform the team of the change of plan, and a decision needs to be made quickly or the opportunity will be lost.

Normally, the manager tries to consult the team as a means of empowering them in the process of decision making, but he also wants to lead out from the front. Clear communication is also important to him, and he recognises the dangers of causing misunderstanding through sending emotionless email, rather than speaking on the telephone.

On balance he decides to call another team meeting, despite the pressures of time constraint. He wants to lead out and feel in charge, and a decision must be made quickly. There is no time for a new round of consultation, but he also wants to maintain good communication and be facilitative. He also wants to be appropriately transparent and so he communicates something of his thought process, in order to give his team a window into the values which led him to this decision. The way he has managed this process has been thoroughly based on the values he honours in his life. He has consulted, empowered, informed, communicated with people and been appropriately transparent. Values have operated at every level of his decision making process.

Separating 'Being', 'Doing' and 'Having' Values

Our values of principle, and our values of personal need together form our core personal values. These core personal values find expression through our own preferred ways of doing things. These preferred expressions of *doing* flow from our core values of *being* (principles) and *having (*personal needs).

This way of understanding our core values and the behaviours which develop from them, helps us to live life in a more balanced and centred way, because our *doing* behaviours grow naturally out of the core principles of *being* that we honour and the core personal needs we desire to *have* fulfilled. If I only focus on my preferences of 'doing', without recognising the underlying values which influence them, I run the risk of becoming unbalanced, cast adrift from the deeper core of who I am.

Making a distinction between our core values and the expression of those values helps us to be more specific about what our core values are, and more considered about the best ways we can fulfil those values in life. The words 'knowledge' and 'learning' offer a good example. Knowledge is not so much an expression as it is a core value; learning is not so much a core value as it is an expression of a core value. So we could say that the underlying *principle* is 'esteeming knowledge', or the underlying *personal need* is 'having knowledge'. We could also say that 'learning', though often thought of as a value, is perhaps better thought of as an activity which expresses the underlying core value of having knowledge or esteeming knowledge.

By recognising a need as a need, I can be more specific in what I need to receive, or in what I need to ask others to do for me, or in what I personally need to put in place so that my own needs are fulfilled. By recognising 'doing expressions' as distinct from 'needs values' I can be more specific in what I must do to fulfil my values. By recognising a principle 'being value', I can be more aware of the ways of being, or be-haviour or be-attitudes which are congruent with who I am, what I honour and how I believe I should live.

> When you consciously know what your core values are, you enhance your sense of personal power because you are more able to live in harmony with yourself, and you are more able to choose actions which fulfil you and create an environment around you which is optimised for your own development and the development of others.

Exercise 2:
Placing your values in categories and in order of importance:

Having read the previous section, you are now ready to look over your list, and decide which category each word best fits within. The following table may help to give you an idea of how this might look, but remember, these are *only examples* of how it might look; your list will probably look quite different.

By looking at how we seek to express our core values, we can gain an insight into our core sense of life purpose, because our core values ideally inspire us to meaningful action. Keep the list you create safe - you will want to refer to it when you begin the exercises in the next chapter.

PRINCIPLES Be Values	PREFERENCES Do Expressions	PERSONAL NEEDS Have Values
	Be my own boss, or manage a department.	Autonomy
Beauty	Be my best / Behold / Give attention to beauty	
	Accountability and Competition	Achievement
Compassion	Care for/Serve others/Listening	
	Shape / Build / Lead	Control
Courage / Justice	Confront evil / Confront injustice	Courage / Safety
Excellence	Be accountable / Do things well / Be my best	
Be responsible	Take responsibility	Have responsibility
Honesty	Authentic/Sincere/Tell the truth	
Knowledge / Wisdom	Learning / Teaching	Knowledge
	Planning/Organisation/Structure	Order
	Perfectionism/Accuracy	Be right
	Routine / Predictability / Planning / Structure	Safety
Understanding	Listening/ Empathy	Understanding
Freedom	Spontaneity / originality	Freedom

Figure 11 ©Richard A. Burwell 2010: Examples of Values in Categories

When you have placed the words from your list into categories, you are then ready to rank them in order of importance, within each of the three categories. Ideally, you will find this more manageable, if you have no more than 10 words in each category. If you struggle to do this, don't worry. The finer distinctions may become clearer to you in due course; but you can still rank your value words in order of importance, even if they are all in the same list.

One benefit of separating out our values from the expression of those values is that when we come to rank 'value words' in order of importance, we don't make a false separation between the value and the expression of that value. For example, if autonomy or independence is a core value, and being my own boss is one possible expression of that value, it could be tortuous trying to decide which is more important – independence or being my own boss! But when I recognise that being my own boss may be an expression of independence, I realise don't need to rank them against each other.

Values Conflict –The Convenient or the Congruent

Sometimes, the convenient or easiest thing to do is not the right or the best thing to do. Sometimes, the urgent demand upon our time is not the most important demand upon us. Sometimes, we find ourselves stuck with an inner conflict – on the one hand 'this' and on the other hand 'that'. When faced with such a conflict, which should we choose and why? The inner conflict is genuine because both possible decisions are based on things we genuinely value. But which one should we choose and how should we express those values in ways which are congruent with who we are?

Sometimes, we make decisions based on fulfilling a need or a want while ignoring a higher value or principle and sometimes the *way* we fulfil that need is not to our best advantage. The actions we take and the things we do are motivated by the things we value, but sometimes those actions are not in harmony with other values which we hold.

For example, we may drive too fast in the car because we value being 'on time', but at the same time, we may value 'consideration' and 'safety for other road users' as well as ourselves, in addition to valuing the road traffic law. Yet we might ignore these other values because they are not convenient and the value of being on time has become more pressing.

Asking the question, "Which is most congruent or most in harmony with who I most deeply am?" may be the beginning of wisdom in what to do. By adjusting our practice - such as leaving earlier and driving more slowly, we find better ways of honouring the value of being on time, and honouring the other values we hold such as consideration for others.

Another example is smoking. The positive intention or value behind the behaviour of smoking may be to relax, but the act of smoking may violate other values we hold. Again, the challenge is to recognise the positive value intention behind the behaviour, and to find better ways of honouring the value. As with all behaviour change, there are degrees of habitual practice which need to be overcome. But recognising the 'principle value' or 'personal need value' behind the behaviour is the beginning to positive behaviour change.

A real challenge we all face is to choose a better behaviour or action, especially in a moment of stress, when the pressure of the moment squeezes us into less helpful forms of behaviour. It's in these moments of stress and confusion that compromise can cloud our judgement if we are uncertain of our true values in life.

When we know the value or positive intention behind a behaviour, we are then empowered to find a better behaviour which more fully supports the value we seek to express, and also to begin to form new habits of positive value expression.

Values Conflict - Embodied and Disembodied Values

As we have seen, our values of principle and personal need must find form in the tangible world of self expression – at home, at work or at play, if we are to live life in the most fulfilled way possible. But not all values which we hold as important are values we necessarily express. There are some values which we struggle to live out because we haven't yet found a way of integrating them with other values which are also important to us.

This tends to occur where two values seem to have an opposite characteristic to each other. This creates a values conflict - an apparent incompatibility between one value and another. Some examples of conflicting values might be freedom and responsibility; individuality and communality; facilitating others and taking a lead.

Another example could be 'security' and 'independence'. Security may be my dominant value, but independence may also be important to me. I may already be expressing security by working in a large company which offers many benefits, but I may not yet have found a way of expressing my value of independence. I may also not even know what my values are, which also increases my sense of confusion.

In this example, the stronger value of 'security' is honoured in my work employment - it is *embodied*; but the weaker value is unconsciously dishonoured - it is *disembodied* because it has not yet found an adequate form of expression in my life. Perhaps an opportunity occurs where I can manage a department within the company, with little involvement from line management. This may offer me a way of honouring both values.

> A disembodied value is a value which has not yet found form within you, which has not yet been fully embraced by you. It may be held by you, but it is not yet living within you.

When I ignore one value over another value, purposefully or unintentionally, this will lead to feelings of unrest. The ignored value is agitating, looking for recognition and expression.

One person I coached recently wanted to launch out on his own and begin a training consultancy, but he was struggling with the decision to resign from his current employment. As we talked, it became clear that there was a values conflict operating at a deeper level. The desire to leave and start out on his own was motivated by the value of freedom, but the struggle to hand in his resignation was motivated by the value of loyalty, expressed in his desire to remain loyal to friendships he had developed at work.

It was especially pronounced because he had left several jobs over several years, and the value of friendship-loyalty had become disembodied. Once the nature of this conflict was recognised, the client was able to 'make a request' to himself, asking that in leaving (the value of freedom), he would also embody the value of loyalty by maintaining the friendships which had become important.

There is a difference between simply holding a value and really embracing it. There is a difference between a value which is embodied through lifestyle expression and a value which is disembodied - finding no expression or integration within you.

Our subconscious will try to inform us of this lack of integration through feelings of frustration, restlessness and dis-ease. These disembodied, unintegrated values will continue to make us feel uneasy until we own them, acknowledge them and integrate them into our life. It is a conflict between values we are living and values that want to be lived. For example, the value of 'understanding', which is embodied through the expression of listening, may in conflict with the combined values of helping, knowledge and communication, which may be disembodied as a result of having little or no opportunity of expression through the talent of teaching.

How to Integrate Conflicting Values

The lack of integration of values creates a disharmony which needs to be addressed. A way needs to be found for you to honour all your values in accordance with the weight you give to them, in relation to the different contexts of your life. The next exercise may help you to re-balance these values and find ways to integrate values which are dishonoured and disembodied.

Exercise 3:
Values Integration:

Integrating your values is about recognising that you don't necessarily have to abandon one value to live the apparently opposite value. There may well be ways in which you can give prominence to one while at the same time honouring the other. The first step is to more fully understand what the conflicting values really mean to you and how you would like to express them.

Write a thorough values description for each pair of values which seem to be in conflict with each other.

This is most effective if you divide your page down the middle, and write your values descriptions alongside each other. Note the use of the word 'alongside' rather than opposite. Having done this, you are in a better position to explore how you might integrate these values, and, if necessary, re-balance them in your life.

<u>figure 12 Values Integration</u>

Dominant Value X Eg Individuality	**Weaker Value Y** Eg Communality
<u>Expressed by</u> Working for myself (the form of expression is different for everyone)	<u>Expressed by</u> Working in a team (the form of expression is different for everyone)
A dominant value is more likely to be embodied in lifestyle expression	A weaker value is more likely to be disembodied, not yet having found an adequate means of expression.
How can I value **x** while also valuing/doing/being **y** ? How can I value **y** while also valuing/doing/being **x** ? In which ways can I do/be/have **x** in a **y** sort of way? In which ways can I do/be/have **y** in an **x** sort of way? In which ways can I express my disembodied value at work? In which ways can I express my disembodied value in my leisure? What do I need to do, to give my weaker value a stronger voice? What do I need to adjust? What contexts will enable me to do this? What changes do I need to make? What do I need to join? What do I need to leave? What do I need to see differently?	
It is also possible that, over time, a natural shift may occur, where the weaker value takes on more prominence and weight, such that it becomes the dominant value – the value which is most important for you to express.	

©Richard A. Burwell 2010: Values integration

Embodying a Value in a Lifestyle Practice

As we have seen, values are a mixture of what we believe to be good and right and of benefit to us and others. But a value will only be fulfilling to us, if it is embodied in our lifestyle through <u>habitual practices</u> which express the value. When a value is not fulfilled, we feel unfulfilled. We may even be very clear in our minds that a particular value is important to us - it may have risen from being just a subconscious influence to becoming a conscious imperative - and yet we may still struggle to express it practically on a daily basis.

It's easier to maintain bad practices than it is to develop new ones. It takes practical and persistent dedication to successfully embody our values in the regular routine of life.

The Oxford Dictionary defines a practice as 'an habitual action'. Some examples of how the word is used are: "He really makes a practice of saving his money," or "That's a great idea. When are you going to put it into practice?" Or "If you want to play well you need to practice." Similarly, a business team might be heard to say, "We've agreed it in principle, now we need to put it into practice." In each case, the practice is based on a deeper underlying principle, value or desire.

> So, we can say that a practice is an action performed often or habitually, which gives form to an underlying principle or value.

Exercise 4: How to express your values in practices which fulfil them:

Using the list of values you discovered for yourself in exercises 1 and 2, choose a specific context, such as your work, or your family life etc, and for each value ask yourself the following questions...

- Do I want to express this value in **x** situation?
- How do I need to _see_ things differently in order to see this value expressed more fully?
- How do I need to _say_ things differently?
- How do I need to _hear_ things differently?
- How do I need to _do_ things differently?
- How do I need to _feel_ about things differently?

Based on the insights you gained from these questions, how do you want to express this 'x' value in 'y' situation? What are the practices you want to apply (eg in work) which will give expression to this value? What actions do you need to do, in order to see this value fulfilled? What are you currently doing that is hindering or stopping you fulfilling this value?

The table on the following page is adapted from ideas expressed by Robert Dilts, in the module 'Fitness for the Future' from the NLP Practitioner course 2009 (PPD Learning Ltd). Robert Dilts is a developer, author, trainer and consultant in the field of NLP.

HOW TO EMBODY A VALUE WITHIN A HABITUAL PRACTICE

The Value	The People	The Location	The Time	The Action	The Obstacles	The Resources	The Accountability	The Practice
(Which) ...you want to embody	(Who) ...you want to express the value with / for	(Where) ...you want to express the value in	(When) ...you want to express the value	(What action) ...you want to take in order to embody the value	...you want to overcome	(Help) ...you need to turn the action into a habitual practice	(Help) ...you need to employ to turn the action into a practice	The practice is defined in reference to the value, the context (who with where) and the time (when) and the activity of what exactly you will do.
Gentleness Patience	For the children	At Home	Especially at tea time and bed time	Listening & holding back my judgement	Stress Tiredness	More rest	My Wife	I will be gentle & patient with my children during meal times & bed times by listening to them more deeply and holding back my judgement
Taking responsibility	N/A	My Computer Emails	First job of the day	Answering new emails and filing them	I enjoy doing developmental work before boring maintenance	Imagine how I feel when all my emails are log jammed. Imagine how I feel when all my emails are answered 1st thing in the day	My Wife (business partner) and 'post it' notes on the office wall saying "do the right thing at the right time"	I will take responsibility for my email administration 1st thing every day, by answering new emails and filing them immediately.
Spirituality	N/A	Anywhere	3 times a day	15 Minutes prayer and meditation after meals	Tiredness Other more pressing pressures	More rest Imagine my life with a more developed spirituality	My Wife and my friends	I will live a more spiritual life by making a practice of praying & meditating for 10 minutes after each meal.
Relaxed atmosphere	The Team The Board etc	The work environment	Before every team meeting	5 minute coffee and pleasantries before the business	Pressure of the business agenda	Build it into the agenda. Give a team member the job of introducing the 'coffee and share' time.	Same as the Resources	We will make it a practice in our business meetings to develop a relaxed environment by chatting for 5 minutes over a cup of coffee before business.

The value is constant, but the activity and the practice which evolves from it is determined by the context (people and location) that I want to express the value within. In a similar way, the obstacles I face and the resources I have at my disposal, and the accountabilities I have available to me are all determined by my context - by the people around me and by the location I am in.

If I apply the value of 'taking responsibility' in the area of my emails, then the action I want to take is to deal with my new emails and file them first thing in the day. But if I apply the value of 'taking responsibility' in the area of team life, then the action I may want to take could be to deal with a team members poor performance head on, and not ignore it for fear of confrontation. In each context, computer emails and team life, the value may be constant, but the action will be different and the obstacles, resources and accountabilities will also be different.

Assuming Shared Values in a Team is Risky

It is normal for us to assume that we share similar values with other people. We naturally look for 'like-minded' and 'like-lifestyle' people because we are all looking for a place to be welcomed and appreciated; a place where we can share who we are without fear of rejection. A temptation is to assume that we have a shared set of values simply because we speak the same language or because our goals looks the same, but looks can be deceptive.

Our desire to feel 'in', to feel 'one of the crowd', to feel 'an insider', or to feel 'on the same page' can even be so strong that we project onto other people the values we want them to have. We ignore the differences and magnify the similarities; we imagine that they are the same as us. We hope that we've found commonality and camaraderie in the journey of life.

The inevitable tensions and disappointments that eventually arise when it becomes clear that we are not as alike as we once hoped, can be managed more easily in a large and diverse community; but when the group we are part of is smaller and the purpose more clearly defined (be it a task group or management team) then the conflict of values becomes much harder to ignore and much more important to address.

> When we don't know what the other team member's values are, or when we don't really understand their preferred way of doing things, it becomes easy to assume the worst, and to judge their motives and attitudes, rather than assume that they are doing the best they can from a different value base.

Often our conflict with others is a conflict of value priority; we may value the same things, yet not to the same *degree*. Or, our conflict may be a conflict of value expression; we may value the same things, but we just 'do it' differently. But when we have a foundation of shared value principles that we agree on right from the beginning, and when we understand each other's personal value needs and each other's preferred way of doing things, we are then in a better position to work the issues through.

I have learnt this truth at real personal cost. Several years ago, a preacher rather enigmatically spoke one Sunday morning, saying, "Beware of people who sound like they are saying the same thing but are in fact saying a different thing. Equally be aware of those who seem to be saying a different thing, but are in fact saying the same thing as you!" My wife and I knew the preacher's words were meant for us, though he didn't know it. We were about to sell our house and move into a new area of the city to begin a project with another couple. We had already spent some time looking at our shared values, but foolishly we had not clarified what those values *meant* to each of us, nor had we clarified which *practices* and *priorities* flowed out of those values.

It became clear over the following year that we were in fact saying different things, despite on the surface, having an apparent unanimity of values. The team never really took root. We had moved our children's schooling, couldn't sell our house, and in the process of trying to convert it and let it into flats, lost £20,000 - all for the sake of a team we assumed we had shared values for.

> Until we have really defined the words we use, and clarified the practices which flow from those values, we can't be sure that the words we share, share the same meaning at all.

The assuming of shared values can occur in any area of life, from marriage to community enterprise, to a business venture to the formation of a small team to starting a new job. It is critical for the long term success of the venture that core values are shared by team members and that they are held at a similar level of priority; that their meanings are understood; and that the way we seek to express those values has a reasonable level of agreement in shared practice. Courtship is the time honoured process for coming to this level of shared understanding. But even in the courtship process, we need to know what we are looking for.

> The courtship process is meant to help us understand the definitions and meanings of the values we each hold as important, and work out whether the values we hold in common and the shared practices which flow from those values are strong enough to hold us together.

The courtship process acts as the precursor to formal partnership in any type of venture. It doesn't need to take forever, but it does need to take place. If we get it wrong, unravelling the tangled web of meanings, misunderstandings and motives is not pleasant. It pays to do values work early. Of course, the presence of conflicting values doesn't mean a partnership can't take place, it just means that you need to weigh up how large the conflict is, and whether your shared values are weighty enough to carry you through. It also means you are going in with your eyes open.

I once worked as a housing support worker for homeless people who suffered from mental health disorders and drug addiction. It was a rewarding job, and I worked with very motivated, selfless colleagues. But I had values conflicts operating on several levels.

I believed my clients needed to be housed in small supported communities, rather than in individual self-contained flats   (*I valued their communal needs* above the 'self contained flat' policy of the organisation). I wanted to work in my own office not an open plan environment where we were all expected to do each other's administration and take each other's phone calls. (*I valued my work space.*) I wanted to give my clients more 'one-on-one' time, but every two months another client was added to my portfolio, and I ended up with too many highly dependent clients (*I valued quality of service* over quantity of those being helped).

As a result, my work environment was stressful. When I was attacked by one of my clients with a baseball bat (thankfully he missed!) it was my cue to leave. It was a symbol of the values conflicts I had been struggling with for two or more years. Had I been more aware of my own values at that time, I might not have taken the job, or I might have been more empowered to raise my concerns more forthrightly and with greater conviction. It pays to do values work early.

Exercise 5:

Choose a context such as your family, work, team or faith community, and list the values which are important to you in that setting. Then describe the practices which flow out of those particular values. Then describe the areas where the people around you do things differently. Assuming the best for these people, imagine what the values might be that motivate these people to do the things they do. Then, if you can do it sensitively, without causing a problem in the relationship, try and explore with them what the value is behind their way of doing xyz. This exercise will give you a better perspective on why things are the way they are for you in that context of your life.

Personal Values and the Values of the Team

When we have a clearly defined set of work or community values which set out what is expected of us, we are helped to know how to integrate with others, and, whether we actually want to integrate with them at all. Knowing our core values and the values of others affects the strength of our sense of place.

When the values of the team are not clearly articulated, personal values come more strongly into play. In a vacuum, our strongest inclinations and motivating values begin to express themselves, whether they are favourable to the organisation or the team or not. If we find that either we or others can't stay, they, or we, are likely to leave unpleasantly. When we leave badly, or when we are not allowed to leave easily - because people won't let go - everyone in the loop is damaged or diminished.

The source of much relational and organisation conflict is the conflict of core values such as: interdependence or independence efficiency or quality, adventure and freedom or safety and security, in addition to the different ways we express those values.

> It is the shared commitment to agreed value principles and the right application of those principles which forms a relational glue enabling conflict to be resolved and understanding to be forged.

Examples of higher value principles in a team setting might be respect, honesty and fairness. Respect requires listening to the honesty of how other people see things and feel things. Honesty requires a courageous, yet appropriate expression of personal feelings, ways of seeing (points of view) and the choice not to be hidden. Without honesty there can be no relationship. The higher value of fairness requires 'just' solutions to honest points of view, but fairness in a situation of conflict cannot be honoured if other principles such as respect and honesty are not also honoured.

Principles may be honoured because they are inherently right, not necessarily because they provide us with immediate benefit - though the benefit will be felt in due course! For example, imagine two people about to jump out of an aeroplane, excited to experience the ultimate exhilaration of freefalling. Adrenalin junkie A says to adrenalin junkie B, "Hey, it's time to put on the chute, bro"! "Not me" says B. "I want to be really free. I don't want to be inhibited in my freestyle. The chute would really get in the way." "Suit yourself, bro!" says A. "See you on the ground."

Of course, we know who is the really free person and the one who is enslaved to death. A harness can be the greatest gift of freedom or a cumbersome infringement on your liberty - it depends on your perspective. A good set of principles can be like a parachute or harness, helping us to enjoy the ride of life and helping to moderate the way we engage with life on the ground!

Commonality-Solidarity-Creativity-Productivity Cycle

When higher values or behavioural principles such as respect, honesty and fairness are recognised within a team, and clear practices are agreed as a way of embodying those values, this creates a *commonality* which then helps to foster team *solidarity* which leads to cohesive team relationships. This encourages an environment of *creativity* because solidarity and team cohesion based on common principles of behaviour provide an environment of safety where creative exploration and problem solving can occur. This enhances *productivity* because work time and energy is focused rather than being dissipated through unproductive conflict. The presence of higher values and the practices which flow from those values also enable an easier parting of the ways, should that be necessary.

> It's the determined and habitual practice of higher values or principles which fosters the sort of unity which creates an atmosphere of freedom, facilitation and fulfilment.

Common Principles of behaviour cultivate an environment of solidarity or team cohesion. Team Cohesion creates a safe environment for the creative exploration of ideas and problem solving. Creativity enhances productive enterprise through reduced conflict, or conflict which is well managed. This can be seen in figure 14.

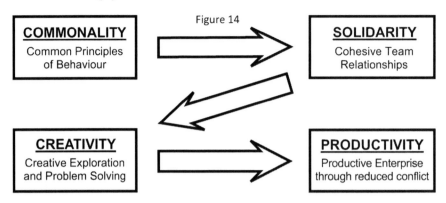

Richard A. Burwell 2010: Commonality-Solidarity- Creativity-Productivity Cycle

Relational conflict threatens self confidence which weakens creative expression and productive energy. Where core personal values are in conflict in a team environment, an appeal to agreed team values and the implementation of higher values, or principles of behaviour enables conflict to be resolved.

Creating a healthy environment where team member values are explored and team values agreed, helps to foster the sort of working relationships and decision making culture which enhances team productivity. When a team or organisation have a clear recognition of higher values which are non-negotiable because they are self-evidently universal, this offers a common bedrock of understanding on the foundation of which further agreement and understanding can be built.

When we recognise that the source of much relational and organisational conflict is the conflict of personal value needs such as risk taking or being cautious, rather than the higher universal values or principles such as fairness and respect, this provides us with a way back into harmony, because the higher universal values are still held in common and can be used to help build understanding.

This process is explored further in the following diagram...

Figure 15

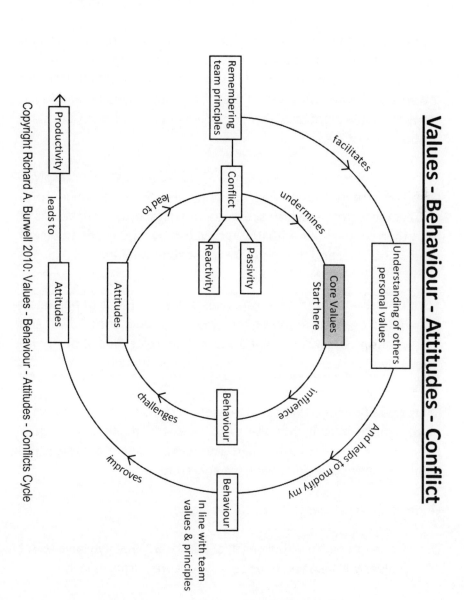

Values - Behaviour - Attitudes - Conflict

Our core personal values influence our behaviour and the behaviour of others. Our core values are also the lens through which we view and appreciate, or fail to appreciate the behaviour of others.

When we fail to understand another's values we are likely to also misunderstand their behaviours, style of working and motives; and this challenges both our attitudes towards them and their attitudes towards us. When an atmosphere of misunderstanding and judgement of motives prevails, conflict is inevitable, and our values are further undermined.

At the point of conflict, we either move into the *passivity* of unresolved unspoken irritation, the *reactivity* of carelessly spoken anger, *or* a courageous *empathy* which seeks to understand the core values of the other person - an empathy motivated by the higher values of respect, honesty and the desire for a just solution (fairness).

> Both passive and reactive responses are expressions of personal power at opposite ends of the spectrum, and both adversely affect our productivity. Empathy is also an expression of personal power which seeks to nurture mutual understanding.

Of course, it may be that the behaviour of fellow team members is quite simply difficult, but the way we challenge their behaviour needs to be moderated through a process which is based on the higher values or principles we have agreed to.

Understanding values is powerful medicine.

The next chapter looks at our sense of purpose. What you have learnt about values will help you to uncover your core purposes in life.

Chapter 3

THE SENSE OF PURPOSE

*This is the true joy in life, the being used for a purpose recognised
by yourself as a mighty one.*
George Bernard Shaw.

*One needs something to believe in, something for which one can
have whole-hearted enthusiasm. One needs to feel that one's life
has meaning, that one is needed in this world.*
Hannah Senesh.

The Purpose of the Ball

When I play golf, I love the moment when I address the ball, facing
it square on, with my club placed strategically an inch away. It's a
moment mixed with anxiety and anticipation. I take a few practice
swings, and then suddenly everything quietens down and I'm in the
zone - all I can see is the ball as it looms large in my consciousness.
I swing and I connect, and for a few brief seconds, I identify myself
with a ball in flight.

Not so lucky was the Scotsman who wanted to demonstrate the new game of golf to US President Ulysses S. Grant. The Scotsman carefully placed the ball on the tee and raised his club heavenward, intending to hit the ball as far as he could. He missed the ball and hit the turf, showering the president with dirt. The ball sat idly, still waiting for the mighty connection. The Scotsman swung again, and again he missed. The President waited through several more attempts and then finally he spoke. "There seems to be a fair amount of exercise in the game, but I fail to see the purpose of the ball!"

The purpose of the ball is a metaphor for life. Often we swing into action, keen to get busy, keen to engage our lives with purpose and make a difference, keen to know - will we fly and how far will we fly? Will we go long and straight or will we miss the mark having hit the turf rather than the ball? Sometimes, it seems that we fail to engage with our purpose fully; sometimes, there is a connection, but our actions are not fully centred on our purpose, and as a result, our lives get skewed to the left or to the right, lost in the long grass waiting to be found again.

For every golfer, the question we ask of the ball as it flies towards its destination is, "Will it land on the green - will it do what it's made to do?" The question of purpose asks the same question of us. Like the ball, the true purpose of our lives is to go long, and fly far, yet the ball may still be waiting for its true purpose to be fulfilled. Our purpose may be lost, waiting to be discovered underneath the soil of previous failed attempts to truly connect.

On other occasions, we find ourselves idle, just standing there, somehow separate from ourselves, looking at our lives, weary from numerous attempts to make the mighty connection, and now not really engaging, not really sure perhaps of what the purpose is. We hold the stick but we are not sure what to do with it, we see the ball, but we are not sure where it is meant to go. A man with a stick may have the potential to swing and hit the ball, but unless he knows that the purpose of the ball is to fly, he is likely to just stand there and wonder; he remains just a man with a stick. The golfer is waiting to emerge; the ball, still waiting to fly.

I googled GOD last week, and got 398 million sites. SEX brought up 618 million sites, RELATIONSHIP gave me 264 million sites. PURPOSE gave me 525 million sites - with a plethora of definitions - so purpose is clearly important! But why? What is purpose, and how can we engage with it? How can we make the all important connection and fly?

In part one of this chapter, we will consider a basic definition of what purpose is, where purpose comes from, and the three different types of purpose we can find. In part two, we will think in more detail about purpose and the related ideas of vision, values and goals. Finally, in part three, we will think about how to discover a stronger sense of purpose for our lives using two mapping tools designed to draw out your core sense of purpose.

But first...

PART ONE

WHAT IS PURPOSE

Purpose addresses the 'what' and the 'who' and the 'why' of our life - whether it's the larger view of our existence on the planet (our core life purpose) or the more localised view of the work that we do (our role specific purpose). Purpose moves beyond the outward activity to reveal the hidden reason and meaning. Purpose explains what I do, who I do it for and why I do it.

Our purpose in life could be a purely hedonistic self-serving purpose, but a purpose which provides the greatest meaning will include a strong element of service towards others. When we seek to have things or people in our life, our focus is on having a difference made to us, whereas a meaningful purpose is more concerned with us making a difference for others in our own unique way. Ultimately, a lasting and meaningful purpose is not about' *having'*, it is about *'being'* the kind of person we want to become and about how this influences the things that we *'do'*.

A purpose which is worthy of our life's potential will touch our emotion, stimulate our reason, stir our imagination and offer us the opportunity for genuine contribution. In other words, a transforming purpose will hold us – body, soul and spirit.

Living from a Sense of Purpose

What is it that grabs you in the morning? What is it that moves you to rise with a ready spirit? It's your purpose! Your purpose is your motivational engine. If you are not grabbed in the morning for self-directed action then you are not living from a sense of purpose - you are living from habitual action only.

It is not easy to live *from* a sense of purpose. The struggle to simply live and perform the daily routine sidetracks us from a more intentional and purposeful way of living. We live on autopilot rather than purposefully piloting; we have 'just a job', rather than finding a purpose within it; we perform the tasks of parenthood in survival mode, rather than seeing before us the great privilege and purpose of being a parent. When we live on autopilot we don't 'take action' - rather we follow a well worn path of habitual action where our heart is not in it. There is a better way to live.

Finding a clear purpose for your life or for the roles and work in your life gives you the courage to live with focus and direction, even in the face of contrary winds seeking to blow you off course. If you have a purpose, you are self-directed, *you* are piloting the plane. You will live each moment with intention and focus, with full consciousness that this is the purpose to your life.

> Your purpose will give you a new perspective on yourself because you will begin to see your contribution differently. Your purpose will define your sense of responsibility; you will begin to see your contribution as necessary. Your sense of purpose will help you to honour your own potential and the relevance of your own contribution. A great sense of purpose will define you.

Everything in life tends towards the route of least resistance, but the route of least resistance is not necessarily the route of greatest reward. We need help to pursue the best when second best is easier to attain. A sense of purpose offers this support.

Living from purpose helps you to press through the pain to win the prize, or to pursue a different prize you had not seen before. Without a sense of purpose you may give up when difficulty obscures the pleasure of the activity; or you might sleepwalk through life, not knowing why you do what you do, nor how it contributes to your greater good, or the good of others.

So, how can we live from a sense of purpose? Living from a sense of purpose requires constant reminders of what motivates us. We need constant reminders because the pressures of our life can cause us to forget the purposes of our life. We need reminders of what we want, what fulfils us, what inspires us, what we are passionate about and what provides us with purpose.

Where does Purpose Come From?

There are two ways you can think about purpose which will help you to further understand the part it plays in your life. The first is to think in terms of a *designated* purpose, and the second is to think in terms of a *discovered* purpose.

i Designated Purpose
Designated purpose is a particularly helpful idea especially if you have a belief in a *higher* meaning to the universe. Designated purpose is a purpose that is *given or offered* to us through a faith system which normally includes three dimensions of responsibility and relationship, operating in three movements.

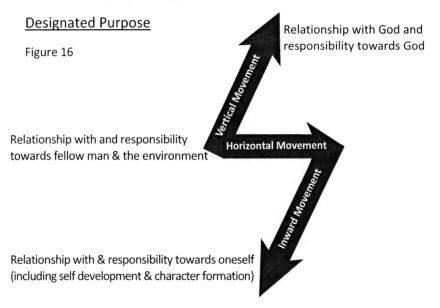

Designated Purpose

Figure 16

Relationship with God and responsibility towards God

Vertical Movement

Horizontal Movement

Inward Movement

Relationship with and responsibility towards fellow man & the environment

Relationship with & responsibility towards oneself (including self development & character formation)

Copyright Richard A. Burwell 2010: Designated Purpose

The vertical movement involves a relationship with and responsibility towards God. *The horizontal movement* involves our relationships with and responsibilities towards our fellow man and creation. *The inward movement* involves our relationship with and responsibility towards our self, especially in terms of self development and character formation.

The belief in a designated purpose leaves plenty of room for the *discovery* of our own unique personal purposes in life. So what is *discovered* purpose?

ii Discovered Purpose

Discovered purpose leads us to explore our unique contributions which are highly motivational and highly meaningful to us, for work, family, local community, faith community and so on. Discovered purpose is related to our abilities, values, interests and an intuitive sense of calling which is hard to put into words. Discovering our own personal sense of purpose is a deep well to dig. It can dawn upon us over a period of time through personal reflection, experimenting with different interests and areas of service, or through moments of sudden insight and revelation.

> We may also be able to articulate an overall sense of purpose which acts like a thread of meaning and motivation woven through every season and context of our life. Such a core sense of personal purpose is greatly empowering and offers us a navigational sense of direction, even when other directions have come to their natural end.

Three Types of Purpose

Within this idea of a purpose to be discovered, it is possible to identify three distinct types of purpose – they are a role specific, season specific and passion-filled purpose. By asking three distinct types of questions, "What are you <u>doing</u> and why?", "What are you <u>learning</u> and why?" and "What do you <u>want</u> to do and why?" we may get an early indication of the type of purpose that operates behind what we are doing, or an indication of the type of purpose we may want to be fulfilling.

Figure 17

Role Specific Purpose	Season Specific Purpose	Passion Filled Purpose
What are you doing and why	What are you learning & why	What do you want to do & why

©Richard A. Burwell 2010: Three types of purpose

I asked myself the question, "What am I doing and why?" some 27 years ago, with particular intensity and desperation. I was working as an X-ray filing attendant at the Leeds chest clinic, and part of my job was to sweep the forecourt in the morning, removing the previous day's rubbish and discarded takeaway cups of coffee, while pedestrians walked by on their way to apparently more purposeful work. It was a 'purpose' question, and it took a while for me to find the answer.

If, on one of those mornings while I held a brush and picked up litter, someone were to have asked me, "Richard, what's your purpose here?" I might have replied, "I haven't the faintest clue, I think I'm lost!" But if they persisted, and asked me again, "What is your purpose here?" I would have answered that my purpose was to sweep the floor *in order that* people were kept safe and the environment would be a happier one. This was my *role specific purpose*. It was not there in the job description when I signed on the dotted line, but it was there to be discovered.

There was another sense of purpose that I discovered while picking litter and filing ancient X-ray reports. This second purpose came as the fruit of some deep searching of soul. It was apparent that my role specific purpose was not meaningful enough to sustain my interest, so I began to ask if there was another purpose I could find in that season of life. In the absence of what I could meaningfully give, I realised that another question I could ask was what could I meaningfully receive? I realised that my purpose was to learn what the season could teach me. My purpose was the *season specific purpose* of what I was learning within it.

Slowly, I gained the insight that my purpose was to learn the importance of service in a culture which dishonours the role of service and menial work.

This insight has enabled me to honour those who toil in menial work knowing that their work does not define them, and that, like me, they have a purpose greater than the work which they do. Knowing what the lesson was, gave me a sense of purpose for that season of my life, and it made the task easier to bear. It gave me the sense that I still had meaningful direction in life, even though the roles and the activities I was engaged in did not seem meaningful in themselves.

What I still hadn't found, however, was an understanding of my _passion- filled purpose_ - the purpose that I was passionate about being fruitful in. This insight was a longer time in coming. Passion-filled purpose or core personal purpose is the insight which holds the most promise for life change and personal fulfilment. It can also be the most elusive to find.

The following story illustrates how we can have several season-specific purposes to our life, and at the same time, a defining passion-filled purpose which integrates all the others.

A father and four sons

A father who had four sons wanted them to understand how the different seasons of life could offer different purposes, and how there was also a core purpose in life which offered the chance to be truly fruitful and fulfilled. So he sent them, in turn, on a quest to visit a rare and beautiful tree in a great and distant land.

The first son visited the tree in the winter. The second son visited the tree in the spring. The third son visited the tree in the summer and the fourth son visited the tree in the autumn. When they had all returned, he gathered them together and asked them to describe what they had discerned to be the purpose of the tree, for each of the seasons in which they had visited.

The first son described how the tree had seemed to lack beauty and how barren the branches were. Then he explained how he saw that the tree was not dead, but that its life was in a state of rest. He began to discern a hidden purpose for the tree in the season he had visited; the season specific purpose for the tree was the *purpose of rest.*

The second son described how the tree was dressed in a canopy of green buds and shoots. He felt that the tree was full of a promise that had not yet found its full expression. He also discerned a hidden purpose for the tree in the season he had visited; it was the *purpose of preparation.*

The third son described how the tree was heavily laden with beautiful, sweet smelling blossoms, and how some of the blossoms seemed to be developing into a fruit he could only imagine was the most satisfying he could ever taste. He also discerned a hidden purpose for the tree in the season he had visited; it was the *purpose of growth* which required patience lest the fruit be picked before its time.

The fourth son described how the tree was ripe with the most luscious fruit he had ever seen. As he looked upon the tree it seemed that the tree was alive with passion and joy in its season of fulfillment. The fourth son also discerned a purpose for the tree which was the purpose all the other seasons had been leading towards. He saw that fruitfulness was its *passion-filled purpose.*

The father said how proud he was that his sons had correctly discerned the purpose of the tree for each of the four seasons of its life - the season specific purposes of rest, preparation, growth and fulfillment - and he explained that ultimately the core purpose for the tree was to bring forth fruit.

The father then encouraged his sons to recognise the many seasons that they would each enter throughout their lives, and most importantly to discern where they most passionately wanted to be fruitful. Their most important task in life would be to find their own passion-filled, core life purpose and to pursue it.

Your Passions are a Sign Post to Your Purpose

Passions relate to what you feel deeply about. They can range from enthusiastic hobbies for your own benefit to areas of altruistic service, and can cover just about any area of interest. Passions in life offer joy, meaning and fulfilment, and may also be a sign post to areas of life purpose; but a passion will not necessarily offer a purpose, or define a purpose for you. However, where a passion intersects with an area of service, you may be looking at a core purpose in life. Passion is related to purpose because where there is purpose there is a heart-felt connection.

> A true purpose in life will be a passion-filled purpose. A true purpose will be a motivating and driving force, energising you to action. There will always be a passion behind a purpose. The area of life where you really want to be fruitful and make a difference indicates the presence of a passion-filled purpose. Passion helps to clarify and define your purpose. To live from a sense of purpose requires reminders of what you are passionate about.

Your passion may serve your purpose

Where a passion is a skill, ability or an area of interest, it is possible that this passion may serve a purpose in life. For example, you might have a passion for clothing and design, but it's what you do with your passion for clothing that determines whether it serves a purpose or not. A purpose implies an area of service for the greater good. So, you may have an emerging concern to alleviate the working conditions of Asian textile workers, and you find that your passion for clothing serves this purpose.

The Great Football Give Away (TGFG) Charity is a great example of a passion for football serving a purpose. The founder, Paul Clarke, and his band of volunteers have now given away thousands of footballs to children in Angola, Malawi, Zambia and Uganda. In a similar way, we could combine our passion for horses or music with our purpose of serving those with learning disabilities, or combine our passion for art with our purpose of serving the elderly in our local community.

Your passion may evolve into a purpose

Your sense of purpose may begin simply as an area of interest, but as you get to know someone personally involved or affected, it may then grow into a concern, and then develop into an issue that you want to address. It may then evolve into a full blown passion to make a difference. Before you know it, your passion may become a purpose directly related to the problem or need or question that you see needs addressing. In this case, your passion becomes your purpose.

Perhaps you don't have a particular interest or hobby like computers or photography that you use to serve others with, but your interest in the environment, for example, evolves into a concern and matures into a passion. This passion for serving the environment becomes your purpose.

How can we know if our purpose is to serve the elderly, or help the unemployed, or to write music to inspire people, or any number of other possibilities? The answer is that a sign post to a purpose is a growing passion in that area. Where we notice within us a passion to serve it is likely that a purpose is beginning to form.

> Some passions can be used to serve our purpose. Some passions become our purpose. Some passions just remain hobbies we are passionate about. But if there is a reason for service behind our passion, there is probably a purpose to be explored.

A passion may emerge out of a trial into a purpose

We are often passionate about areas of life where we have experienced a problem, an injustice, a tragedy or a failure personally and we want to be part of the answer to the problem we see. We know the territory; we have something to say and something to contribute. From the ashes of tragedy, failure or brokenness, our pain may rise like a phoenix, transformed into a passion to be part of the solution, and a new purpose is born.

When you know who or what you are serving with passion, you have probably then found your purpose. Where true purposes have been found, passions have been released. If I'm not passionate about my purpose, the chances are it's not a core life purpose, just a role specific purpose which I am required to fulfil. A true life purpose will be something I am truly passionate about, which energises me and motivates me to make a difference in that direction.

We have already suggested that purpose addresses the *what* and the *who* and the *why* of our life - whether it's the larger view of our existence on the planet (our core life purpose) or the more localised view of the work that we do (our role specific purpose). Purpose also gets beyond the outward activity to reveal the hidden reason. With these thoughts fresh in our mind, now let's think about how vision, values and goals connect with our core purposes in life.

PART TWO

THE SUBTLETIES OF PURPOSE, VISION, VALUES and GOALS

Thinking about what purpose is can be confusing because there seem to be so many different ways of talking about it. Words like 'purpose', 'vision', 'values' and 'goals' are often used within the same sentence almost interchangeably. However, the distinctions between these words, though subtle, are important, and once understood, help us to be clear about what we believe our purpose to be. The following pages explore these distinctions.

Metaphors of the motorway and the building site

A journey is a good metaphor for thinking about our purpose because it draws in the other related elements of goal setting, values and vision quite naturally. Every journey we embark on begins with a purpose which motivates the journey. For example, the statement, "lets drive to the coast and have a day out!" has a purpose within it. We are not simply driving to the coast; we are driving to the coast for a reason.

Every journey has some rules of the road – we could call them principles. For example, keeping within the speed limit concerns the principles of obeying the law and being responsible. Similarly, every journey is influenced by the style, or the way we travel. For instance, do we drive quickly, slowly, forcefully or gently? And do we drive on our own or with others? Our values will determine these things.

Every journey also has some goals to reach on the way to the destination. For example, in planning the journey, we set ourselves goals of rest and refuelling, so that we don't get too tired or run out of petrol before we arrive.

Finally, for every journey we make, we have a vision of what it will be like when we get there. The statement ,"I can't wait until we jump in the sea, eat an ice cream and play ball on the beach," suggests some prior thought about what we want it to be like when we arrive.

So, to summarise the elements found in the journey illustration, purpose sets the direction of your life and is the motivational engine which drives you. Values are the way you drive and the way you do things when you get there. A goal is a milestone of achievement on the way to fulfilling your purpose and attaining your vision. Vision is what you do when you get to your destination.

A building site is another useful metaphor for thinking about purpose, because it also draws in these other dimensions of what it means to fulfil our purpose. Every building has a reason behind it. The architect cannot plan the design adequately without asking the developer what purpose or function the building is to serve. Every builder has some principles and values behind the way he builds; for example, safety may be seen as more important than speed. Every foreman has some plans to follow and some goals to achieve on the way to seeing the building erected.

Every architect has a vision he is working towards in line with the purpose of the building that the developer commissions. Ask an architect what his vision is, and it will be crystal clear. "I see a beautifully designed, elegant, and functional building, which is also the smartest, tallest and safest building in town; I see people admiring it, and the workers who work within it content, in a functional but pleasing place of work."

It may sound like his vision tells him what to build, but actually, the form the building takes (vision) follows the function (purpose) the building is to fulfil. Vision follows purpose as form follows function.

The fulfilment of your purpose will involve the expression of your values, an adherence to your principles, the employment of your abilities, and the attainment of your goals guided by your vision of the best kind of life you could live. We will explore these ideas in a little more detail over the next few pages.

Figure 18

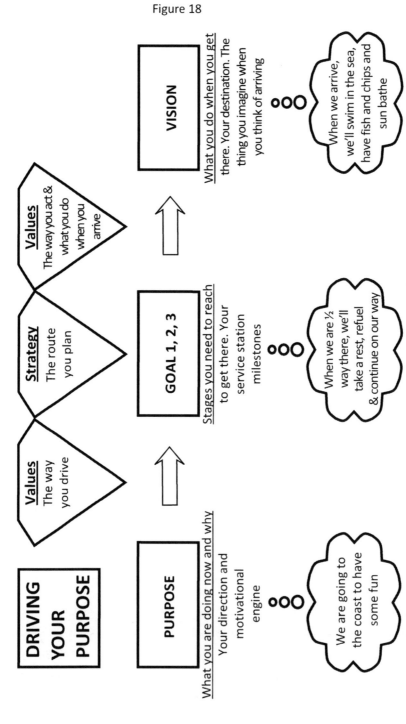

Purpose and Vision

A purpose is a motivating outcome big enough to energise action and perseverance. An outcome answers the question, "What do you want to happen?" and a purpose answers the questions, "Why? What's the reason? What motivates you in this?" A vision answers the question, "What specifically do you want to see?" or, "How do you want it to look?" When an action embodies both passion and direction, it becomes an action with purpose. Without passion, it is an action performed from force of habit with no heart, gradually running out of steam. Without direction, it is an action performed with no focus, quickly missing the point.

A purpose offers the deeper reason behind the action. For example, what might be the purpose of me repairing my son's bicycle? If my purpose were just to restore the bike, it might not be a big enough reason for me to complete the task, especially when other responsibilities compete for my attention, or mechanical problems get in the way. But if my purpose is to restore the bike *so that* he can enjoy riding it again, that may be a big enough reason to motivate me. For a purpose to be a true purpose, it has to have a big enough reason behind it. A purpose gives you a reason.

As I work at restoring his bike *so that* he can enjoy riding it again, I begin to imagine him riding it and a vision begins to form. Now I can see a vision of my purpose fulfilled. I can see my son having a wonderful time on a beautifully restored bike. Now I'm really motivated! Purpose and vision work hand in hand.

For life direction, the questions you ask are really important

There are two main ways people approach the question of life purpose. One is by way of the heart, and the other by way of the head. One question can be phrased, "What do you feel hearted towards?" and the other, "What do you have a vision for?" Both questions are necessary, but getting the order of the questions right is essential. This is because we can conjure up a vision on any subject and imagine how it might look great, and even get really inspired by the vision we see, but if it is not connected to our heart-reason for being, then we may spend our time building towards something that we have no lasting motivation for. On the other hand, we cannot conjure up a purpose in our heart that carries real meaning for us. Our heart motivations are there to be uncovered and discovered, not conjured or created.

> By understanding our purpose, we can begin to define our vision because a true vision extends forward out of a true purpose. Crafting a vision which extends from our purpose helps to keep us on track towards fulfilling our purpose.

If you craft a vision before you know why you are in a particular place, or doing a particular activity, the vision may lead you to build towards something that isn't entirely you. You have to know what track your purpose has set you on first, if your vision is to guide you effectively.

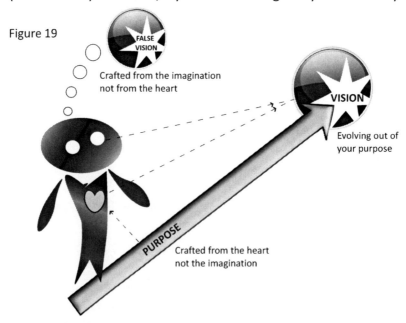

Figure 19

FALSE VISION
Crafted from the imagination not from the heart

VISION
Evolving out of your purpose

PURPOSE
Crafted from the heart not the imagination

Copyright Richard A. Burwell 2010: Crafting a vision out of purpose

> Your purpose is the motivation you carry with you now in the present moment. It is a state of being in the continuous present that holds you to account. It is a present tense *feeling* that keeps you motivated. It is a present tense sense, moving you towards a vision which extends out of your purpose.

Once you know what your purpose is for being somewhere, or doing something, then you can identify where that purpose is taking you and what you want the end result (or vision) of that purpose to look like. You can begin to envision the best possible future extending out of the purpose which you are expressing now. You can take your purpose and project it into the future, imagining what the ideal future will look like when you have fulfilled your purpose. In the example of my son's bicycle, my vision is a happy boy riding his bike with a big smile on his face.

When I start with what's in my heart and what motivates me, I am more likely to end up with a vision that is in harmony with who I am. The vision in my head flows out of the purpose in my heart. If the vision for my life grows out my purpose in life, it is far more likely to be a vision I will attain; it is far more likely to be a vision I will find joy in living towards.

It is worth mentioning at this point, that sometimes we don't know what's in our heart - we may have become disconnected from our own heart motivations. Nevertheless, we may still find ourselves imagining and envisioning the future. If this is the case, it's possible that our visions may be a window into our heart motivations. We should be careful, however, not to run with just any vision, but to test the vision to see if it really flows from the heart. If it doesn't, then ultimately we will not have the heart for it.

Your purpose describes what you do, who you do it for and why you do it, but it doesn't describe the end result that your purpose is moving you towards - that is the realm of vision. For Van Gogh, his purpose was to paint, but his purpose of painting still required a vision of what each individual painting would look like. Van Gough said, "I dream my painting and then I paint my dream." But notice - he already knew that he should be painting. That was his core purpose. The dream or imagination of each painting grew out of the purpose of his life which was to paint.

There must have been many times when Van Gogh's vision of a paint ing did not materialise in the way that he saw from his imagination. These 'failed visions' did not stop him painting however, because the underlying motivating purpose of his life was to paint. He simply dreamed a new vision, extending out from his life purpose of painting.

When your purpose is clear, your vision will begin to form in harmony with it. A pipe dream is a wish (or unformed vision) that hasn't taken root inside you because your purpose may not be clear to you. A purpose will harness you, it will propel you, it will hold you to the vision that you have begun to see.

Vision is a future tense panorama rooted in the direction which purpose has set. Vision is a future tense *seeing* that keeps me inspired. Vision describes the future I see in the best possible terms. Vision covers subjects like reach and reputation, quantity and quality, and can be enhanced by including the details of what I imagine *seeing*, *hearing* and *feeling* in my ideal picture of the future. On a personal note, I have managed to persevere through to the conclu- sion of seeing this book published by combining the motivational engine of purpose rooted in my heart with the inspirational vision of the book in my hand and the hand of others. Seeing it complete and well received has kept me on track towards fulfilling my purpose.

Vision is sight of something in the future yet to happen. It answers the question, '"What will it look like when it's all in place, when I've fulfilled my purpose, achieved my goals and honoured my values?"

Purpose and Values

If a purpose sets the direction you travel in and is also the engine which drives you, and a goal is a milestone, or service station on the way to fulfilling your purpose, and a vision is what you do when you get there, then values can be seen as the *way* you drive on the road to fulfilling your purpose, achieving your goals and attaining your vision. They are also the way you live when you get there.

To expand this idea, your values determine the way you travel through life: fast, slow, within the rules or outside of them, forcefully, gently, conservatively or extravagantly, meanderingly or directly, communally or independently, honestly, responsibly, carefully, creatively, methodically, spontaneously, respectfully, compassionately and so on. Your values are the way you carry yourself - your *personal style.* Your personal values add colour and fragrance to the way you live out your sense of purpose.

> Your core values will be applied in every context of life, but they will find particular freedom and room to flourish where your core purpose is given room to develop.

Your purpose will involve the expression of your core values. A purpose which does not give room for the expression of your values will not be a true purpose for you. Values such as courage, integrity, service, freedom, safety and so on, are not the same as your purpose; they are the *way* you choose to express your purpose and may be a sign post to your purpose.

For example, you may highly value compassion and understanding, and you express these values through listening and find yourself drawn towards the counselling professions. You may highly value knowledge expressed through learning and teaching, and have a passion for empowering the poor, which leads you to teach in the inner city. Where others do it as 'just a job', you may express your purpose through your teaching profession. Or you may highly value courage and justice, expressed through confronting evil and injustice, and find yourself drawn to law enforcement. Your personal values inspire the decisions you make, and may also be windows into your purposes in life.

Your purpose and values together help to define your vision. A vision is a projection of your purpose and values into an ideal future where your values are fully honoured and your purpose fully lived. Purpose and values go hand in hand on the way to defining the vision you are aiming for.

Values not only determine the quality of the journey you are travelling now, they also determine the quality of the vision you are aiming for, because the values you aspire to now, help to determine the fabric of what you see in your vision.

Purpose and the Setting of Goals

> Your sense of purpose is an inner drive that *propels* you forward, whereas a goal is more like a defined objective in the future which *pulls* you towards it. A goal pulls you forward by demanding actions which move you closer to the vision you see. Purpose offers you a sense of meaning; goals offer you a sense of achievement. Goals do not give purpose; instead, goals enhance the motivation that purpose provides.

When you reach the milestone goal of a service station, it's then that you get rested, refuelled, recharged and remotivated to fulfil your purpose and attain your vision. The achievement of a goal keeps your purpose powered. Perhaps one definition of burnout is never reaching your service station goal. If you fail to reach a goal, you may begin to lose heart, because the journey seems to take so long with little sense of making headway and achieving milestones on the way. Your purpose runs out of power.

When we fail to set goals and reach them, we begin to lose heart; we lose connection to the purpose which motivated the journey; we begin to lose the point. When there are no goals to reach, there is no encouragement that our purpose is being fulfilled or that our vision is any nearer to being reached.

> It's really important that we set goals for ourselves which are achievable because achievable goals lead to an attainable vision.

An achievable goal is a SMART goal (specific, measurable, achievable, relevant, and timed), but it is also a value-centred goal. If my goal is not congruent with my values, and not in sympathy with my purpose, several negative results may occur. First, I may become stressed because my values are being ignored. Second, I may become derailed from my purpose, lost to the true point of the journey. And third, I am unlikely to fulfil even the goal I have set, because it is neither supported by my core values, or my true purpose. Setting goals in line with my purpose and in harmony with my values is really important.

A goal is a defined objective to be achieved. It has an end point to reach and is action-oriented. Your purpose motivates you to achieve your goals, and your goals affect your sense of achievement on the journey.

> Goals help to provide a definition to your purpose, a definable way to assess whether you are fulfilling your purpose.

One client I coached began to see the power of goals in the fulfilment of purpose. Here is a transcript of the conversation.

Client: "I feel I've never done enough, I feel there's always something else. I want to get out of what I'm doing because of the daily grind..."

Coach: "What do you want to get out of?"

Client: "Feeling that I'm just finding ways to make it work, to make it manageable in the midst of the chaos. It feels like every day is now until eternity."

Coach: "How much definition does your life have?"

Client: "Not much."

Coach: "What would give you more definition?"

Client: "Having some goals, but I'm reluctant to, because I don't want to make prejudgments about where things are going. I don't want to be so programme driven."

Coach: "What type of goals might help to provide some more definition to your life, without making you feel programme driven?"

Client: "I want to make a difference. So I think it would be good for me to think about where I want to make a difference and what really motivates me."

Goals help to give a sense of definition to the journey we travel, like a service station or signpost on a motorway. The purpose of the journey is to get from A to B, but without some clear and definable goals, a motorway journey would indeed feel like 'now until eternity'. A lack of goals may contribute to a person's lack of definition in life; and the inability to celebrate a milestone achievement when a goal has been reached, may also contribute to the feeling of 'I've never done enough'.

We've spent several pages considering the definitions of these terms. The following table draws out their characteristics.

Figure 20

Purpose vision values goals - Definition of terms

Purpose	Vision	Values	Goals
Why we are here	**Where** we are heading	**Way** we will get there (operational values) **Way** we want it to be (aspirational values)	**What** we will do to get there
Meaning		Manner	
Propels me forward	inspires me	Influence me	pulls me forward
offers a reason	offers a future	offer a meaning	offer achievement
drives me	directs me	guide me	draw me towards them
Intentional	Inspirational	Influential	
offers motivation	offers guidance	influence what I do & the way I do things	demands action
offers a meaningful present	offers a compelling future	offer shape and form	offers challenging objective
is to be lived	is to be attained	are to be expressed & honoured	are to be achieved
I am driven by my purpose	I aspire to my vision	I am shaped by my values	I am challenged by my goals
I live from my purpose	I live towards my vision	I fulfil my values	I achieve my goals
I embrace my purpose	I attain my vision	I acknowledge my values	I achieve my goals
your purpose just is!, its about who you are	your vision maybe, its what may become	your values are to be lived	
holds you steady	lifts you up	listened to	aimed for

Copyright Richard A. Burwell 2010. Purpose vision values goals - definition of terms

The Parable of Metaphorical Man

Having reflected in more detail on the importance of vision, values and goals as they each relate to our sense of purpose, come with me on a journey of the imagination as we meet metaphorical man, and imagine yourself in his shoes...

Metaphorical man is made of metaphors! He has a heart, but it is a metaphorical heart - he calls it his *'purpose'*. It helps him to get out of bed in the morning. He has a pair of eyes, but they are metaphorical eyes - he calls them his *'future vision'*. They help him to see where he is going. He has a mind, but it is a metaphorical mind - he calls it his *'values.'* They help him to make decisions he is comfortable with. He has feet and hands as well of course, but they too are metaphorical - he calls them his *'goal getters'*. They help him do the tasks he has to do in order to fulfil his heart purpose and get where his vision directs him. Life works well for metaphorical man, but it wasn't always the case. On one particularly frustrating week, he began to lose his metaphors...

On the first day, he lost his heart. He managed to drag himself out of bed, but it just felt that whatever he did, his heart wasn't in it. He could see where he thought he should be going, but the passion had just drained away and his vision seemed distant and meaningless. He knew what tasks he had to do but he was bored and couldn't *feel* the point. When he finally got home from a purposeless day, he settled slowly into his arm chair and lost himself in hours of television, watching other people live the adventure he had some-how lost.

The following day felt different. Having found his heart, he jumped out of bed with new purpose energising him into action; he was motivated again. Yet still, something wasn't quite right. This time he had lost his vision! He knew what he was meant to do, he had people to visit and tasks to perform and he was feeling excited about the day, but he had no view of what he wanted it to look like at its best.

He tried to imagine a picture of what his tasks should look like, but it was just foggy and very unclear. He got on with his jobs with his normal energy and purposefulness, but somehow, his lack of vision for how his day could be, failed to inspire him to do his best. He had purpose and meaning, but he had lost inspiration! He also kept bumping into things that he would normally have foreseen on a better day. He began his day enthusiastic and full of purpose, but gradually began to lose heart again, because he just could not see where it was all heading.

On the third day he thought, "That's more like it, now I've got my purpose and I can see where I'm going!" The day began well. He got on with his normal routine and everything was easy, until he was faced with his first big decision. "Oh no!" he thought, "I've lost my mind! I don't know how to make the best decision. My values have gone missing." This time, metaphorical man was purposeful, energetic and had a clear picture of how he wanted his day to look, but he wasn't sure of the best way of getting there. With every decision he made, he felt strangely uneasy, as if he hadn't been true to himself or honoured the things that were important to him. When he finally got home, he couldn't sleep; he hadn't been in harmony with himself or his conscience all day.

The next day arrived and this time, metaphorical man was confident – he'd learned his lessons. Today was going to be a day of purposeful action with a clear sense of where he was heading and what it was all to look like, and with his values guiding his decisions. But it never seemed that he made any progress. Yes, he *was* full of energetic purpose, his heart *was* beating nicely. He *could* see where he wanted to be, his vision *was* clear and he *did* know the values that were important to him and the principles that would guide his decisions, but he simply didn't know where to start. He made a number of attempts to get going, but they didn't seem to work out as well as he hoped. It seemed like the day dragged on forever.

It soon became comically clear to metaphorical man, that he had lost his hands and feet! He was simply unable to engage his energy with useful activity and set any goals to achieve.   In losing his metaphorical hands and feet, he had lost his goal getting ability. He wasn't able to channel his purpose, his values or his vision into any strategic action. He ended his day very frustrated that so little had been achieved!

That night, metaphorical man resolved never to lose his metaphors again. He determined to make sure that he put them on each morning and that he still had them at the end of each day. He knew that he couldn't live to his full potential unless his heart was beating full of *purpose,* his eyes were focussed, with his *vision* clear, his mind was in place with his *values* guiding every decision, and his hands and feet were well connected, fully able to take the *strategic action* necessary to achieve his *goals*.

Exercise 1:
Forward Planning for Tomorrow:

Having read the parable of metaphorical man and seen yourself in his shoes, now try forward planning the day that is coming up for you tomorrow by thinking through the following questions.

What is your purpose for the day? What will you be doing and why?
Answer motivationally; describe the reason and the meaning.

What is your vision for the day? What is its best possible outcome?
Answer inspirationally; describe what you hope to see, hear and feel.

What are your values for this day? How should you like to live?
Describe the main values you hope to be guided by.

What are your goals for this day? What do you want to achieve?
Answer SMART (specific, measurable, achievable, relevant, timed).

You can also use these questions for each main event, activity or meeting that you may have.

When Other Purposes Demand your Allegiance

Many years ago, I worked on a building site as a brickie's mate. My job was to supply the brickie with a constant stream of quality bricks so that he could build well and fast. My role specific purpose was to help in building visually pleasing and architecturally sound houses, so that home dwellers would be content and safe. Similar to my previous role at the Leeds Chest Clinic, this role was not written in the job description, but it was there to be discovered. My role specific purpose was part of the larger purpose of building the new housing estate. When the weather was bad, I was helped to persevere as a brickie's mate when I kept in mind a mental picture or 'vision' of the completed house I was working on. It helped motivate me to do a good job.

These external purposes were not the heart and soul of who I was. They did not define me. I had a stronger, underlying personal purpose which was beginning to emerge beyond that which the job provided. I couldn't articulate it very clearly then, but in essence, it was to motivate and inspire people towards personal growth and spiritual development. It became clearer over time, that I would accomplish this through individual and small group facilitation, teaching, training and coaching. I wanted to facilitate insight and understanding in people, in order that they might be empowered for transformational change.

While I worked on the building site, my *core life purpose* was still finding a way to express itself in the context of my role specific purpose of being a brickie's mate. I was subconsciously looking for opportunities to share insights with people in order that they would be helped in personal development. Of course, this core life purpose was not my job, and it did not need to become my job, in order for it to find an opportunity for expression.

A core life purpose may be to make music which inspires people, or to be an outstanding mentor, or to write poetry and communicate a message through it, or to enter politics or be a fantastic parent, or help young people navigate the rocky road of adolescence, or any one of a thousand purposes which offer you a reason and a meaning and a benefit to others. They *could* become your career, or they could find a release through voluntary means. You may seek to find ways to fulfil a core personal purpose in and through your paid work, but even if you cannot, you will still seek ways to express your deeper meaning and purpose beyond the paid role which may fail to fully define you.

These core personal purposes may also find their full meaning within a faith community or in association with others who share a similar worldview to yourself. If one of your core purposes in life finds an expression in paid work this may provide you with more focus and immediate reward and perhaps, in an ideal world, it may be the best option to be paid for the expression of your core purpose(s). However, it may also be unhelpful, and diminish the natural joy you have in expressing your purpose, by assigning a monetary value to it. We are all unique and we must each find our own way to fulfil our core life purposes.

We each operate within varying families, businesses, clubs, institutions, sports communities or faith communities that also have their own organisational purpose – whether it's clearly defined or not. When we belong to a community or business venture of some kind, this can often help to infuse us with a strong sense of purpose. This external purpose may resonate with us, and cause us to feel part of something important; something that we wish to give our energies to. The venture we join has a purpose which existed before us, and which offers us a home and a meaning. However, sometimes, being involved in someone else's purpose may complicate the process of us finding our own core purposes(s). It doesn't need to, but it may do.

When these organisations or groups are led by a strong or vocal leader, who expects high commitment to the organisation's purpose, but with little opportunity to find our own purpose within the organisations purpose, it may be harder for us to define or discover a purpose which grows from within us, as distinct from a purpose which we align or attach ourselves to. This is especially true if the organisation or group has limited interaction with other groups beyond it; but if the purpose is a big one and the vision large enough, our own personal purpose may more easily find a home there.

It's essential for us to define our own sense of core personal purpose(s) in addition to the purpose and vision of the business we are employed by, or the organisation we are members of, so that we are then able to contribute our own purpose to the purpose of the whole. Or at least so that we are able to live out our own purpose separate from our involvement at work. A key question is, "How can I find ways of fulfilling my own sense of purpose within the wider purpose and vision that I am part of?"

If we don't know what our purpose is, we are likely to become bored and frustrated, but not know why. If we do know what our purpose is, but can't find ways of expressing it in our current settings, then we may need to make some purposeful changes to the way we order our life, in order to make room for our own sense of purpose to flourish. We owe it ourselves and to those our purpose is waiting to serve.

Other people will always shout for their need, or their dream to be first in line. It's too easy to adopt someone else's purpose and vision, while leaving the treasure of our own purpose still hidden, waiting to be discovered. Knowing our own core purposes in life will help us to determine where we should focus our energies.

There are many competing claims to our energy and our ability - this is why it's important that we recognise what our core purposes in life are, and what our personal purpose is in a particular context or season of life. We will want to give our best effort to our main purpose.

Purpose and Potential

In the grand scheme of life, 'calling' comes before capability, 'purpose' comes before potential, 'meaning' comes before means. This is as it should be. If life were determined by your perception of your potential you may miss your purpose by having too low an opinion of yourself. A nine year old who 'feels the call' to be a doctor doesn't consider her capability first, and the boy who feels called to build aeroplanes doesn't weigh his sense of potential first. Rather, they both sense their innate purpose, and their potential grows with every year that follows, in the space their sense of purpose provides.

> If you focus first on what you think you can do, you may miss the very thing your heart aspires to do. When a sense of your purpose comes first, you are *called up* to fulfil what you see; you step up to the plate, you take your place and in doing so find the means. Your potential is found in the fulfilment of your purpose. Your potential is for a reason. Your potential is for your purpose.

Our potential may inform what our purpose is, but it does not need to define it. We should look at our purpose first, lest a poor view of our potential limit the purpose we see for our lives. When we see a grand purpose for our lives, our potential will grow in the space it provides. If you are possessed of a great purpose you will go out of your way to grow your potential. Your sense of potential grows within the grandeur of the purpose you feel.

Being a father or a mother is a case in point. If I feel the grandeur of the purpose that being a father can offer to me, then my potential to be a great father is likely to grow in proportion to the sense of purpose I feel. If my sense of purpose in being a father is obscured by self interest, then my potential is unlikely to grow any larger. The principle of the goldfish in the goldfish bowl will come into effect. The fish (potential) will grow only as large as the space which the bowl (purpose) provides.   Our potential only needs to be as large as the purpose it serves. The bigger the purpose the bigger the potential required to fulfil it. A great sense of purpose will grow within you a great sense of potential.

When your Purpose Feels Tired and you are Losing Heart

There are times in life when our purpose becomes tired and we seem to miss the point and lose heart. Our initial motivations no longer inspire us, and we lose connection to our reason why. It may be that we no longer have passion for the work we do, or the purpose that once inspired us now fails to fire us; the passion we had for our purpose is in danger of being lost.

Purpose is action and motivation (reason) combined, driving us forward towards our goal. But what happens when we drive ourselves forward, even when we've lost touch with our reason why?

In times of tired purpose, the danger of burnout is very real and hard to recover from. Our career, hobby or voluntary work seems pointless, meaningless and joyless; we end up purposeless, passionless, compassionless, weary, hopeless and energy-less. So what can we do to keep our purpose well-oiled and fully fuelled, and prevent the onset of burnout?

Reflect Regularly on your Purpose

Check the passion (fuel) gauge
It is possible to become so engrossed in the activity of driving our purpose forward, that we simply forget to check the passion gauge and before we know it, we've run dry and run down. It makes sense to check the passion gauge every so often, because, like an engine without petrol, purpose without passion cannot spark the engine. When we run the tank low on fuel, the engine fires off poor quality petrol. Driving the engine low on the dregs is no way to drive; driving our purpose low on passion is no way to live. Low passion

leads to tired purpose leads to poor performance. However, we can refuel our purpose with passion by having a clear vision of the way we dream things can be.

It is also possible that we may still have passion for our purpose, but *the way we express* our purpose and the *specific activities* we engage in may not energise us in the way they once did. By remaining open to better ways of doing something, we keep our experience fresh. Don't assume that what you are doing, or the way you are doing it, is the best way to fulfil your purpose. There may be other ways. Find ways of expressing your purpose which energise you.

<u>Check the values (oil) gauge</u>
Is your current way of expressing your purpose fulfilling your values? Have you begun to take on new activities which, though designed to fulfil your purpose, are not really in alignment with some of your core values? What could you do differently, that would still keep you on track with your purpose, but enable you to stay in tune with your values?

<u>Set achievable goals</u>
When we set achievable goals, we are motivated and encouraged to keep going because we believe we can make it - the next goal is not too far away. When we set achievable goals, our journey to the attainment of our vision is divided into manageable bite-sized portions.

When we don't set goals which are achievable, or when we simply don't set goals, we then have little in the short to medium term which motivates us, or which encourages us to keep going. The result is that our journey seems endless, with no chance for celebration, achievement or rest.

Eventually, we lose heart, lose the point, get lost or break down. Consider how your strategy and the individual tasks which make up your strategy are moving you closer to achieving your goals and fulfilling your purpose, and how motivating those goals are.

Celebrate success, and rest on the foundation it provides

When we reach an achievable goal, we are able to celebrate our success and take a brief moment of rest. Being able to celebrate the success of the past enables us to rest on the foundation of what has already been achieved. When we don't celebrate our success, however small, we drive ourselves forward like a workaholic, straining for the next achievement, but never really recognising it when it comes, because we don't give ourselves the opportunity to enjoy it.

When we celebrate our achievements, taking appropriate moments of rest, or sabbath, we allow ourselves to look back and say thank you for the good of what has already occurred. An appropriate level of self congratulation is healthy psychology. Also, an appropriate level of self discipline reigns in runaway perfectionism and insists on us resting, even though we may not feel that what we have done is good enough.

Refuel the heart with renewed vision

Life sometimes has a tendency to knock the wind out of our sails. In these moments we can begin to lose a sense of purpose. This is because purpose is *within* us and may be knocked out of us. Vision, however, is not in us, it is *before* us, and an inspiring vision can be used to reignite our passion and refuel our purpose, so long as it is in harmony with our deep motivations.

It is in the moments of foggy purpose that a clearly defined vision can help to keep us on track. The vision is less affected by circumstance than our sense of purpose is. So by keeping our vision before us, vision may help to re-energise and re-awaken our purpose.

> Purpose will drive you, energise you and motivate you. Vision will inspire you and guide you, but it is purpose which powers you forward, pushing you past the hurdles and obstacles which confront you each and every day.

When you recognise you are beginning to lose a sense of purpose, it's then that you need to look again, to see again, and to envision what you want your life to look like.   Purpose is then re-awakened, motivation rekindled.

Embrace the future with faith

When we embrace the future with faith, as opposed to fearing the unknown and expending the energy of anxiety on the fear of what may never be, we are more open to new possibilities, new ways of working and indeed, new purposes for our life.

A fear of the unknown can hinder us from ceasing the old activity which has lost its purpose and prevent us from finding a new purpose which offers new meaning. The antidote is trust, and a belief that there is indeed a new point and purpose to our life which is waiting to be discovered - trust that we have a unique contribution to make in a new area of service.

The final section of this chapter will help to clarify how we can keep our purpose healthy; which purpose to have a rest from or let go of; in which ways our present purposes may be evolving into something new, and how to clarify what our core life purposes actually are.

PART THREE

DISCOVERING A SENSE OF PERSONAL PURPOSE

There are some people who just seem to know what they have always wanted to do, or were meant to do. A sense of self direction seems to emanate from them; purpose has always seemed clear to them. They are probably in the minority.

> For many, a purpose will dawn on our heart in incremental stages, almost like the process of waking up. It's not clear at first, the feeling is groggy and the vision unclear. We are not fully conscious to what it is or the implications it will have upon us. Like early morning consciousness, we have to let it emerge.

Personal purpose is something we may recognise in hindsight, as we observe the patterns of our life choices and the things which have brought us meaning and a sense of significance. Personal purpose is something we grow into rather than grasp upon. However, there are questions we can ask which can help to facilitate the emergent awareness of a personal core purpose in life.

The remaining pages of this chapter will lead you through a series of reflective questions, designed to help you navigate this process of discovery and reflect on the patterns, choices, feelings and experiences which may point you in the direction of your purpose. We will begin with the 'Kairos Compass' and conclude with a multi-dimensional mapping tool.

As with the exercises in previous chapters, I encourage you to use a journal as you work your way through the questions. Insight which is journalled is more effectively rooted in our life. A journal is the interface between conscious and subconscious thought, creating the springboard for more effective and congruent action.

The Kairos Compass: Gaining Perspectives on your Purpose

The Ancient Greeks had two words for time. The first was *chronos*, the second was *kairos*. *Chronos* refers to time which is in sequence, hence the word 'chronological' which we use today. *Kairos*, on the other hand, refers to the right or opportune time, that is, a moment of time in the flow of chronological time in which something important or significant happens. A *kairos* moment can be missed or fulfilled.

Our purpose(s) in life has a *kairos* quality to it. Just like a *kairos* moment, we fulfill our purpose within the flow of chronological time, and like a *kairos* moment, our purpose can be missed or fulfilled. When we fulfill our purpose, something special happens.

Figure 21

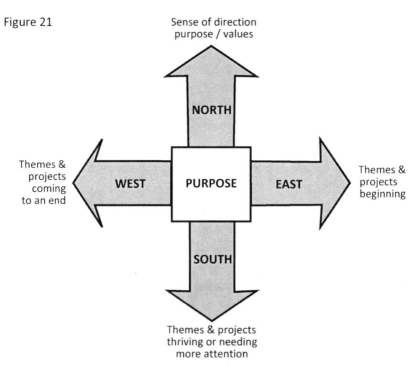

Copyright Richard A. Burwell 2010: The Kairos Compass
Adapted from 'Windows of Your Life' By David Runcorn Spirituality Workbook p117

Using your journal, answer the following questions. It may help to choose a work context, or just your life in general. Some questions will resonate with you more strongly than others.

Looking to your True North

What are your true north values? What gives you the clearest sense of direction? What gives you a strong sense of purpose? What keeps you on track? What are you certain of? What is so utterly important to you that you need to give your attention to? What do you return to when you feel unstable or lost or directionless? What are the past and present themes of your life which still hold meaning for you?

Looking to the West

What is coming to the end of its day in your life? Which themes of your life no longer hold the meaning they once did? Is this because the season is changing, or because you haven't given them the attention they required? Which projects have you been working on, but now want to move on from? Which aspects of your community and work involvement no longer offer the meaning they once did? What should you be thankful for, but let go of? What should you have a temporary rest from in order to engage more meaningfully with later?

Looking to the South

As you look south, what is growing in your life? Which areas offer room for development? Which opportunities in life and work are developing well that you want to give more attention to? What are the elements of your life that keep you feeling nurtured and significant? Is there anything dying that you want to keep alive and well watered?

Looking to the East

As you look out at the dawn of a new day in your life, what do you want to prepare for? What do you want to welcome? What do you have a faint whispering of that you need to tune into? What do you *need* to welcome? What would it take for this necessity to become a desire? What can you begin to see on the horizon, even if it's not very clear to you yet? What do you hope is coming, but haven't yet dared to dream for?

Now draw together the themes which are clear to you from your answers to the previous questions. What do you notice?

Discovering your Core Purposes Multi-dimensionally

Traditionally, psychology has studied three aspects of the mind related to our ability to think, feel and act. These are cognition, affection and conation/volition. The term cognition was originally used to refer to the intellect in terms of what we know, process, understand, file away and retrieve, but it now has a more expanded use.[23]   Intuition is also a faculty of the mind or soul, and is the ability to perceive something without the use of rational thought. [24] The term affection describes our feelings and emotions; the term volition describes our freedom of choice or the will to act and conation describes our sense of self direction connected to and influenced by our thoughts, feelings, intuitions and actions.[25] The chief question in the study of personal conation is 'why?' addressing issues of personal intention, motivation and self direction.

However, research into these faculties has tended not to pursue the affective, conative and intuitive dimensions of mind as much as the cognitive. In this respect, E.R. Hilgard has observed that,

> "Cognitive psychology is ascendant at present, with a con-current decline of emphasis upon the affective-conative dimensions...In the process, some dynamic features such as drives, incentive, motivation and curiosity have been more or less forgotten." [26]

As a result of this over-emphasis on the cognitive function, less is known about the way the other functions influence us, and this has meant that the way we talk about a sense of purpose in life has been reduced to a more popular, less rigorous form of speech. But the Google search on 'purpose' which I referred to earlier, reveals just how important the sense of purpose in life is.

By looking at our action/behaviour, our rational thought, our emotional feelings and our intuitions (non-rational thought), we can ask the question 'why?' and find the hidden purpose which motivates us and which offers us a sense of self direction. Conation and volition are closely entwined. If conation is the 'why?' behind the action, then volition is the will to act based on the 'why'.

Our sense of purpose is exactly this – it is a *sense*; it is hard to measure. It is a deep instinctive knowing that is discerned through a combination of signs, impressions and reflections which are informed by our reason, affection, intuition and action, but which cannot be solely identified with any one of them.

What we _think_ about our life, what we _feel_ about our life, what we _intuit_ about our life and what we _will_ or choose to do with our life and abilities and what we actually do, all influence our sense of personal purpose. In the journey towards a stronger sense of personal purpose, our thought processes (cognition), will touch our *reason* (rational thinking), our *affection* (feeling), our *intuition* (non-rational thinking), and our *volition* (willing) leading to *action*.

Our reason helps us to judge, compare and evaluate information, facts and experience. Our affection helps us to interpret our emotions and attachments to everything, in particular, our passions, our pains and our pleasures in life. Our intuition helps us to know things instinctively through non-rational thought, by dreams, visions and hunches, often using the imagination. Our volition involves our intentions, decisions, choices and actions, and relates to the question what *will* I do and what *do* I do with my abilities, time, resources and opportunities?

By reflecting on our thoughts, feelings, dreams and actions, we will create a multi-dimensional map which signposts the purposes we are moved to fulfil. Together these four areas become a sign post to our personal purposes in life. With these thoughts in mind, please create four headings in your transformational journal, and answer the questions associated with the following diagram.

MULTI DIMENSIONAL MAPPING TOOL FOR FINDING YOUR CORE PURPOSES IN LIFE

Copyright - Richard A. Burwell 2010: Mapping Tool for Core Life Purpose

Diagram:

- Doing — Action
- Non rational Thinking — Intuition
- Purpose (Conation) — The why? Behind the what? Inc volition - the will to action
- Thinking — Reason
- Feeling — Affection

A core life purpose will engage your affection moving you emotionally; it will engage your reason stirring you intellectually; it will engage your intuition inspiring your dreams, it will engage your volition moving you to action. A core purpose in life will touch your emotion, stimulate your reason, stir your imagination and offer you the opportunity for genuine contribution. A transforming purpose will hold you – body, soul and spirit.

Doing (Action)

Which responsibilities, activities or abilities give you a sense of significance, fulfilment, and meaningful contribution? Answer separately for each word if this helps.

What do you really value doing? Why?

Describe the sense of purpose and meaning you feel in these responsibilities activities and abilities.

Answer the above questions for times in the past in blocks of 5 or 10 years

If you didn't have to work for money & you could have any ability, what contribution would you make? What have you always wanted to do?

What do you think is expected of you by others? Does this represent the real you connected to your true sense of purpose? If this isn't the real you, what might it be?

What do you expect of yourself? Does this represent the real you, or is it a false self?

If you were fully connected to your purpose, using your abilities, time & resources in the most fulfilling way possible, what would you be doing?

When are you at your best? What are you doing? What meaning do you find in this? When have you been at your best?

If you found that you had 6-12 months left to live, what would you do with your life and time?

Thinking (Reason)

What thoughts do you find yourself coming back to time and again?

Which subjects stir your intellectual interest?

What unfulfilled ideas do you find yourself thinking about in restful moments?

What do you enjoy learning about?

During difficult times what have been the ideas and themes which have focused your mind helping you to persevere through the difficulty? Why?

When you think about your purpose, what do you think is the natural and logical core purpose for your life, given what you already know about yourself?

What rationalisations do you put in the way of you fulfilling the purpose(s) which are in your heart to fulfil?

How would you feel if those reasons against fulfilling your purpose were removed? If there was no obstacle hindering you?

What would you then do? What are the core values here that could be applied in other areas of life?

Non rational Thinking (Intuition)

Don't think too deeply about these questions, go with your 1st response.

What inspires you and draws you into another version of your life?

What hopes and dreams did you once have which you have let go of? Think back in blocks of 5 or 10 years.

In reflective moments what do you dream of doing? When you day dream what comes to mind?

Imagine a future where you could do any work you wanted. What would you do and why? What skills would you have and why?

If you were guaranteed to succeed what grand dream would you dream? Who are you helping, benefiting?

What are you actually doing, saying in these dreams and visions? Who are you helping, benefiting?

What is it about these dreams that inspires you? What do they give you?

If you imagine doing heroic things what are they? How would you like to be remembered? What legacy would you like to leave?

What are the key themes in these 'flights of fancy' which contain elements of truth about who you are and what you want to do?

What do you secretly think may be your true purpose(s), which you have never shared with anyone?

Feeling (Affection)

Which subjects and areas of life stir strong passion within you? What do you get heated about?

What gains your emotional involvement?

What do you feel is missing in your life? Be specific.

At work what motivates you? With friends what motivates you? On your own, what motivates you?

What do you not enjoy doing? What's the opposite of that for you? What do you enjoy doing? Why?

In the present, think about times when you are happiest, when are you most content, when you are most motivated / energised. What are you doing? Describe the sense of purpose, meaning and significance you feel in these moments.

Answer the above question for times in the past in blocks of 5 or 10 years.

Have you been affected by injustice, major disappointment, crises, or personal brokenness? As you think about these times, could one of these be an area where you want to make a difference, to be part of the solution? Could a passion be stirring within you in this area? Could you find a purpose here?

If you were given the chance of a lifetime what would it be?

Having answered the questions in figure 22, and using your transformational journal, please answer the questions below:

In reference to the questions on rational thinking how would you begin to describe your purpose?
In reference to the questions on intuitive dreaming how would you begin to describe your purpose?
In reference to the questions on affective feeling how would you begin to describe your purpose?
In reference to the questions on active doing how would you begin to describe your purpose?

PULLING IT ALL TOGETHER:

Looking at all the key activities, roles, responsibilities themes, feelings, hopes and dreams, which you have recognised as you have completed the 'Kairos Compass' and the 'Multi Dimensional Mapping tool', which words, phrases, pictures and sentences stand out for you most strongly? List them in your journal.

Comparing all these words and phrases how would you describe your core sense of life purpose or the various senses of purpose which are important to you? Refer back to your list of core values from Chapter 2, and see how they dovetail with your developing sense of purpose. Let your core values inform and shape the way you begin to define your sense of purpose.

Write a Purpose Statement:

Finally, write a 'core purpose statement' for yourself, like a job description, which you would find meaningful and significant. This will be a job description that 'calls you up' to the fulfilment of it; one that inspires you and motivates you to be more and to be the best you can be. You can write one core 'purpose description' for your life, or several 'purpose descriptions' for various areas of your life. Make sure that you write your purpose statement with the _personal_ pronoun, '_I_', in the _present_ tense, '_I am_', and make sure it is _positively_ worded.

The power of a personal, positive and present tense description is that it empowers you _now_. Your subconscious mind hears the present tense statement and says to itself, "OK, if that's who I am, then I am going to be it!" When the subconscious hears a future tense statement like "I will be, or I intend to be", or "I want to..." it feels like the perpetual carrot on the end of the stick, always visible but never quite in reach. The future tense intention mocks you rather than empowering you. To say, "I intend to be loving," subconsciously means "I'm not loving now," and it's almost okay if I'm not. It lets you off the hook!

It is your 'present tense _now_ identity statement' which is the empowering identity! When I say, "I am," my subconscious begins to feel it and believe it, even if my rational mind argues against it. The present tense, positive "I am,"' statement is not a lie, it is a command that the subconscious must respond to. If my purpose statement says, "I want to inspire people," what my subconscious hears is, "I want" and all I have done is reinforce my desire. If, on the other hand, my purpose statement says "I inspire people," then my subconscious hears the embedded command "inspire people!" and then I begin to do what I want to do.

What you write now concerning your sense of purpose will be an empowering statement, but it may not be the last word on the subject. The discovery of purpose is a process; it is like a journey or quest to be embarked on, not a project to be completed. There are layers of depth to who you are and what you are capable of doing and achieving, and what you feel called to fulfil. I encourage you to live with the insights you have gained in this chapter for several weeks or months. Notice how they settle within you, or if they don't. What you notice during this time of reflection will be further information which will help you to discern the various purposes you feel to be important to you.

Chapter 4

THE SENSE OF POTENTIAL

If I were to wish for anything, I should not wish for wealth and power, but for the passionate sense of the potential, for the eye which, ever young and ardent, sees the possible. What wine is so sparkling, so fragrant, so intoxicating, as possibility.
Søren Kierkegaard, Diapsalmata.

Experimenting with your Potential

I remember my school science experiments measuring potential. They involved weights of varying shapes and sizes suspended from differing heights, and coiled springs waiting for expansion. The experiments were all designed to measure the potential energy waiting to be released. The potential was in there, in the object, it was just waiting for permission for the experiment to begin; waiting for the experimenter to exercise belief that something would happen.

In a similar way, your personal potential is your *possibility for growth, waiting to be exercised.* Your personal potential is waiting for the experimenter (you) to let the experiment begin; to exercise belief that something great will happen; to exercise belief that there is greatness within you waiting to find its opportunity.

The Parable of 'Sense of Potential'

Imagine with me, a speedboat race. You are one of the pilots and your boat is called 'Sense of Potential'. You arrive early and find that you are first on the lake. The water is calm, the sun shining and the crowds cheering. You begin to feel that your boat is aptly named. You feel a surge of optimism, and you believe that you can win this race.

One by one the competition arrives in their loud and exciting boats. You notice the flashy names painted with bright and flamboyant colours. You see the customised foils and the go faster stripes, but you are not deterred. You maintain a sense of your own possibility, knowing that winning the race is not just a matter of the size of the engine; it's the potential of the pilot to do extraordinary things that will ultimately count.

As the boats arrive, a whisper is heard among the crowd, and all heads turn to see the latest arrival, 'No Comparison'. Everyone seems to agree - if looks are what you win by, this will be the one to beat. But as the other pilots turn their gaze away, preparing for the race ahead, the pilot of 'No Comparison' also begins to look around at the competition, and begins to wonder...

Suddenly, the starting pistol fires and engines roar. The innate capacity of every boat is given an opportunity to prove itself. You were first on the starting line and now you are first to speed away. Your senses are fully focussed on the capacity of your boat and your potential to get the most out of her. Though you may not be the best pilot, you haven't put a ceiling on your potential to win the race. You know that you will do your best.

At first, all eyes are on the boats as they accelerate down the lake, but then the crowd begins to notice just one boat remaining on the starting line. It's 'No Comparison'! The crowd begin to talk among themselves, "What went wrong? It was the fastest boat on the lake. There should have been no comparison." But now the boat is idle, gripped by a strange inertia.

When the pilot is asked, "What happened?" he explains that as the boats began to arrive, his sense of potential drained away in the face of all the unfavourable comparisons that he began to make between their boats and his. The more he made, the more he became preoccupied with the power of the other boats around him, and he lost sight of the potential he once felt for his own opportunity to win. The pistol fired, but he couldn't move. As he lost his sense of potential, he lost his ability to act.

Meanwhile, the other boats speed down the lake. The pilots are determined to fully exercise the potential of their boats and to be the best they can be. After several laps, two boats pull away from the others. In the lead is 'Past Results', closely followed by 'Sense of Potential'.

'Past Results' is truly an outstanding boat, with many medals to her name. The pilot has many years experience and has been in this sort of position before. He still has more potential to explore, but now in the lead, he begins to wonder whether his boat has reached her capacity, and indeed whether he has too. His mind begins to wander as he thinks about the results he has already achieved. He rests on the success of the past, rather than reaching out for the reserves of potential he still must take hold of if this race is to be won.

You, however, have little experience but your self belief is strong. As you see the finish line approaching, you reach for reserves of capacity in your boat and for the courage to go faster. You navigate the bend at high speed. As each second of the race passes, you find that your own sense of potential to win has increased.

In the heat of the race, you reach into the realms of the possible, pushing at its boundaries, believing for more, almost reaching past the possible, hoping to perform even better than you can dare to believe. This is the meaning of your name 'Sense of Potential'. You don't know whether your boat has more or less capacity than 'Past Results', you don't know whether the other pilot has more ability than you to drive better, but what you do have is a belief in your own possibility to win - you have a sense of potential - you have a sense of the possible, and it is this sense of the possible which enables you to outperform the other competitors.

In a moment, you are head to head with 'Past Results', but *you* have the momentum and you speed past the finish line first. Your 'sense of potential' is fully realised and the crowd erupts in wild applause. In your name, they see their own potential to succeed.

Capacity and Potential - Definitions

In the story, the pilots trusted in different aspects of what they brought to the race. 'No Comparison' and 'Past Results' both focussed on their previous experiences and abilities and in their engine capacities, but the pilot of 'Sense of Potential' trusted in his innate possibility to win. For him, the result was open-ended; it was not predetermined by the greater capacities of the other boats, or the abilities of the other pilots. For him, his sense of potential had priority over all other considerations. It was more than simply believing he had capacity - he believed that he had the potential to fully use his capacity, and without that self belief, he would have failed to do so. He knew the difference between capacity and potential.

Capacity and potential can be confused, and though similar in concept, the difference is subtle and yet profound. The Oxford Concise Dictionary states that potential is 'the possibility of *something* coming into being' and capacity is 'the maximum amount of *something* that can be contained or produced.' *(Italics mine.)*

Both personal capacity and personal potential are concerned with development, but they look at development from different ends of a development scale. Potential begins at the beginning and sees the opportunity of growth; it sees the possibility of something good happening; it looks ahead and sees the possibility of something coming into being.

Personal potential is an open ended concept. It raises my expectation of what is possible and lends itself more easily to the important area of self belief. Capacity sees development from the perspective of the maximum limit that can be reached. It is a closed concept and, without a strong sense of potential, may cause me to limit my expectation of what is possible.

The story of the speed boat race illustrates that there will always be someone with more capability and capacity than me or you - this is the unavoidable reality of life's inequality. But ultimately, the amount of our capacity and the extent of our capability is not the determining factor in how much we achieve. Rather, it's what we believe is possible that ultimately determines what we pursue and therefore, what we achieve. Additionally, the capacities of the boats were fixed, but in life, we have the possibility of increasing our capacity by adding more capability as we update ourselves with new experiences, new knowledge, and new skills.

The level of our sense of potential will determine two things. First, the degree to which we use our full capacity, and second, the degree to which we expand our capacity by adding to our ability.

> If I think of my capacity alone, I may put a limit on what I can achieve. If I think of my potential alone, I may place unrealistic expectations on what I can achieve. When I think about my capability in addition to my sense of potential, I add in the raw material that potential uses to reach my capacity.

The more capability I add to my life, the more my capacity seems to grow and the greater my sense of potential seems to become. A virtuous circle of self development is formed which begins with my sense of potential. If I can only see the limits of my capacity and capability, I will need to grow in the self belief that a sense of potential offers. When I see only my potential, but lack the ability to realise it, I may need to grow in my capability by adding new experiences, knowledge and skills that give legs to my potential.

In the challenge of life, I want to think about my possibility not my maximum amount of capability. Capacity puts a cap on my ability, whereas potential opens the door to possibility, or lifts the lid on what can be achieved. When I start with possibility I am encouraged to begin the journey of personal development, achievement and service.

Applying these ideas to the world of personal development, we can say that we do have the capacity to develop and improve, and yet the important issue is not *how much capacity*, but rather how much of a *sense of potential* to develop our capacity do we have?

When the famous Cellist, Pablo Casals reached 93, a reporter asked him, "Why do you still practice three hours a day?" He replied, "Because I notice myself getting better." [27] He saw his potential to improve, and he believed that he still had the possibility of adding to his capability.

The question of our sense of potential is a question of how much do I believe in my inherent possibility to grow? My sense of potential is an aspect of my self belief, and it is far more important than how much capacity I actually have.

Potential is a universal principle found in everything - whether it's the potential of a chemical or nuclear reaction, the potential of a seed, latent with the possibilities of growth, or a new born baby, primed with the potential to develop into someone who brings great benefit to their world. Everything has the *potential* to develop in some way. There simply needs to be an *activating agent* like gravity, water or nutrients.

> The activating agent in personal development is self belief. It's the *sense* of your potential which turns the potential lying dormant within you into energy awakened, ready to be released through you.

Sense of Potential and Self Efficacy

In 1977, Psychologist Professor Albert Bandura published his seminal paper: "Self-efficacy: Toward a Unifying Theory of Behavioural Change." Since the publication of this paper, the subject of 'self efficacy' has become one of the most important subjects amongst psychologists. He writes,

> 'Perceived self-efficacy refers to beliefs in one's capabilities to organise and execute the courses of action required to manage prospective situations.' [28]

In other words, self-efficacy is the belief in one's capabilities to succeed. What Albert Bandura refers to as self efficacy and self belief, I am referring to as the sense of our potential to fully explore our capacity, and to see our capabilities come into being. Speaking of his concept of self efficacy, Bandura writes,

> 'People's level of motivation, affective states, and actions are based *more on what they believe* than on what is objectively true.' [29] (Italics mine).

This is a profound insight. What we believe is possible significantly affects what we are able to do. Self belief has just as much bearing on what we are able to accomplish as our abilities have. Without a sense of your potential, the possibility of your capacity being fully activated is much reduced.

> We could say that our self belief is the measure of our actions and behaviours more than our abilities are. Our identity determines our behaviour! It is almost accurate to say, "If I believe I can, I can, and if I believe I can't, I can't." In this respect, King Solomon said, "As a man thinks in his soul, so is he." [30]

If we take two people with exactly the same physical and intellectual capacities, they may have very different senses of potential. The one with a higher sense of potential will go on to achieve far more than the other person. The person with a weak sense of potential is more likely to experience inertia; the person with a stronger sense of potential is more likely to take action.

When our sense of potential is weak, we simply lack the self belief to activate the capacities we possess. When we suffer from a low sense of our potential, we withhold our talent through lack of self belief. Not only do others miss out on what we have to offer, but we miss out on the joy of expressing our gift.

Your potential for growth can be applied in any area of life, such as sport, business, art, writing, speaking, listening, understanding, and so on. The important thing is not so much whether you have natural ability or high or low capacity in any of these areas, but whether you apply your sense of potential with decisive action.

The application of a sense of potential will always take you further than you have gone before. The application of your self efficacy will lead to self actualisation; it will lead to a fulfilment of who you are and what you are capable of becoming. That you have capacity and potential is without question. The question is how much of a *sense* of potential do you possess, and are you applying it with action?

The Wrong Sort of Comparisons create a Low Sense of Potential

Sometimes, we lose connection with the sense of our own possibilities because we fail to use our talents and abilities sufficiently, and thereby, we forget what we *can* do. Sometimes it happens in the absence of encouragement, and we begin to wonder if what we *have* done has really made a difference. But perhaps more than any other reason, it's because we compare ourselves to other people. The pilot of 'No Comparison' was a victim of this sort of mistake.

> The temptation to compare ourselves with others starts out as an attempt to encourage ourselves. The motive feels right, but the result is all wrong! Whether we are the winner or the loser in the comparison, we lose our sense of potential every time.

When we compare ourselves with others and come out on top (an arrogant comparison), we then have no incentive to grow or develop any further. We lose a sense of our potential to grow, because we don't feel that we need to! Arrogant comparisons stunt our growth as we say to ourselves, "I don't need to grow."

When we compare ourselves with others and come out the loser (a pessimistic comparison), we may lose a sense of our own potential by saying, "I'll never be like him/her." This limiting belief robs us of a connection with our own potential in the face of the superior abilities we see in others. It is self deprecating and self defeating, and very demotivating. Pessimistic comparisons and arrogant comparisons both rob us of the possibility to develop any further; either we feel we don't need to or we feel we can't.

Optimistic comparisons on the other hand, inspire us to see our own possibilities for growth. With an optimistic comparison, we see someone else's achievement or ability and we are inspired to do the same. Optimistic comparisons create an anticipation which says,

"I want to do that too and I believe I can!" We don't lose heart, we find heart motivation, and see our own possibility in the other person's success. Pessimistic comparisons are futile.   Henry Van Dyke recognised this when he said, "Use what talents you possess: the woods would be very silent if no birds sang there except those that sang best." The only type of comparison worth making is an optimistic comparison which inspires aspiration and which ignites our sense of potential.

Perseverance is the Sign of a Strong Sense of Potential

Our expectations are often greater than our initial appropriations – we rarely get what we want the first time of asking or the first time of trying. It's probably fair to say that for most people, experiences which don't meet our expectations are far more numerous than those which do. We have to work for our success, and experimentation and perseverance are perhaps the two qualities which ensure success more than any other. But, what is it that causes us to experiment in the first place, and what is it that enables us to persevere in the face of failure or disappointment?   The answer is 'a sense of potential'.

A great example of this is Thomas Edison, the perfecter of the light bulb. Edison tested over 3000 filaments before he finally found a practical and efficient light bulb. Anecdotally, a reporter is reputed to have asked, "How did it feel to fail thousands of times?" Edison replied, "I didn't fail thousands of times. The light bulb was an invention with thousands of steps." That's great perspective, but it's founded on a great sense of potential. Right perspective helped Edison to persevere; but it was a sense of his potential to succeed in making a light which worked, which helped him to keep going through each one of those 3000 steps.

People persevere because they believe they can do the thing they've put their mind to. If we didn't believe we could, we would simply give up. A belief in our potential to succeed is what keeps us going.

The chronology of President Abraham Lincoln's career illustrates this power of self belief. Although he was considered a successful politician, he nevertheless experienced a large number of defeats and disappointments on the way to his greatest success.

* 1809 Born. Little formal education in childhood.
* 1818 Mother dies of milk sickness - Abraham is 9 years old
* 1828 Sister dies in childbirth (Sarah Lincoln)
* 1832 Loses job – the store he worked in goes out of business
* 1832 Defeated in run for Illinois General Assembly
* 1832 Buys another store with business partner
* 1833 Store Fails in business Abraham badly in debt
* 1834 Elected to Illinois General Assembly
* 1835 Fiancée dies
* 1836 Re-elected to Illinois General Assembly
* 1836 Nervous breakdown
* 1837 Partner in a law firm
* 1837 Rejected - Proposal to Mary Owens is rejected
* 1838 Elected to Illinois General Assembly for 3rd time.
* 1838 Defeated for speaker of House of Representatives
* 1840 Engaged to Mary Todd
* 1841 Suffers from Depression
* 1841 Breaks off engagement to Mary Todd
* 1842 Marries Mary Todd
* 1843 Defeated for nomination for U.S Congress
* 1846 Elected to Congress
* 1849 Rejected for Commissioner of General Land Office
* 1849 Leaves politics to practice law
* 1850 2nd son Edward dies. 3rd son William is born
* 1851 Father dies
* 1854 Elected to Illinois State Legislature
* 1855 Defeated for U.S. Senate
* 1856 Defeated for nomination for Vice President
* 1859 Defeated for U.S. Senate
* 1860 **Elected** President by the age of 51. [31]

No doubt Abraham Lincoln persevered because he knew he had the potential to succeed. History abounds with the stories of others who have persevered through to the point of success, despite significant discouragements.

For example, one of Albert Einstein's teachers described him as "mentally slow...and adrift in his foolish dreams," but now Einstein is often regarded as the father of modern physics. He received the 1921 Nobel Prize in Physics, and is best known for his Theories of Special and General Relativity, publishing more than 300 scientific works. After Fred Astaire's first screen test, the MGM director wrote a memo, dated 1933, saying, "Can't act. Can't sing. Slightly bald. Can dance a little." Yet, he went on to become a Hollywood legend. Walt Disney went bankrupt 4 times before creating the Walt Disney Empire which has brought entertainment, hope and employment to so many people; and J.K. Rowling's first 'Harry Potter' manuscript was rejected by 12 publishers before becoming the first in a series of 7 successful books and films.

All these people certainly had capacity, but so did many others who didn't make it. So what is the key factor that made the difference to those listed here? It was their sense of potential to succeed, to grow, to develop and improve. It was their self belief.

A Strong Sense of Potential Inspires Powerful Decisions

Many of the decisions we make occur on autopilot - personal hygiene and eating habits are good examples. These are decisions which have become habitual and instinctive, passive and automatic. The decision to live a certain way was made long ago, and a lifestyle developed around the original choice. But other decisions are more complex, or affect the immediate direction of our lives, and require greater energy and self belief to move us forward. These are active and often powerful decisions.

Powerful decisions are made in circumstances that involve *competition* in business or sport, *conflict* in relationships, *context changes* involving a job or house move, and *comfort zone challenges* like public speaking or deadlines to meet, or changes in lifestyle like diet and exercise. Strong self belief empowers us to make decisions which *face* the issues or challenges before us, rather than turn away from them and take a more passive posture. A strong sense of potential will motivate us forward to face such situations with confidence.

The alternative to making active and powerful choices in challenging situations is that we succumb to the stronger person in a conflict, or avoid a conflict altogether. We may avoid a context change and refuse to change job or house. We may avoid a competition or passively succumb to the other contestants or we may avoid the challenge to change our lifestyle and refuse to do something new that we've never done before.

Every decision at some level requires a certain degree of self belief - a belief that what we decide, what we do and what we say will have a result and will effect a change in some way. Whatever the situation, wherever a strong decision is required, a strong sense of potential is also needed to undergird that decision. Figure 23

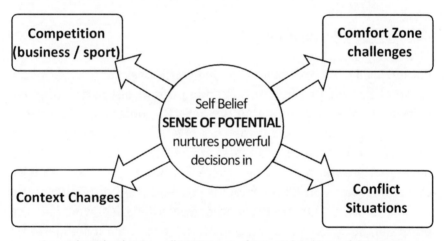

Copyright Richard A. Burwell 2010: Sense of Potential and Powerful Decisions

The power of decision operates in the context of self belief, grows in the soil of self belief, is attracted by the lightening conductor of self belief, and breathes in the air of self belief. Self belief almost invites powerful decisions. Of course, decisions can be made without strong self belief, but they tend to be decisions motivated more by self-preservation than self-actualisation; they are decisions motivated more by the desire to get 'away from' the problem, rather than a desire to face the problem and overcome it.

If there is no underlying belief in your potential to succeed in the thing you decide for, there is nothing for your decision to connect with. The power of the decision is dissipated, because there is no sense of potential to harness the decision which is made. This is the limiting effect of a limiting self belief. Limiting self beliefs limit the way in which we exercise power in our life because they limit the wholeness of heart we can apply to a decision. We will explore this idea in part two of this chapter.

The belief that you have in your potential to grow, develop and improve is more important than the ability you actually have, or the amount of capacity you ultimately have, because without self belief you will probably not exercise the ability you have at all.

Potential and Personal Power

Paradoxically, you can have a strong sense of potential, but a low sense of personal power. This is an important distinction to make. Sometimes we may *know* that we have the potential to do something, but the environment may hold us back, preventing us from exercising our decisions, talents and abilities. How many times have you been in a situation where you knew you were able do something, but you didn't know if you had the permission to do it, or you were actively prevented from doing it? You had the potential, but you lacked the power. In some way, it seemed that the context hindered you. However, it's also possible for an environment to be so empowering, encouraging and releasing that our sense of potential *grows* within it. We will explore this idea of personal power in the next chapter.

Your Sense of Potential is the Key which Unlocks the Door

Having a sense of your potential is the difference between hope and hopelessness, optimism and pessimism, an empowering self belief or disempowerment. A sense of potential empowers you to start living to your full capacity. The poet Virgil wrote that, "They are able who think they are able." Your sense of potential is the key which unlocks your capacity. Your sense of potential activates you into making decisions and performing actions.   Your sense of potential converts dormant ability into dynamic activity.

So putting your potential to work through decisions which move you forward is essential to personal development. The potential is in there, the key is within you, but you need to have a sense - a belief - that it really is. You need to believe in the adequacy of your own potential, or key, to open new doors of opportunity and experience, to see new abilities developed, and aptitudes turned into exceptional skills.

The sense of your potential is a belief in your possibility to learn, to grow, to develop and improve in almost any area of life. It's a belief that you are capable of so much more.

> Our sense of potential is so important because without it, we won't believe that we can develop in any area of life. It is the one sense of self which unlocks growth in all other areas — whether self esteem, self direction, self knowledge or self actualisation.

How can we Increase our Sense of Potential?

According to Bandura there are 4 main sources for self efficacy.[32] The first of these is what he calls 'performance accomplishments', where the experience of success increases one's self belief. The second is 'vicarious experience' gained through modelling the behaviour of others.   The third is 'verbal persuasions' where encouragers help to enhance self belief through positive words of encouragement, and the fourth is 'physiological and emotional arousal', and in particular, our mental perception of how we feel and how we expect to perform.

I will address these areas from the perspective of self development and team development using my own headings of *Mastering Success; Modelling Excellence; Messages of Support;* and, *Mental Conditioning.*

Mastering Success
When we set ourselves goals which are just a little beyond our current ability, but which are still achievable, we are stretched enough to give ourselves a sense of achievement. The result is that we feel more able than we did, and our sense of potential is increased. As the saying goes, "Success breeds success." Our sense of potential is increased as we continue to improve and do better.

When we avoid tasks which are difficult for us and only accept easy challenges, we ultimately reduce our sense of potential, or at least cause it to plateau out. However, taking on tasks much too great for our experience or skill level will cause us to fail, and repeated failure will reduce our belief in our ability. Finding new tasks which are just beyond us, but which are still attainable by us, is the key to mastering success and growing in our sense of potential.

Our sense of potential needs to be fed and watered through repeated success gained by trial and effort, and by learning the positive lessons of failure. Our sense of potential will be starved by too many easy wins, and bruised through repeated failure where the only lesson was "not good enough!" Our sense of potential will also be starved through lack of opportunity to experiment. Even a fully developed ability is still a potential until it's used. When abilities are not used and lie dormant over long periods of time, our confidence in them begins to evaporate and our sense of potential in that area begins to weaken.

Modelling Excellence
Imitating good practice and observing the types of behaviour which work well in order to gain similar results, is as old as civilisation itself. The Judaeo/Christian tradition refers to this as discipleship; tradesmen and those working in industry refer to it as apprenticeship; and

more recently, NLP and modern psychology refer to it as 'modelling'.

Our sense of potential is increased as we closely observe someone who has already achieved success in an area of life we want to grow in. By observing them, we see the precise pathways that led to their success, both the practical elements of what to do, and the psychological and physiological elements of how they handled themselves, and especially how they navigated the inevitable failures and disappointments that came. It could be in the area of finance, personal relationships, public speaking, managing a team, stopping smoking and so on. As we see how it's done, our expectation of also being able to do it is also enhanced. "If he can do it so can I!"

Having observed every aspect of how the successful person lives, thinks, makes decisions, relates to others, prepares, deals with disappointment and so on, we are then in a position to model their excellence. We are unlikely to copy them precisely, but as we model them, we find that our sense of potential increases as we find new ways to do things which bring new results.

Messages of Support
The environments we live in, the people we are a surrounded by and the words they speak over us – or don't speak over us - all contribute to our inner sense of potential. It makes sense for us to seek out places where we are recognised, respected and appropriately praised, and where we are honoured and helped to become all that we capable of becoming. A supportive environ-ment is not just one where we can receive praise and affirmation, but also one where we can receive genuine feedback on perform-ance. It is important for us to intentionally seek out a fair balance of *helpful critique* which gives us   information for improvement that we can build on, and *helpful praise* which encourages us, letting us know what worked well, so that we can reproduce it next time.

The reality is that most of us are insecure at some level of what we do and how we interact with others. This innate insecurity is made worse, when what we do and what we say is met with silence. Silence is typically interpreted as a negative comment, even if other people actually appreciated our contribution. Silence from the observer or recipient is meanness of spirit. When we take the role of observer or recipient, let's be courageous enough to say what we appreciated and if the contributor is willing to hear it, let's also offer some suggestion on how they can improve. Common courtesy implies that the recipient should honour our effort with appropriate praise, and as the contributor, we should honour the recipient with our willingness to learn how to give them a better contribution next time.

Mental Conditioning

The way we *feel* affects both the way we approach our tasks and the way we perform them. If we feel emotionally stressed, anxious, or upset, these emotions will strongly affect our sense of readiness in being able to accomplish what we need to do. If we feel physically unwell, we will inevitably feel less capable, and perform less capably. Headaches, neck tension, dizziness, and stomach aches all affect our sense of potential and the quality of our performance, but they can also find their cause in emotional stress, which in turn can find its cause in the way we think.

Making sure that our mind is conditioned for success will help our emotions and bodies to be more conditioned for success also. NLP refers to this as 'States of Excellence'. The way we think determines to a large extent the state or the condition we are in. Mental conditioning doesn't just affect our sense of potential; it impacts on all aspects of our self beliefs – including our self esteem, self direction, self knowledge and self actualisation. Our mental conditioning is a key aspect in how our self beliefs are strengthened, and will be the subject of the second part of this chapter.

WHAT ARE SELF BELIEFS AND HOW CAN I STRENGTHEN THEM?

When we talk about self beliefs, we need to make a distinction between 'worldview beliefs', which may be secular or religious views of reality; and 'self beliefs', which are ideas or opinions we hold about ourselves. Self beliefs are generalised statements about what we see as true for ourselves. They help us to make sense of our experience. They offer us a kind of map describing our experience of reality.

Self beliefs may be either true or false, but the fact that we hold them means that they hold us – for good or ill. Self beliefs have a strong influence on our thoughts, behaviours and feelings, and can also be influenced by the worldview we accept as true.

We can see some examples of *empowering* self beliefs in the following I am statements: 'I am honest', 'I am kind', 'I am confident', 'I am fair', 'I am intelligent', 'I am good with my hands', 'I am beautiful', 'I am able', 'I have a purpose', 'I am loved', 'I am worth knowing' and so on.

Some self beliefs are closely related to our values, such as honesty, fairness and kindness. Normally, we would say that we exhibit the personality traits of the values we hold as important. For example, 'I value honesty - I am honest', 'I value responsibility - I am responsible', 'I value understanding – I am understanding' and so on.

Disempowering self beliefs can be seen in the following examples: 'I am clumsy', 'I am scatter brained', 'I can't do that to save my life', 'people don't understand me', 'I never get it right' and so on. Of course these self statements are not *always* true of us, even if they do have *some* foundation in fact; this is why they are generalisations. There are always exceptions depending on different circumstances. We make generalisations in order to make sense of our experience, but often the generalisations we make about ourselves are negative.

The things we believe about ourselves, act as a tramline or railroad for our actions and behaviours.

> A limiting self belief sets the parameters or limits of possibility that we see for our lives. A limiting self belief conditions us to expect negative behaviours and outcomes as normal, and positive behaviours and outcomes as unattainable, even though they are really within our reach. However, an empowering self belief conditions or programs us to expect high standards of behaviour and performance. It raises our expectation of what is possible.

Self beliefs operate in different areas of our lives. I have referred to five areas specifically: Self esteem, enhanced by my sense of place; self direction, enhanced by my sense of purpose; self knowledge, enhanced by my sense of the principles, preferences and personal needs which influence me; self efficacy, enhanced by my sense of potential; and self actualisation, enhanced by my sense of personal power.

Their effect can be seen in the following table...

EMPOWERING and LIMITING SELF BELIEFS

Intrinsic
Empowering Self Belief

Self Esteem
I have intrinsic worth and value. I have high self esteem in some areas or each area of my life.

Self Direction
I have purpose and I am full of purpose and self direction.

Self Knowledge
I can know and understand myself so I will try. I am worth knowing.

Self Efficacy
I have potential, I am able, I can do it, I can grow, develop and improve.

Self Actualisation
I have the power
I choose to
I take or make the opportunity, I believe I can, so I do.

Temporary State affected by Circumstances

Self Esteem
I am praised - so I feel good about myself. I am accepted, appreciated, respected - so I like myself.

Self Direction
My job etc offers me direction and purpose so I feel on purpose.

Self Knowledge
My attempts to understand myself are bearing fruit so I feel more inclined to continue the quest.

Self Efficacy
I did well, so I feel more able, my sense of potential is stronger.

Self Actualisation
I'm facilitated to…
I'm encouraged to…
I'm invited to…
I'm given room to…
I'm given opportunity, so I make positive choices.

Self Esteem
I am not praised - so I feel bad about myself. I am not accepted, appreciated or respected so I don't like myself.

Self Direction
My job etc feels pointless without meaning, so I feel lost and without purpose.

Self Knowledge
My attempts to understand myself are not bearing fruit I feel more confused & less inclined to continue.

Self Efficacy
I did not do well, so I feel less able, my sense of potential is weaker.

Self Actualisation
I'm not allowed, I'm not encour-aged, facilitated, given room or opportunity so I feel I can't so I don't; or I feel controlled so I do things out of obligation.

Intrinsic
Limiting Self Belief

Self Esteem
I don't feel I have any intrinsic value or worth I have low self esteem I'm useless.

Self Direction
I have no purpose
Its pointless
I'm pointless.

Self Knowledge
I can't know or understand myself. I will not bother trying. I am not even worth knowing.

Self Efficacy
I have no potential. I'm not able I don't think I can I can't improve.

Self Actualisation
I'm powerless, I have no confidence, so I can't decide, or, I do things out of obligation & feelings of 'ought'.

A self belief becomes intrinsic to who we are by being nurtured from a very early age, and by repeated and continuous imprinting throughout life by virtue of affirming or discouraging experiences and statements made over us by ourselves or others.

Where do Early Self Beliefs Come From?

Prenatal and early childhood is a formative time when core self beliefs are formed within us. The positive and negative experiences we have as babies and children, and the positive and negative statements which are spoken over us, form the foundation on which our early self beliefs are constructed.

Prenatal psychology has begun to establish that life in the womb is a formative experience. Dr T. Verney, in his book, "The Secret life of the Unborn Child" refers to how newborn babies in a nursery were frequently exposed to a tape recording of a human heart beat. He records that: "[they] ate more, slept more, cried less and got sick less." Imagining the baby's in-utero experience, he writes,

> "The reassuring rhythm of its beat is one of the major constellations in his universe. He falls asleep to it, wakes to it, moves to it, rests to it. Because the human mind, even the human mind in-utero, is a symbol-making entity, the foetus gradually attaches a metaphorical meaning to it. Its steady *thump-thump* comes to symbolise tranquillity, security and love to him. In its presence, he usually flourishes." [33]

Positive self beliefs are formed from early moments in the mother's womb, as affection and attention are given to the baby through feeding, holding, soothing voices, music, and through the regular sound of the mother's beating heart. These messages of reassurance continue from the first moment a baby is held through to all the subsequent times it is given positive attention.

These positive experiences contribute to an underlying store of positive self beliefs. A baby cannot rationalize its experience, or think critically about what happens to it, but assuming that it has good parents, a baby has positive self beliefs nurtured within it right from the beginning.

As the baby becomes a child, it begins to internalize negative experiences of disappointment and failure as its own fault or as examples of personal limitation. These non-affirming experiences affect the child's self belief. The child's conscious mind is still underdeveloped, and therefore his/her ability to rationally consider what is true and false about him/herself is limited. The conscious mind is less able to act as a guardian or accurate interpreter of experience. Statements spoken over the child are received as truth uncritically, and this may work to the child's advantage if the statements are positive, or to their disadvantage if they are negative.

Although childhood is a key time in the formation of self beliefs, self beliefs are continually being formed or confirmed throughout our lives, and the conscious mind is a primary instrument in their formation. As adults, the challenge we face is to navigate our way through the continual bombardment of negative experiences and not allow them to infect our core self beliefs with negative self-appraisals and negative expectations of what is possible.

Equally, we must allow ourselves to be affirmed by positive experiences in life, reinforcing our core self beliefs through the words we listen to and the way we interpret the experiences we have. If we are to navigate this journey successfully, and develop empowering and accurate self beliefs, we must learn to use our mind actively and effectively.

The Relationship between Self Talk and Self Beliefs

Self talk is inward thinking towards ourselves about ourselves. It is _influenced_ by the things we believe about ourselves, and _reinforces_ core self beliefs already embedded within us. Self talk also _influences_ the things we believe about ourselves and can _reconfigure_ core self beliefs into positive or negative, accurate or inaccurate self-perceptions.

Self talk is normal. Although people who talk to themselves have often been caricatured as mentally unstable, the reality of course, is that self talk is simply the outward manifestation of the inward self *thought* which is occurring nearly all the time.

What's really important isn't so much *whether* we talk to ourselves, but *what* we say when we do. The most mentally healthy people are those who talk or think towards themselves with positive affirmations, rather than with the negative self talk which passes for a lot of our internal dialogue.

The Trojan Horse of Negative Thinking

In Virgil's epic Latin poem, *The Aeneid*, the tale is told of the 'Trojan Horse'. After a fruitless 10-year siege of Troy, the Greeks build a huge figure of a horse and hide their best soldiers in it. They leave it on the battle field along with a Greek warrior called Sinon, who pretends to have deserted the Greeks. Sinon strategically misleads the Trojans, saying the Greeks are tired of the war, and that the horse is an offering to the Greek goddess Minerva, to ensure their safe voyage home. Meanwhile, the rest of the Greek army pretends to sail away, hiding in the bay of the Isle of Tenedos:

> "The Greeks grew weary of the tedious war, and by Minerva's aid a fabric rear'd which like a steed of monstrous height appear'd...Thus they pretend, but in the hollow side selected numbers of their soldiers hide: With inward arms the dire machine they load, and iron bowels stuff the dark abode..."

The Trojans pull the Horse into their city as a trophy of their apparent victory. The Greek army then sails back under cover of darkness, with 'the monstrous steed' now within the city, and Sinon unlocks the horse:

> "Sinon, favor'd by the partial gods unlock'd the horse and op'd his dark abodes; restor'd to vital air our hidden foes."

The Greek soldiers emerge from the Horse, and open the city gates:

> "A nameless crowd succeed; their forces join t' invade the town oppress'd with sleep and wine. Those few they find awake first meet their fate; then to their fellows they unbar the gate... The fire consumes the town, the foe commands; and armed hosts, an unexpected force, break from the bowels of the fatal horse." [34]

Thanks to the 'Trojan horse, the city of Troy falls. For us, every negative thought which is received into our mind becomes a Trojan horse robbing us of our self belief. Once the horse is within the city walls, the damage is done. One negative thought welcomed in, leads to a flood of others behind it.

Instead of being actively on guard and checking the intention of the horse, the Trojans passively let it into the heart of their defenses. They were passive to the danger which the Greek horse posed. In a similar way, our conscious mind can be passive to the negative self talk which would destroy our self belief. Rather than being actively on guard we are asleep to the danger which our negative self talk poses. Negative self talk is a Trojan horse because we don't always recognize what's happening. Once the negative thought is in, it takes some serious fighting to get the thought removed.

Active and Passive States of Mind

When I speak of the conscious mind, I want to differentiate between an *active* state of mind and a *passive* state of mind. Understanding the difference will help us to see how our states of mind affect the formation of self beliefs (see figure 25). An active state of mind is one where we become attentive to the thoughts that are flowing within, and where we begin to direct the flow of our thoughts, rather than simply being caught up within the flow. The Philosopher and Psychologist William James writes that,

"[Attention] is the taking possession by the mind, in clear and vivid form, of one out of what may seem several simultaneously possible...trains of thought.[35]

A passive state of mind in contrast, is a semi-inattentive state, where the stream of thought flows within us, but where we are passive observers at best. We do not take possession of the flow; the flow of thoughts takes possession of us.

The Stream of Thought

There is a stream of thought which is constantly flowing within us. When our mind is in a passive, inattentive state, we are caught up in the stream and directed by its flow, we are inattentive to where the stream is leading, Our mind is in passive mode - we are being led, we are not leading.   In contrast, when our mind is active, we are more likely to determine what we think about, to guard the space in our head, and to specifically direct the flow of our thoughts in healthy and empowering ways.

> If we want our thoughts to empower us, we must be certain to maintain an active state of mind, and keep at bay the Trojan horse of negative self talk.

As an example of how we may be inattentive and passive to the stream of thought in our mind, imagine yourself in a queue at the supermarket when someone pushes in front of you. Suddenly, from that one event, a whole train of thoughts are set in motion. "What should I say to him? Dare I say it? Doesn't he care I've got my baby with me? What if my baby fell? Nobody really cares about me..." and so the thoughts continue, like a thread of cotton, unravelling from a piece of cloth. The thoughts create a flow of thinking which you haven't directly initiated. You are not directing the flow; you are *in* the flow.

A minute later, you come to your 'senses', and say to yourself,

"How did I end up thinking about this?" Somehow, you have ended up in Malibu on holiday, having an argument with an imagined queue pusher who doesn't speak English! Meanwhile, the real queue pusher has long since gone, and the check out girl is talking to you, but you are not registering their conversation. You are too full of negative thoughts and emotions about being pushed to one side. You probably couldn't even say how you ended up with the last thought in your mind. The previous sixty seconds have been full of *passive inattentive* thought, as opposed to *active attentive* thought. You were not fully attentive or alert to the negative process of thinking that you passively engaged in.

Here's a different scenario. You are at work and your manager walks by saying, "Can I see you in my office in five minutes please?" Immediately, panic grips you as you imagine the boss giving you a verbal warning for the report that you handed in late, and one negative scene after another plays across the inner screen of your mind. But as you walk into her office, you see that she is smiling and she hands you a new project, saying, "Good work on the previous report. It was a bit late, but well done!"

Suddenly, you realise that you've spent the last five minutes passively allowing worry and limiting self beliefs to form a stream of negative thinking in your mind. Because your mind was in a passive state, you failed to question the direction your thoughts were flowing in. You were conscious, but you were not actively aware of the process. You were caught up in the stream; you were not directing its flow.

The thoughts we accept into our minds drop into the pool of the subconscious, to rise helpfully or unhelpfully at a later date. They become the food we feed from or the soil we are sustained by. King Solomon wrote "As a man thinks in his heart, so is he." [30] and elsewhere, "With the fruit of a man's mouth his stomach will be satisfied; he will be satisfied with the product of his lips. Death and life are in the power of the tongue." [36]

When we fail to take active control of our thinking, our mind may passively hear a negative statement said about us, by our boss, for example. Or, we may experience something happening to us, as in the case of the queue pusher, and being in a passive state, we fail to constructively assess the words spoken or the experience felt. The words or experience are 'received' uncritically, and may become part of our self thought framework - especially if there's a recurring pattern to the words which are spoken over us, or to the experiences happening to us.

> Our active attentive mind is our gatekeeper, or guardian, ready to examine any potential 'Trojan Horse' for its malign or benign intent. However, passive unthinking acceptance of negative self thoughts allows them to become a 'Trojan Horse' of destruction in our life, when they are not arrested at the gate by the active attentive mind.

It is the job of our mind, our reasoning faculty, to evaluate the experiences we have and the words we hear, and to filter out the inaccurate negative once it's recognised. It isn't possible to maintain attentive thought continually - it's far too mentally taxing to manage such concentration all the time - but we do need to bring our attention back into an active state of mind regularly, if we are to maintain an effective guard or sentry at the door. The longer our mind passively and uncritically accepts negative thoughts into its domain, the sooner it slides into habitually negative ways of thinking. The negative thinking which gets in and takes root will grow into limiting self beliefs, robbing us of our true potential.

In wartime, enemy aeroplanes fly over foreign lands dropping bombs of destruction. The country that is attacked must have its radar turned on, and have fighter aeroplanes ready for action. If the radar is off, the enemy fighter has free access to create chaos. For a moment, try picturing enemy bombs as negative self thoughts bringing destruction whenever they are allowed to fall on the mainland of your mind. See your own fighter planes as positive affirmations which cancel out these bombs of self- destructive thinking. See your conscious active mind as your radar defence system protecting your thoughts, maintaining peace of mind and preserving the territory of your subconscious self beliefs.

As air force command you must only allow into the subconscious, thoughts which serve you and which build up a positive reservoir of self beliefs. When your mind is in a passive state it is then that bombs of negative self destruction *will* get through. If you don't keep vigilant, you will suffer the lie you believe in the morning for the rest of the day, or even for a lifetime.

Of course, sometimes the thought which serves us may be a helpful critique. It may *seem* to be negative, criticising our behaviour and making us feel bad, but if we learn from its lesson, the outcome will be positive. A *helpful critique* is specific to an action or behaviour we can change; a *destructive generalisation* is a generalisation which defines us negatively with no means or hope of change. A helpful critique may sound like, "What you said or did wasn't good because...and here's what you can do about it..." A destructive generalisation may sound like, "You *are* stupid", or "You *never* get it right." We need to shoot down destructive generalisations and respond to helpful critiques.

> Over time, negative self thoughts become 'sewn into' the fabric of our self belief system *when we agree* with the message they've been communicating. This is the essence of how limiting self beliefs are formed. *We stop opposing the negativity;* we give our allegiance to it. We hear the negative self talk and we think, "That's right." We offer no resistance, and the negative self talk begins to make its home within us. It becomes a limiting belief that we hold as true - the negative belief now holds us.

These concepts are shown in the following diagram...

Figure 25

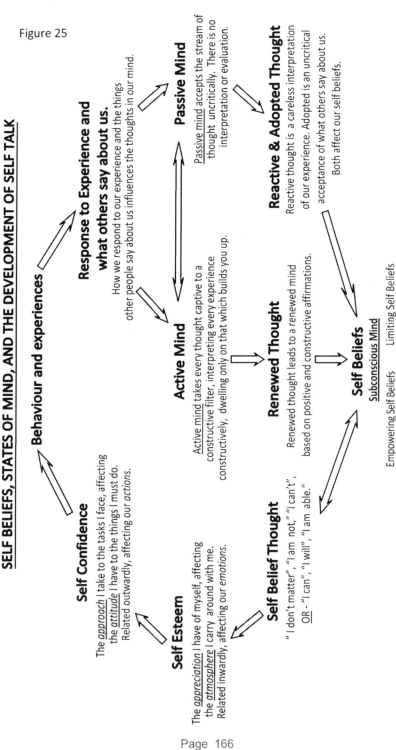

SELF BELIEFS, STATES OF MIND, AND THE DEVELOPMENT OF SELF TALK

Behaviour and experiences

Response to Experience and what others say about us.
How we respond to our experience and the things other people say about us influences the thoughts in our mind.

Passive Mind
Passive mind accepts the stream of thought uncritically. There is no interpretation or evaluation.

Self Confidence
The *approach* I take to the tasks I face, affecting the *attitude* I have to the things I must do. Related outwardly, affecting our *actions*.

Active Mind
Active mind takes every thought captive to a constructive filter, interpreting every experience constructively, dwelling only on that which builds you up.

Reactive & Adopted Thought
Reactive thought is a careless interpretation of our experience. Adopted is an uncritical acceptance of what others say about us. Both affect our self beliefs.

Self Esteem
The *appreciation* I have of myself, affecting the *atmosphere* I carry around with me. Related inwardly, affecting our *emotions*.

Self Belief Thought
" I don't matter", "I am not," "I can't", OR - "I can", "I will", "I am able."

Renewed Thought
Renewed thought leads to a renewed mind based on positive and constructive affirmations.

Self Beliefs
Subconscious Mind
Empowering Self Beliefs   Limiting Self Beliefs

Copyright Richard A. Burwell. 2010: Self Beliefs, States of Mind and the Development of Self Talk

Our Thoughts are Where The Battle is

> Empowering self beliefs need to be sustained if we are to preserve our freedom, just like agricultural soil needs to be nurtured to retain its fruitfulness. We need to keep the soil fed with nutrients and keep the weeds out of the way. Positive self beliefs need to be encouraged and the thoughts we entertain in our head are either going to be the Trojan horse of destruction, or the strong tower of protection. Our thoughts are where the battle is.

Let's take another example of how negative thoughts may develop. An employee called Bill, wakes up in the morning with the thought, "I can't face today - all those telephone customers are going to give me a really hard time." As he eats breakfast, the negative thought firmly embeds itself, and he begins to think about the different type of people who will call. He gets into his car and begins driving to work playing the negative thought through in his mind. He is in passive mode - he is not directly initiating the negative stream, he is following in the flow of it.

As he drives to work, he is not really concentrating, because he is passively caught up in this negative meditation of a bad day at work, and a few people hoot their horn at him. It doesn't help. He sits at his desk, answers the first call with in a gruff, monotone, joyless voice and the customer doesn't feel valued and subsequently complains. Bill's initial expectation for his day is confirmed, the limiting thought that he began his day with has become a self-fulfilling prophecy. The rest of the day follows the same theme, reinforcing his original negative expectation.

Someone else prepares for a work presentation, and thinks, "I'm useless at presentations." Someone else gets ready for a party and thinks, "I'm not really liked by other people." We could find a thousand examples like these. But here's the important point - did you notice how the thoughts were framed? Most often, they don't come to us in the second person, they come in the first person. They don't come at us as a 'YOU' statement, they come in the form of an 'I' statement. This is really tricky. So many limiting thoughts appear to us as *us* talking to ourselves.

The negativity doesn't accuse us by saying, "Look Richard, you'll never make your targets, why bother trying?" because if they did, you'd stand up to them and argue your case. Who likes being told what to think and what to do, or what you can't do? No one! But the reality is that so many limiting thoughts tend to be more like *me* talking to *me*, saying, "I'm not going to manage this," or "I'm rubbish at that," and so on, and we think that because we thought it - it must be true! But once we believe the limitation, the rest of the day becomes a sad depressive meditation on the negative thought that has been sown.

In his book, *The Power of the Plus Factor*, the late Dr Norman Vincent Peale tells the story of when he was walking through the tiny streets of Kowloon in Hong Kong. He came to a tattoo parlour, and began looking through the window at all the examples of tattoos that could be chosen. He saw an anchor, a flag, and a mermaid amongst many others. He writes,

> "What struck me with force, were three words that could be tattooed on one's flesh, "Born to Lose." I entered the shop in astonishment and, pointing to those words, asked the Chinese tattoo artist, "Does anyone really have that terrible phrase, 'Born to lose', tattooed on his body?" He replied, "Yes, sometimes." "But," I said, "I just can't believe that anyone in his right mind would do that." The Chinese man simply tapped his forehead and in broken English said, "Before tattoo on body, tattoo on mind."[37]

We need to recognize the constraint of limiting thinking as a constraint indeed and fight for our freedom. Simply don't let that limitation on you. No good is going to come from it. Life's too short to let limiting thoughts limit our life.

RENEWING THE MIND

In A.D.57, St Paul said to his readers in the City of Rome, "be trans-formed by the renewing of your mind." [38]   This was cognitive behavioral therapy some 2000 years ago. Elsewhere he taught his readers that wrong thinking will capture them, unless they were first to capture wrong thinking, so he urged them to 'take every thought captive' and bring them into the obedience of the truth. Although he wrote these words within a specifically Christian pastoral context, it is clear that the power of our thoughts to transform us or imprison us has long been understood. If we don't renew our minds by dealing with negative, self limiting, self deprecating thoughts, the negative will deal with us.. So, how can we renew our minds into a more positive way of thinking?

The following pages contain exercises and further reading to take you through a process to achieve this. Please give yourself enough time to tackle each section to make it really profitable for you.

Self Beliefs and Patterns of Thought, Emotion and Behaviour

Self beliefs are embedded into the foundations of who we are, having been formed through patterns of thought, emotion and behaviour over many years.   Self beliefs are so ingrained and subconscious that they are not immediately apparent to the conscious mind. Like an oil painting, their patterns are hard to see up close. A direct enquiry question like, "What are my self beliefs?" is unlikely to reveal much to you.

To discern them, a more subtle form of approach is required. We need to step back and see ourselves from a more evidential and observational point of view, by looking for *patterns of thinking*, *feeling* and *behaving* which may be sign posts to the hidden self beliefs which influence us. When we notice limiting patterns of *thinking*, *feeling* and *behaving*, it is likely that these recurring patterns are the fruit of hidden roots of self belief.

Exercise 1:
Recognise patterns of thought, emotion and behaviour:

Use the wheel of life template below, and work through each of the segments in the wheel, asking yourself the following questions using the 3 patterns of *thought*, *emotion* and *behaviour*. Persevere with the questions until you have a satisfying answer.

What are the <u>recurring thoughts</u> I have concerning this area of my life? What do these thoughts say about my view of myself?

What are the <u>recurring feelings</u> I have concerning this area of my life? What do these emotions say about my view of myself?

What are the <u>recurring actions</u> I do, or don't do in this area of my life? What do these actions or omissions tell me about my view of myself?

Figure 26

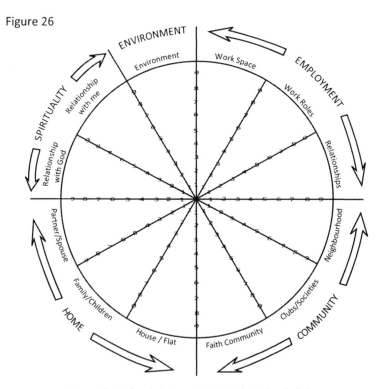

Copyright Richard. A. Burwell 2010: The Wheel of Place

Exercise 2: Have a D Day or Decision Day:

During the Second World War in 1944, the Allies invaded France on the Normandy beaches. The Nazi's had overrun Europe, but the Allies had decided that 'enough was enough' and the 'D Day' offensive began in earnest. (The term 'D Day' is a military term which simply denotes the day in which an attack will begin.)

However, it was not until 'V.E. Day', or Victory in Europe Day, eleven months later, that the end of the war was declared. You may find it helpful to use these profound and historic days as symbols for your own victory in overcoming negative self talk. You may wish to declare that 'enough is enough' of negative thinking and limiting self beliefs, by declaring your own 'D Day' and affirming that limiting self beliefs will no longer rule you. You could set aside one whole day to observe your patterns of thinking and begin your own battle for freedom.

As the day begins, determine to listen for every occurrence of negative self talk that you speak over yourself. Carry a small note book with you through the day, and intentionally note down every negative sentence you hear.

> To do this is a declaration of freedom and deliverance. This is why it's a D DAY! A day of decision. No longer will you be subject to a diet of words which are destructive. From now on you will begin to sustain yourself with more positive fare.

Once you have your list, compare it with the results of Exercise 1 above. You can then decide which self talk you want to deal with first. You may need to revisit this exercise on subsequent days, to help you attune yourself to the hidden self talk you unwittingly allow yourself to be influenced by. You could also set your own V.T. Day, - victory in thoughts day - eleven days (not months) later. Set yourself a target for reconfiguring the limiting self talk that you may be bothered by, and celebrate the changes you have seen. But first, once you have had your 'D Day' then work your way through the exercises beginning on page 176, with the expectation that you will have a V.T. Day eleven days (or more) later. Of course, the time frame is not really important, but it does give you a challenge to really work at the changes in thinking which may be necessary.

Limiting Beliefs can Create a Bad Mood:

The table below suggests some examples of limiting self beliefs, and the effect they can have on you in terms of your action and behaviour and your disposition and mood.

BELIEFS	ACTION	DISPOSITION	MOOD
B	**A**	**D**	**MOOD**
I can do it tomorrow	Procrastination	Day Dreamer	Distracted
It can't last / the bubble has to burst	Self Sabotage	Dream Denter	Deflated
I'll never do that / my sights are set too high	Demotivating	Dream Stealer	Deflated
I can't decide / I don't know what to do	Indecision	Ditch Straddler (fence sitter)	Distressed
I can't change / I'm stuck in a rut	Inertia	Ditch Dweller	Despair
I'm no good	Self Destruction	Ditch Digger	Depressed

©Richard A. Burwell 2010: Effects of Beliefs, Actions & Dispositions on Mood

Characterise Limiting Self Talk

In Co-Active coaching, Whitworth, Kimsey-House and Sandahl refer to limiting self talk as the "The Gremlin Effect". They write:

> "The Gremlin is always there to point out your weaknesses, your fear, your failure - to reinforce your self limiting judgments. He's there to hold you back and hold you down". [39]

Dan, one of my coaching clients (not his real name) suffered from the gremlin to an extreme degree...

Dan: "Sometimes I think other people think I'm a nuisance, so I go to bed as a safe place and hide away. Other times I feel rejected, not wanted, or I question, 'Am I going to fit in?'"

Coach: "May I offer you a thought, just for you to consider?"

Dan: "Yes."

Coach: "My sense is that you feel bullied by the negative thoughts, how do you respond to that idea?"

Dan: "Yes, in fact I would say I'm very easily bullied."

Coach: "In which other ways do you feel bullied?"

Dan: "The thoughts leave me feeling vulnerable and quiet. I give in easily, they demoralise me."

Coach: "What could you do when a negative thought comes up?"

Dan: "I need to face it and not back away."

The insight that Dan had been bullied by his critical self talk, and that he was retreating from it, helped him to realise that there was an alternative approach. Seeing that he could face the critical self talk head on, was a strong empowerment to him. Finding a name for the problem, but not labelling himself with it, was the beginning of a breakthrough in the area of limiting beliefs.

By giving negative self talk a name, such as the gremlin or the inner critic, you are attempting to separate yourself from its influence; you put yourself in the role of director. You are in charge.

When we give negative self talk a name or a characteristic we begin to have power over it. Whenever we name something, we begin to define its boundaries. Something which remains unnamed can take on a life larger than it deserves. By naming or characterising our limiting self talk, we cast ourselves in the role of creative director. We can begin to reconfigure the negative into something more positive and worthy of us. Dan recognised that he needed to face the negative self talk and not back away. Learning how to face the negative self talk effectively is really important. So how can we do this?

The Internal Monologue of Limiting Self Talk

The almost constant internal monologue that we have have towards ourselves goes on unrecognised and undisturbed most of the time. We are hardly conscious of it. This is fine when the content of the monologue is positive and affirming, but it can often be negative and highly disempowering.

The negative monologue has power over you just as long as it remains a monologue. As soon as you begin to address it, it's no longer a monologue, but a dialogue that you can turn the tables on. You turn tables on the negativity by asking it questions, because the one with the questions is always the one with the power. Questions help the conscious mind to take control and determine that a more positive stream of thought is flowing. You can gain power over your negative monologue by asking what the intention or desire is behind the negativity. For Dan, the thoughts that people saw him as a nuisance actually masked his real intention and desire - which was to be useful. The critical voice sabotaged this intention.

As we have seen, negative self talk can often sound so reasonable that we come to believe it and no longer challenge it, but by characterising limiting self talk we are able to see it in its true light – certainly as a critic, but perhaps also as a misguided attempt at self protection, achievement or service to others.

The Positive Intentions of the Critical Voice

Critical self talk on first glance appears to be just this - nothing more than a bully seeking to hurt us. However, on closer inspection, the inner critic may have a positive intention behind its negative exterior.

For example, the statement "I'll only make a fool of myself if I stand up and say something" is certainly a limiting statement, but the positive intention may be self protection. Similarly, the statement "I never get it right" is certainly self destructive in its effect, but there may be a positive desire of achievement locked in behind it. Recognising the positive intention or desire behind the negative statement is one way you can honour that part of you which looks out for your safety or desires your success. The method is bad, but the motive is good. By recognising the possible positive intentions of negative self talk, we are able to honour our own intentions towards ourselves, rather than despising the way we talk to ourselves.

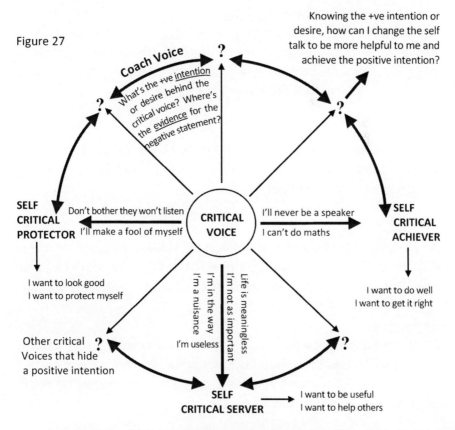

Figure 27

Copyright Richard A. Burwell 2010: Positive Intentions of the Critical Voice

Exercise 3:
Reconfigure a limiting self belief into an empowering self belief:

As we have seen, a limiting belief asserts dominance over you - it tells you what you can and cannot 'do' 'be' or 'have'. But it's a usurper which you can challenge and change. You can do this by asking questions which help you to consider the limiting self belief from different perspectives.

We have already thought about asking what the possible positive intention or desire may be behind the critical voice. But there are other questions which can help us to reconfigure the negative self talk and critical voice into becoming an affirming one.

For example: What's the _evidence_ for it? What long term _effect_ is it having on you? How do you _experience_ it? And how can you _exchange_ the limiting belief appropriately? Choose an example of negative self talk in your life, and work through the following questions, writing them down in your journal.

Evidence
What's the evidence for the negative self belief? What examples can you think of which disprove this limiting belief? What examples of success can you think of?

Effects
What will be the longer term effects of this limiting belief? What Will be the results or consequences of this limiting belief in your life? Consider your answer in terms of what you see, hear and feel.

Experience
What do you experience or feel now, as a result of this limiting self belief? How does this limiting or negative self belief affect you? How does it make you feel? Consider your answer in terms of what you see, hear and feel.

Exchange

What are you going to exchange this limiting belief with? What can you resolve to say that is more supportive of you? What would be an appropriate, believable and comfortable self belief to exchange for the limiting self belief? Although the new belief may not feel comfortable, it must not feel alien! How can you phrase it in a way which feels right? Make the new affirmation positive, in the present tense, and personal eg. "I am talking/succeeding/overcoming," etc. Say what you are doing in this new affirmation, not what you are not doing.

Exercise 4: Reinforce the New Empowering Self Belief:

Having made a choice to *reconfigure* a limiting self belief into a more appropriate and empowering self belief, we then need to *reinforce* it. We can do this by following the same process of consideration which helped us to change the limiting self belief.

Evidence

The difficulty we may have as we introduce a new empowering self belief into our life is that we may not have direct evidence of success or ability in the area we want to grow in. We've not done it before, so how can we find any evidence that we can? The answer is that we do have evidence and experience of success in other areas of life that we can borrow from and learn from. We can apply those lessons and experiences into the situation where our negative self talk affects us.

NLP teaches that the behaviours and ways of thinking which gave us success in one activity can be applied in another activity to help us achieve similar success; and that the feelings we enjoy from the success activity can be recalled and reapplied in the activity we struggle in. The 'state' or feelings of excellence from one activity can supercharge us in another activity.

For example, we may be very fluent in one to one, face to face conversations, but not very fluent in conversations on the telephone. The limiting belief may say, "I'll never feel confident on the phone." So, the first step is to change the limiting belief into an empowering self belief and look for evidence that will support the new affirmation.

The empowering belief we wish to create may say, "I am confident on the phone," but this may not feel comfortable to us yet as we don't yet feel it. So we re-work the new self belief to say, "I am already confident in face to face conversation, *I will be* confident on the phone." This is a halfway house affirmation. It is not present tense - it is framed as a future expectation - but it may be the best we can manage.

Next, we need to look for evidence to support this affirmation and also to look for the success behaviours that we can carry over into telephone conversations. By finding the elements of success in the one to one, face to face conversations, we can carry over some elements of the success situation to the situation we are struggling in. The behaviours and feelings from the first activity then become resources which can be re-applied in many other settings.

If you are fluent in face to face conversations, you may find that closing your eyes and picturing the person you are talking to helps you to recreate a similar setting in your mind, even though you are on the telephone. You may notice that face to face conversation usually involves you being very expressive with gestures. Carrying these gestures over into the phone conversation may help you to relax. You may notice that your breathing is relaxed in the face to face setting, but tight and shallow on the phone; by choosing to breathe more fully, you may be helped to converse more easily on the phone.

Now, think of examples in your life where you have done well. What were you doing in these situations that enabled you to do well? Think in detail about the elements of your success. Which elements of these successful situations do you want to carry over into the new situation? These become your resource experiences, and 'evidence' you can apply in helping you to construct a new empowering self belief.

Effects

Now ask yourself, what will be the effect on you, of having a new empowering self belief fully embedded within you? How would you do things differently or instinctively? How different do you imagine your future is going to be for you, as a result of this new belief? What would you do naturally, if this new empowering self belief felt natural to you? When we imagine the future effect of an empowering self belief, or of something we hope for, we find ourselves mentally rehearsing success not failure.

The more you mentally rehearse doing something in the future the more believable it becomes. In fact, studies have shown that mental rehearsal actually improves ability. The beauty of mental rehearsal is that you can imagine doing it perfectly, and you can enjoy the feeling of anticipation which this brings. In contrast, the more we imagine failing (a mental rehearsal of failure), the more we anticipate failure happening. The more we believe we will fail, the more predisposed we are to fail, the more we are likely to _do_ the failure we _see_ in our imagination.

The benefit of positive mental rehearsal or visualisation was shown powerfully in 1958 in a study conducted by L. Verdelle Clark at Wayne State University, Detroit Michigan. In the study Clark divided basket ball players into three groups. The first group threw practice basket balls for one hour every day for one month; the second group threw no basket balls for one month and the third group simply visualised throwing basket balls for one hour every day for a month. The group which had practiced showed a 24% improvement, the group which had not practiced showed no improvement, but the group which simply visualised throwing basket balls improved by a staggering 23%! [41]

Other studies have since been conducted on the benefit of mental rehearsal on pre-performance routines in sport for tennis, basket-ball, football, volleyball, bowling, gymnastics, skiing and diving with similar effect.

The following exercise is a variation on the NLP *New Behaviour Generator* exercise established by John Grinder in the late 1970's and formalised by Robert Dilts in the early 1980's. [42]   It is also supported by the mental rehearsal studies referenced above. This exercise can be used for any area where you have a limiting self belief which hinders your performance.

As an example, let's say that your desired self belief is, "I believe I can drive a car confidently and pass my driving test," (in contrast to "I don't believe I will ever drive a car confidently, or pass my driving test").   At first, you may want to think of someone you know or have seen who already drives well. So, you imagine you are watching a film of this person driving a car confidently. You notice everything about how they do it – their body posture, their hands, how they move their head to see in the mirror, everything.

Now, see yourself driving the car; this is a mental image of how you want to be, achieving your goal. As you see yourself in this way, you are picturing yourself in a dissociated way, either above yourself or to the left or right. You picture yourself doing everything that you should be doing as if you are watching a film of yourself driving. In this film, you are living out this self belief of driving confidently with self belief fully active and strong within you, reinforced by the affirmation, "I can drive." This can work with any self belief as long as it doesn't depend on other people to make your self belief a reality.

Now, step inside yourself doing these actions which represent your new self belief. You are now associated - you are inside yourself. You are now seeing everything with your own eyes and the actions and the feelings are your own. You are not watching a film of yourself doing these actions, you are now 'in yourself' doing them. As you create this mental picture or movie, fill in all the detail you can. Include the sights, sounds and the feelings - even the smells and tastes, if appropriate. Be very aware of your feelings and repeat your self belief to yourself as you do the actions in your imagination, for example, "I am driving the car confidently." Notice how it feels to be this new person. You are creating a mental map of the 'future you' with a new self belief fully active.

Creating this mental map will help your subconscious see this new self belief in action. It will become more believable. Visualise this several times to really get the picture clear. As you focus on the results of what you hope to achieve you are creating mental pathways of subconscious expectation. You are beginning to embed the self belief into your subconscious mind. You have already seen yourself behaving with this new self belief in your imagination - it's already more believable than it was. A new empowering self belief is now being formed within you; a new self identity is being formed which will begin to affect your behaviour and performance.

Experience
Step out of this imagined scenario. What do you experience or feel as a result of this new positive expectation? What impact is the new expectation having on you right now? In which ways are you feeling different and seeing yourself differently? Try using descriptive language. This is an imagined feeling of success, created as a result of imagining an embryonic new self belief in action. Although it is imagined, it is still an experience which can motivate you to see this new self belief fully formed within you.

Walk around as this 'new person' with this new self belief beginning to emerge. Enjoy the feelings this brings. Practice and repeat until your hope becomes an expectation which grows into a new self belief and begins to change your real life experience.

Exchange
New self beliefs, like a new pair of shoes have to be worn, even if they are not yet fully comfortable. They only become comfortable as

you wear them in and walk out in them. The first steps of a new self belief, like the first steps in new shoes, are slightly awkward and stiff, yet also pleasing. You feel better about yourself. New self beliefs require new types of decisions and new patterns of behaviour. What *decisions* will you make to help embed the new self belief? What *actions* will you take to help embed this new self belief? What are you going to exchange your old behaviour with? What might be a first step you can take to help you establish this new self belief in your life, making it more real to you, helping you to wear it in? What appeals to you about this first step? When are you going to take it? What else do you need to do?

Exercise 5: Remind yourself of the new empowering self belief:

Old disempowering self beliefs form well worn paths and expectations. Like driving a car on autopilot, we naturally go where we have always gone unless we clearly and intentionally re-mind ourselves that we are going in a different direction today!

Life is so full of responsibility and complication, that unless we purposefully remind ourselves of the new self belief agenda, we will probably forget. We will naturally fall into old well worn grooves and habit patterns of thought and behaviour. Embedding the new self belief will take perseverance and practice. We will be helped if we find ways to remind ourselves of the empowering self belief we wish to grow within us.

The following questions may help. What can you associate with the new belief that will help you to remember it? What will you *do* to remind yourself of this new self belief? What will you *say* to remind yourself of this new self belief? What type of words can you say? What type of pictures can you use? What type of music will help to remind you?

Reforming negative self beliefs and negative patterns of thought is a process of development and learning. There will be success and there will be moments when success is elusive. Learning to ask positively framed questions can help you to overcome the effects of negative experiences and will set you up for future success. Technically, you may call your lack of success a failure, but emotionally this is very unhelpful as it reinforces the negative self beliefs you are trying to reform. It's far better to talk about a learning opportunity than a failure.

The following questions may help. How well did I do it? What worked? What didn't work? How could I do it better? What can I learn from this experience?

The Power of Positive Self Affirmations:

If our self beliefs are empowering we will want to make them more concrete in the positive language we use, but if those beliefs are disempowering, we will not want to give them a voice. Instead, we will want to reshape them, and the language we use is a powerful tool in doing this.

> The word pictures we use in describing ourselves, focus our expectation and create environments of possibility or impossibility. The words we speak over ourselves truly are the nutrients which nourish us or the contaminants which poison us. How we think and what we say is incredibly important. Negative self talk narrows the field of possibility. Positive self talk and empowering self beliefs create worlds of possibility.

Susan Jeffers, in her book 'Feel the Fear and Do It Anyway', suggests that we embrace a more powerful vocabulary. So rather than saying "I should", say "I could"; instead of saying "It's a problem," say "It's an opportunity." [40] Below you will find a few more variations on this theme of disempowering and empowering self beliefs expressed in the form of words we use. Look at this list and identify which statements you may fall susceptible to in the left column, and its antidote statement in the right column.

I can't	I can
I am not allowed	I'll do what's necessary
I ought to	I choose to
I am not worth	I am worth
I don't know enough	I do know enough
I never will	I will
I am not able	I am able
I'm rubbish at this	I'm learning how to do it better
I always get it wrong	I'm learning how to get it right

A few years ago, after experiencing several consecutive disappointments, I became uncharacteristically pessimistic. As a result, I began to notice that my internal conversation with myself was increasingly negative, both about myself and about my future. This negative self talk was robbing me of hope, joy, and determination. In particular, I noticed two negative statements which were both un-provable and unproductive. The first was, "The best has come and gone." The second was, "I'm too old for my dreams to happen now." Once I recognised these unwelcome intruders, I decided to change the conversation from negative self-destructive monologues into opposite positive self affirmations. "The best has come and gone," became "The best has yet to come and I will be my best," and, "I'm too old for my dreams to happen now," became, "I'm wise enough to handle them when they do."

Although I can't guarantee that the things I hope for will actually come to pass, what I can guarantee is that if I fill my mind with positive self talk and high expectation, I will be more open to the positive opportunities which present themselves, as opposed to keeping my mind on what I think are missed opportunities. And anyway, it's just a happier way to live.

Positive self affirmations are not meant to be arrogant or unrealistic affirmations. A positive self affirmation does not mean that I say, 'I am the best', or 'better than others'. This would be an unhelpful comparison. Instead, a positive self affirmation invites me to say 'I can', without requiring me to specify how well I can. Skill level and degree of success are for others to judge. I simply need to believe that I am able to grow, develop and improve.

Thankfulness Strengthens our Sense of Potential

Being thankful for what has already occurred raises our expectation of what is possible and for what may yet occur. Thankfulness for the good of the past nurtures optimism for the future; it positions us to see solutions when they arrive because we are hopeful, based on what has already occurred. Thankfulness increases our sense of potential, because it raises the idea that there are resources available to help us from outside of ourselves. We can't easily be negative when we are filing our head with positive. Thankfulness is a powerful antidote to negative thinking.

On 11th November 1620, the ship, *Mayflower,* dropped anchor in Provincetown harbour, Massachusetts with its 102 passengers ready to begin their new colony, in *New England*. Half were pilgrims fleeing religious persecution; the rest, economic migrants seeking their fortune. Their first winter was very severe. After 66 days of voyage they were unprepared for the winter which came, and by the end of March half of them had died through cold, disease and malnutrition. In his journal, Governor Bradford referred to it as the 'starving time'.

The harvest that year was good, and for the first time since they arrived they had plenty of food. Governor Bradford announced it was time for thanksgiving, and from that simple moment of thankfulness, the American day of Thanksgiving was born.

Thankfulness is all about perspective; what side of the problem are you looking from? From the upside, you are on top of the problem - from the downside, you are beneath it. From the upside you can see the negative issue in perspective from all angles. You are in a better position to find a solution because your mind is optimistically poised. Thankfulness is the ultimate form of defiance against a world which would try to squeeze the life right out of us. The person who is thankful looks for the upside and in doing so, finds themselves on the up. Based on their studies on gratitude, Dr Robert A. Emmons and Dr Michael E. McCullough write,

"...gratitude not only makes people feel good in the present, but it also increases the likelihood that people will function optimally and feel good in the future." [43]

With this in mind, try the next exercise on generating gratitude.

Exercise 6:
Generating gratitude:

For the next five minutes record as many things as you can think of to be thankful for in your journal. Write them all down. Be really specific, and don't think anything is too small or too trivial. When you have made your list, try standing up and reading them with a loud voice. The loud voice is important because it is symbolic of conviction and determination, and it will help to get the message of positivity into your subconscious. It's not that your subconscious is deaf, it just needs a little more help to listen. Speaking into your chin, with a whisper, isn't convincing enough.   After each thankful statement, try breathing in deeply, and feel the thing you are thankful for, breathe out and move onto the next one. I guarantee you'll feel good after you've done it.

I will close this chapter by quoting from Professor Frank Pajirez:

"Empirical evidence supports Bandura's contention that self-efficacy beliefs touch virtually every aspect of people's lives—whether they think productively, self-debilitatingly, pessimistically or optimistically... As a consequence, these beliefs can powerfully influence the level of accomplishment that people ultimately realize. Self-efficacy is also a critical determinant of the life choices people make and of the courses of action they pursue." [44]

The sense of potential we feel or the self belief we possess for any area of our life, determines the choices we make, the actions we pursue and the achievements we attain. We do not need to be constrained by limiting self beliefs - they can be changed.

Chapter 5

THE SENSE OF POWER
(Self Actualisation)

We had just moved house to a beautiful four storey Victorian end-terrace on the edge of the inner city in Leeds. We were excited about our new place - the size, the stained glass windows, the staircase, the possibilities. We loved the valley woods nearby, and the park not far away. This brand new place to live empowered us.

Not many months after moving to our 'castle in the city', I found myself faced with an unusual scene. Driving home with my family one day, passing through the valley woods we saw two cars blocking the road at right angles to the oncoming traffic. Two men were fighting each other and their girlfriends were standing at the side shouting them on.

As I assessed the scene at 40 miles an hour, adrenalin took over, and rather than slowing down, I speeded up - concerned that they might kill each other. I banged my hand on the horn, screeched to a halt, grabbed my car crook lock for protection, dived out of the car and ran to the fight scene. I started shouting at the men to stop and began trying to pull them off each other. Within 15 seconds the men had stopped fighting, and rather than turn on me, got back into their cars, girlfriends in tow and drove off down the valley road.

What made me act so boldly? Several things came together that morning, giving me a sense of personal power, a sense that I could make a difference. For instance, I knew the valley road well, I often walked it late at night, it was 'my place' and they were fighting on 'my turf'. Also, seeing them fight each other brought a principle value of mine to the surface – I had to *take responsibility.* I couldn't just ignore the fight. Another principle also came to the fore – *protecting people.* These two principle values provided me with my purpose in that moment; I had to stop a fight, possibly in order to save a life. I also believed that I had the potential to make a difference. Various of my senses of self had come together and I was empowered to take action.

This wasn't to be the only unusual experience I had while living in this area. Over time, other challenging situations began to occur. I saw a man hit another man with a baseball bat 100 metres from my house (my second baseball bat experience), so I went to investigate, but too late to stop the assailant; and then there was a family dispute between my neighbour and his drunk cousin. I could hear the shouting and fighting and went to investigate. When I heard that he had hit my neighbour's young son, I challenged him, and found myself having a wrestle on the front yard.

Around the same time, a gang of drug pushers began congregating at the back of our house, plying their trade with impunity. The police told me not to confront them, but seemed to do little to arrest them. I was enormously disempowered by this invasion of my space, and also by the advice to keep quiet.

It felt like my voice had been silenced. However, after several weeks of covert observation and phoning the police, the gang never returned.

Life seemed to settle down for a while, until, on another occasion I was walking my daughter to school one morning, when I saw a man break into a car, just 200 metres from my home. I challenged him to stop, and he pulled out a knife and threatened us before running away. It became the last straw. I had often gone for late night walks in the local streets, but now I no longer felt like a king living in my castle. I felt threatened and fearful. I no longer felt empowered by the place and area I lived in. We realised it was time to move. My 'place' had affected my 'power'.

I tell these stories to illustrate how the different senses of self can affect each other. This same principle operates in many arenas of life. Managers for example, can be aware of how an employee's sense of place in the office they work in, or the team they work with, can significantly affect their sense of personal power which affects *whether* they make decisions, *when* they make decisions and *how effective* those decisions will be. Similarly, the degree to which the principles and values of a team are understood or agreed by team members can affect the *way* in which decisions are made and the confidence with which they are made.

This final chapter will explore the nature of powerful decisions, the sources of personal power, and the landscape of personal power as it affects our ability to express ourselves effectively, take action appropriately and achieve the results we intend.

PART ONE

POWERFUL DECISIONS AND THE SOURCES OF POWER

What is Personal Power?

Personal power is often described in terms of its external effect, and especially in terms of influence over people. But if this is all it is, then personal power is no more than control and manipulation. I believe that personal power relies on forces which are far more collaborative, internal and virtuous than this. We need a new way of looking at personal power and how it impacts us and other people at the level of personal development and self leadership if we are to embrace it and benefit from it.

> If we see personal power as something to be afraid of or if we view it suspiciously, assigning bad motives to those who seek it, we will deny its operation in our own lives and fear its expression in other people. If we understand it, respect it and appropriately seek it, we will be well positioned to use it for our own benefit and serve others with it.

Understanding the nature of personal power and the way it operates in us and through us is essential if we are to function effectively in our relationships with other people, and especially in team settings. So, what exactly is personal power? How is it expressed in us and through us, and what do we mean when we say, "I feel powerful" or, "I feel powerless?"

Personal Power

Personal power is the intangible energy to do something and the will to do it. In other words, personal power is our *force of will* to do something. Personal power is required to express who we are and to make visible the talents and abilities we have. But what happens when we come across situations where our power of expression is denied or hindered; when there is a lack of *permission* to express our power of decision and action? Perhaps there is an internal conflict within ourselves and at some level we have not given ourselves full permission to do something. Or perhaps other people have withheld their permission; we don't have *authority* to do what we have planned to do. In situations like these, a lack of permission and authority hinders our ability to express our power. Clearly, personal power requires another component to be truly effective.

Authority, Permission and Power

Authority is the right or permission to do something. A policeman may have power in himself to act, but if he has no permission from the state to act (symbolised by his uniform), his sense of power is diminished by his lack of authority. Only when he receives permission from the state does he have the authority to act. A policeman has a sense of power based on the authority he has been given in conjunction with his force of will to do something. Take away his permission or authority and you diminish his sense of power.

> When we have authority we have the freedom to act. The power was already there, but the restraints have been removed. The freedom may be given to us from outside ourselves, as other people give us their permission, or, the freedom may come from within, as we give ourselves permission to do something in our sphere of authority and responsibility.

When I believe that I have the right and authority to do something, this freedom makes way for my personal power to operate with full effect. When I say, "I feel I have no power in this or that situation," I normally mean that I feel I have no authority or right to do something or say something. I may well have the energy and the ability, but I lack the conviction that I am allowed to. Either I haven't given myself permission, or permission has been withheld from me by other people in authority.

This is why personal power is so distrusted, because so often the one who has the power maintains their power by withholding permission from others. It is not that the withholding of permission is wrong in itself; there *are* necessary spheres of authority and responsibility in the world. The problem with permission-withholding is that the leader who withholds permission often fails to adequately consult, facilitate, communicate and provide other avenues for people to express themselves. Together, these inadequacies create a permission-withholding *culture.* A permission-withholding culture in families, societies and organisations is deeply disempowering.

The Sense of Personal Power

I have a *sense* of personal power when I believe that I have the *energy* to do something, the *will* to do it, and the *permission* to do it. When we say that we 'have a sense of personal power', we are bringing these two concepts of power and authority together. We are saying that we believe we have the force of will to do something and the authority to do it. It is a sense of enablement; it is the power and the freedom to turn a decision into action.

A sense of power for action is only fully released where people are facilitated and empowered and permission is given, and this is why the other senses of self (place, principles, purpose, and potential) make such a difference in whether we have a strong sense of personal power or not.

> When we are accepted in a place, when our principles are in alignment in a place, when our purpose is recognised in a place and when our potential is honoured in a place, then our personal power is likely to be given full expression in that place.

The Exercise of Personal Power

As we have seen, when our senses of place, potential, purpose and principles are strong, and the environments we operate in are 'permission-giving' rather than permission-withholding, then our sense of personal power is likely also to be strong.

> When our senses of self are strong, we naturally have the heart for living; we naturally have a stronger sense of personal power for expressing the glory of who we are. When our personal power is strong, we know that the decisions we make will make a difference. We know that they will have an effect and that there will be a result.

Everything we do is accomplished by virtue of our sense of personal power. Through our personal power we action our purpose, potential, and principles for living. We are known to the world and ourselves through the exercise of our personal power, and ultimately, it is the power of the self which coaching seeks to encourage and to engage with. Built upon the first four senses of self, our sense of power becomes the deciding factor in whether we are able to make choices which lead to life fulfilment.

It's the exercise of our personal power which determines the extent to which we are known by others, the extent to which we influence others, the extent to which we allow ourselves to be influenced and the extent to which we are appreciated by others. How we enhance our personal power and how we exercise it is really important.

Personal Power and the Power of Decision

Our sense of personal power is expressed through making decisions which lead to action and even the choice not to act can be an expression of power if it is based on a positive decision. If we don't make decisions and if we don't take action on those decisions, we don't have personal power. We may protest that we do, but our lack of actionable decisions tells the truth. Only the power of decision, and the actions which follow those decisions, reveal whether we have a sense of personal power or powerlessness. Anthony Robbins refers to 'the power of decision' when he writes,

> "What *precedes* all of our actions? What *determines* what actions we take, and therefore who we become...? The answer, of course is ...the power of decision." [45]

The 5 Components of Wholehearted Decision Making

In the previous chapter, I suggested how a strong sense of potential nurtures powerful decisions, helping us to believe in the efficacy of the decisions we make. But this is just one component of whole-hearted decision making. A wholehearted decision needs five elements to take your decision forward, from initial intention to decisive action. These elements are:

1. The strength of *passion* or level of desire that you have for something - you need to *want* the thing you are deciding for.

2. The strength of *permission* that you have – what is the level of consent or conflict within yourself and with others for the decision?

3. The sense of *potential* or self belief that you have in your ability to succeed in the decision.

4. The commitment or *promise* that you make to yourself and others to do what's necessary to see the decision succeed; and

5. The *perspective* that you have on the decision. Have you considered the consequences of taking this action and the consequences of not taking this action?

> Active and powerful decisions are undergirded by passion or desire, by permission or consent, by potential or self belief, by promises or commitments to self and others, and by a right perspective which helps you to know if it's the right or best decision to take.

Where one element is missing or weak, a decision becomes half hearted. Either you don't want it passionately enough, or you don't believe you are allowed to do it, or you won't allow yourself to do it, or you don't believe that you are able to do it, or you are unwilling to commit yourself to doing it, or you are unsure if you should do it!

The 5 Components of Wholehearted Decision Making:

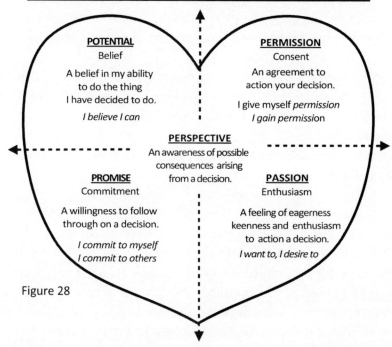

POTENTIAL
Belief

A belief in my ability
to do the thing
I have decided to do.

I believe I can

PERMISSION
Consent

An agreement to
action your decision.

I give myself permission
I gain permission

PERSPECTIVE
An awareness of possible
consequences arising
from a decision.

PROMISE
Commitment

A willingness to follow
through on a decision.

I commit to myself
I commit to others

PASSION
Enthusiasm

A feeling of eagerness
keenness and enthusiasm
to action a decision.

I want to, I desire to

Figure 28

© Richard. A. Burwell 2010: The 5 Components of Wholehearted Decision Making

To make a powerful decision we need to make sure that we are making it with a whole heart not half a heart. We can strengthen the quality of our decisions by asking the questions in the next exercise:

Exercise 1:
Applying the components of powerful decision making to a decision you are struggling with, but want to make:

Passion and Enthusiasm: What motivates you about this decision? As you imagine the positive consequences of this decision, what do you see? What do you hear? What do you feel? What excites you about this decision? How strong is your passion for the decision? How strong is your enthusiasm to do this thing?

Permission and Consent: Have you given yourself full permission to make this decision? What might be the internal conflicts that you are experiencing in regard to this decision? What do you need to do, to gain any necessary permission from other people? If you can't gain permission, are you willing to reassess your decision or, are you willing to carry the consequences of doing it anyway?

Potential and Self Belief: How strong is your sense of potential to do it? How much do you believe you can succeed? What previous success can you draw upon to reinforce your self belief in this particular decision? What do you need to say to yourself to strengthen your sense of potential to do this thing? What do you need to stop saying to yourself, to stop sabotaging your self belief?

Promises and Commitment: How strong is your promise to yourself to take this decision? How strong is your commitment to yourself to follow through on the decision? What might be hindering you from being fully committed to this decision? What resources do you need to help you follow through with this decision? How great is your commitment to do this? How much are you identifying yourself with this decision? Would it help you to make any promises or commitments to other people, in relation to your decision? Where your decision involves others, how strong is your commitment to them to follow through on the decision? Is there someone you would be willing to be accountable to, to help motivate you in following through on this decision?

<u>Perspective and Conviction:</u> A wholehearted decision is not a blind decision. In fact, the more you consider it from various angles, the more you are likely to become convinced – for or against the decision. Cartesian questions[46] are a very effective way of helping you to gain a full perspective on the possible outcomes of taking or not taking a particular decision. 'What will happen if you do x? What will happen if you don't do x? What won't happen if you do x? What won't happen if you don't do x?'

Your Gentleness Makes Me Great

Because making decisions is frequently difficult, and so many aspects of our lives seem to be in resistance to us, making a decision requires a strong exercise of power, either to overcome our own resistance, the resistance of others or the resistance of natural circumstances. The danger we face here though, is that in exercising the power of decision, we fail to exercise the power of restraint, and instead of our power serving people, our power ends up usurping and dominating and we are all diminished.

There is a line in one of the songs of Ancient Israel, relevant as a maxim for us to live by today, 'Your gentleness makes me great.' [47] The principle behind this simple line is quite profound. When we are gentle, we provide other people with a safe place to develop. Our gentleness gives other people the room to grow. When we exercise our personal power in the choice to be gentle towards our family, friends and colleagues, we create an environment where they can take risks without fear of being rubbished or ridiculed. We create a culture that nurtures growth because the culture is gentle towards new ideas.

> Gentleness creates favourable conditions for growth, but a harsh climate kills the chances for a good harvest. Rather than allowing our power to dominate and control, we allow our power to nurture and protect.

Gentleness is not weakness. Gentleness towards other people does not mean that we ignore issues that need to be addressed. Gentleness does not mean an absence of firmness; nor does it imply a poorer standard or a lower expectation. On the contrary, a culture of gentleness is generated where you want to see standards rise and productivity increase. Rules can still be enforced gently; discipline can still be implemented firmly. Gentleness is the way we implement the vision. The vision is still cast, but the culture which sees it fulfilled is a gentle culture which makes everyone great.

A gentle leader or father or mother can still exercise discipline, but they do it with firmness not harshness. At work, when other members of the team observe the gentle spirit with which discipline is exercised, they are encouraged because they are no longer fearful of being dishonoured or diminished. They know that the leader is for them, and seeks their success. Even their failure is dealt with kindly, but it is *still* dealt with. Gentle firmness is the culture in which greatness becomes possible.

> Gentleness is seen in the ability to hold a fragile flower without crushing it; to plant it _wisely_ in soil full of nutrients; to shelter it _compassionately_ from the harshness of the wind; to prune it with _restraint_, with an eye for its full potential, and to have the _wisdom_ to know when enough pruning is enough. Gentleness is the exercise of power with *wisdom, compassion* and *restraint*. Your gentleness makes me great!

Sources of Personal Power

So far in this chapter, we have considered personal power as it relates to authority, permission, decision making and gentleness. Now I would like us to think about where the sense of personal power is sourced from, and to relate this back to the other senses of self we have considered in previous chapters.

In the same way that the *source* of our physical power does not lie in the strength of our arms and legs, but in the power of our heart to spark our body into action, so the primary source of our personal power lies at the *heart* of who we are – our sense of self. Our sense of personal power is supported by our <u>internal</u> self beliefs (see figure 29) which in turn nurture our senses of place, purpose, principles and potential.

Our self beliefs can have a powerful effect on our self esteem, affecting our sense of place, and they can have a powerful effect on our self direction, influencing our sense of purpose. Self beliefs can affect our self knowledge and our ability to know the principles and values which guide us, and they can affect our self efficacy, determining the sense of potential we possess. When these internal senses of self are strong, our sense of personal power is equally strengthened.

Our sense of personal power is also supported by <u>external</u> factors, such as our relationships with other people, the tasks we engage in and the resources we have at our disposal. These external factors also nurture our senses of place, purpose, principles and potential and consequently, our sense of personal power.

Figure 29   **Sources of Power**

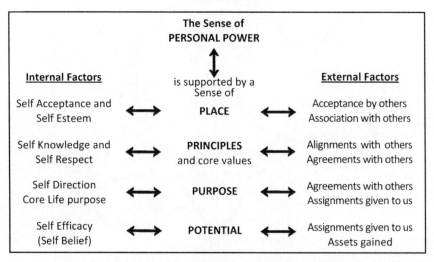

Internal Factors	The Sense of PERSONAL POWER is supported by a Sense of	External Factors
Self Acceptance and Self Esteem	PLACE	Acceptance by others Association with others
Self Knowledge and Self Respect	PRINCIPLES and core values	Alignments with others Agreements with others
Self Direction Core Life purpose	PURPOSE	Agreements with others Assignments given to us
Self Efficacy (Self Belief)	POTENTIAL	Assignments given to us Assets gained

Copyright Richard A Burwell 2010: Sources of Personal Power

The next diagram describes the external sources which facilitate the nurturing of personal power, shown by the inner ring.

Each of these sources – the degree to which we are accepted and affirmed; the degree to which we have positive associations with others; the degree to which we find ourselves in positive alignment with others; the degree to which we are able to make powerful agreements with others; the degree to which we have worthy assignments to fulfil; the degree to which we are resourced by assets of various kinds; the degree to which we have the opportunity to achieve and to which we succeed, and the degree to which we are able to abandon our power for the greater good - all affect our sense of personal power.

Each of these sources of power is to be sought and welcomed.

Sources of Personal Power:

Figure 30

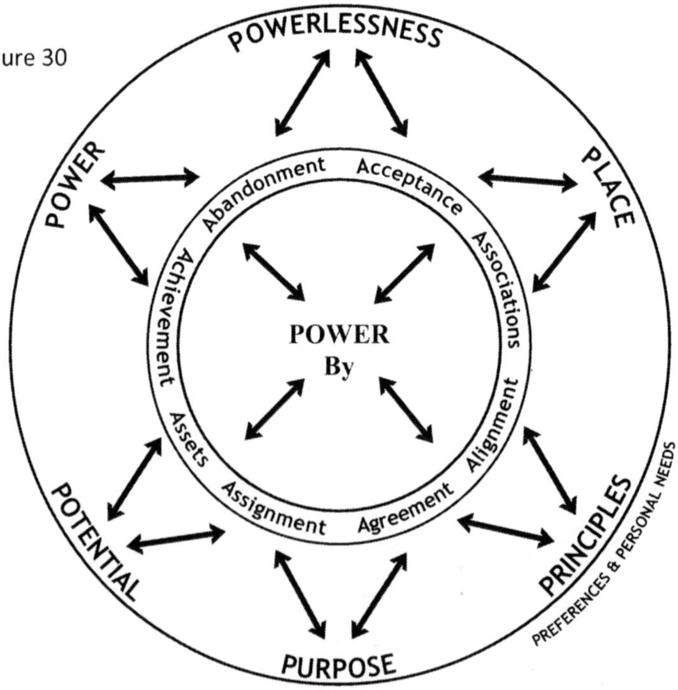

Copyright Richard A Burwell 2010: Sources of Personal Power

<u>Acceptance</u> is an essential condition for the nurturing of personal power. Personal power is nurtured in environments or places where we are accepted and affirmed. This is natural and will always be the case, no matter how mature we may become. Where acceptance is removed, the ground is taken away from us; there is no safe place to build upon or experiment within. Acceptance refers both to the outer dimension of finding a place where we are welcomed and also to the inner dimension of self acceptance. As we grow in self acceptance and self esteem, our sense of personal power will grow.

<u>Association</u> with other people who are more experienced than we are, and who can share their expertise with us, is another important aspect of growing in personal power. When we associate with them, their power and influence can rub off on us. When we spend quality time with them, the 'rubbing of shoulders' enables a sharing of weight-bearing capacity. The strength they carry in their shoulders is duplicated within us. When we find and maintain positive associations with resourceful people, we enhance our own growth in personal power. From the strong base of powerful associations, we are empowered to serve others who are less powerful.

<u>Alignment</u> with ourselves and the people we work with is another source for personal power. When we are aligned with our own primary values we are able to live with integrity, inner harmony and poise, and thereby limit internal resistance against ourselves. When we are aligned with the values of our colleagues, we are able to live and work in an environment free of unnecessary conflict. Alignment with personal and team values creates an inner and outer harmony which facilitates the growth of personal power and the expression of personal power. As we align with core values, we are guided to a wise and virtuous exercise of power. Of course, the process of coming into alignment with other people always involves some degree of conflict, but the pain is normally worth the prize.

<u>Agreement</u> with other people also nurtures personal power. Agreement creates a synergy which maximises the expression of power and the outcome that can be achieved. Agreement may involve agreeing to shared principles and values in a team setting, or agreeing to a shared purpose, which may involve a sharing of resource, a sharing of intention and focus, and a sharing of support and commitment. Agreements can include a strong resolve to do something and this resolve may be with others or simply an inner resolve we make with our self. Agreements may also involve gaining permission from other people to do something that we have proposed to do, but which may require their permission.

<u>Assignments</u> are not strictly a source of personal power, but they do focus our power in a particular direction, giving us a sense of direction or purpose. Where there is no assignment, power is dissipated. When our personal power is focused for a purpose it is amplified, in much the same way as the power of water flowing down a pipe is intensified. Compare this with a dispersed and directionless flow. A man without work appears powerless and may also feel it. A man on assignment, working to a purpose, appears powerful and harnessed. His power which was dissipated is now harnessed and directed.

Assignments also enhance our sense of potential which nurtures our sense of power. When we are given assignments, or when we decide on assignments for ourselves, our sense of potential is honoured; we are believed in and we feel affirmed in the task to be completed. To the extent that our sense of potential is enhanced, our exercise of power will be greater.

<u>Assets</u>, used as a broad term, refer to life resources rather than simply business resources.[48] Assets cover 5 major areas, namely time, health, people, knowledge/skill and materials. Some personal assets can be increased; others are fixed. Assets can be used very effectively and also misused. Assets are resources that may be a

source of personal power, and when we haven't got them we feel disempowered.

An asset can also be wrongly thought of as the most important element of personal power, but this is not the case. For example, even a man with many assets (talents, ability, skill, time, people support) may not have the *power of decision* to use them; he may lack a sense of power from which he makes powerful decisions. In contrast, a man with fewer assets may have a stronger sense of self which reinforces his power of decision. Such a man may accomplish more than the man who seems to have more. For tools on finding power through assets/resources see pages 207 - 211.

Achievements are also a source of personal power. There are two dimensions to achievement, namely outward achievements of education, lifestyle change, career development, sports competition, relationship development and so on, and inner personal achieve-ments, such as attitude changes, and self belief growth, which are more hidden and which undergird the external achievement more visible to others. When we achieve, we feel powerful and believe that we can do it again, even better, next time. Success breeds success.

It's important that we are able to celebrate our achievements without embarrassment because an appropriate celebration of achievement actually enhances our sense of power. The celebration of achievement brings validation and honour and this is an empowering experience. Of course, praise and celebration should follow *genuine* achievement, and when this occurs, the sense of personal power we feel is an experience rooted in reality.

Abandonment can be both an internal choice and an external experience. Periodically, we may choose to let go of something meaningful to us (internal choice) or, we *may be,* in fact, abandoned, left alone or ignored by other people (external experience). At certain points in our life, it may be necessary to abandon our own personal power for the greater good, or so that we are better able to receive a re-infusion of power having been detoxed from an attachment to personal power which may have become polluted by ego-greed.

Achievement is a good thing, but if we hold to our achievements too strongly, we run the risk of identifying ourselves too closely with our success. Our identity then becomes a 'success identity', that is, an identity defined by our pursuit of success, and our inability to face failure or defeat. When we are no longer successful, we then lose our identity because our identity was so closely attached to the success we have lost. Our willingness to let go of power and the pursuit of success, makes us less susceptible to these dangers.

Our sense of power is a utility to serve us, and is not to be sought in its own right. As we learn to hold our achievements - and the sense of personal power which grows from it - more lightly, we will be more ready for the next challenge which comes. Being able to abandon our attachment to power and achievement is a necessary protection to us and those we serve. I expand on these thoughts in pages 225 – 228.

Whether we make the choice to let go, or other people make decisions which cause us to be abandoned, we will experience powerlessness as a result. This is an opportunity for us to re-engage with the internal journey of self acceptance and self esteem, and the external journey of finding new places which receive us, and new associations which support us and which we can offer support to. By growing in self esteem and self acceptance, irrespective of the achievements we gain, we will find it easier to abandon our attachment to success and the feelings of power we experience in the future.

Where Has All the Power Gone?

Whenever we have a weak sense of belonging, whenever our purpose may be unclear and the principles of engagement uncertain, whenever limiting beliefs rob us of confidence, or past experiences contribute to a low expectation of who we are and what we may become, it is likely that our sense of personal power will be affected. But this is not an exact science. We are each affected by experience and circumstance differently. Even if one of our senses of self is weak, the other senses may compensate for this lack. For example, we may still have a sense of personal power, even if we have a weak sense of place because we may have a really strong sense of purpose, or the principles which guide us are still able to spark us into action.

I remember working with one man who had become homeless through a traumatic experience in business. Brian (not his real name) had been the managing director of a midsized company, but sadly, his fellow directors had acted deceitfully against him, and he was removed from his position losing many of his key sources of personal power. Brian's principles had been violated, his sense of place in the business ripped away and his senses of purpose and potential deeply shaken. As a result, his sense of personal power was significantly reduced. And yet, even from this desperately low moment, and the homelessness which followed, he managed to maintain some residual sense of power which was rooted in the strong sense of the principles which guided him.

Brian was determined to prove his case, and he was determined to maintain his honour and integrity. This became his new purpose. He was down, but he was not out. I don't know how his story ended, but I remember the intensity of his desire to recover his loss. He was seriously diminished, but he was not defeated. There was still a fight left in him, and the fight was born out of the strong principles he held. Though everything had been taken from him, the principles which guided him became the source of his power to rebuild his life.

A homeless person will probably experience this sense of powerless-ness more acutely than anyone else. They are understandably weakened in every sense of self. Their sense of place is contested, their sense of purpose – if they've managed to hold onto one - is mocked by their homeless and unemployed condition, their sense of potential is challenged by their lack of outward success, their primary values of principle and personal need are under stress, and as a result, their sense of personal power is deeply affected.

Nevertheless, the improvement in just one sense of self can have a positive effect on each of the others. We can see this with the homeless "Big Issue" sellers on the streets of our major cities.

By joining the ranks of other Big Issue sellers, a homeless person is given a new sense of place, of _acceptance_ and _association_; their principles are no doubt reinforced as they begin to take responsibility for themselves and as they _align_ their own values with the values of the 'Big Issue' team. Their sense of purpose is reactivated with the _assignment_ to sell magazines, and as people buy the magazine, their sense of potential and personal power is strengthened with the _achievement_ of selling successfully. As a result, the process of their re-empowerment has begun.

It's important, I think, if we are going to help a 'Big Issue' seller, to actually buy their magazine, not just give them money. In buying from them, we affirm their purpose – they are successfully _selling_ to us; we affirm their potential – they _are_ able to do it well; and we affirm their primary values – they don't want to live on handouts, they want to _make a living_ by their own effort and ability.

Another example of how each of the '5 Senses of Self' can impact each other can be seen in the school staff room. Ideally, teachers who have a strong sense of place in the staff room have a context where they can feel accepted, appreciated and understood. The staff room can be a safe place where they build strong associations with other teachers and where they are in alignment with shared values.

The staff room can be a place where their purpose is strengthened and their sense of potential encouraged through a clear knowledge of the <u>assignments</u> they have to fulfil and where their <u>achievements</u> are celebrated. The staff room can also be a place where the personal <u>assets</u> or resource of knowledge and skill are enhanced. In short, the staff room can be a place where their personal power is reinvigorated. From this place of strength, they can then 'take ground' in the classroom, extending the boundaries of learning, and also, improve the sense of place that the children are able to learn in.

Supportive and Resistant Assets/Resources

From the categories above, I will focus here on assets, as these are fundamental to our level of effectiveness in achieving our goals, and thereby, the extent to which we feel empowered.   We can think of assets as the resources we need to fulfil a task. These assets can be either general *life* resources, or specific *work*-related resources.

> How well we develop our resources, manage our resources, and discern the right time to use our resources determines whether they are supportive of us or resistant to us. When we harness the resources at our disposal, they come 'on side' working with us and for us. Making sure that our resources are 'on side' with our values, purpose and goals is an important element in achieving the outcomes we want. When our resources are in synergy with us, we are empowered by their support.

Figure 31 below offers one example of assets/resources that could be supportive or resistant for one individual, family, team or organisation at one moment in time. All the examples are generic. Take a look at this diagram and get a feel for how this individual is both supported and resisted.

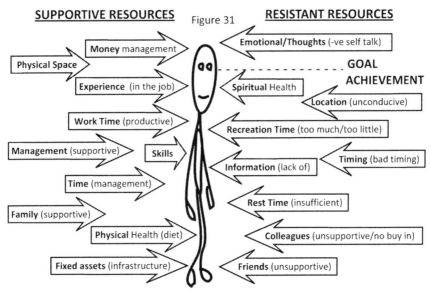

SUPPORTIVE RESOURCES   Figure 31   **RESISTANT RESOURCES**

Money management

Physical Space

Experience (in the job)

Work Time (productive)

Management (supportive)   Skills

Time (management)

Family (supportive)

Physical Health (diet)

Fixed assets (infrastructure)

Emotional/Thoughts (-ve self talk)

GOAL ACHIEVEMENT

Spiritual Health

Location (unconducive)

Recreation Time (too much/too little)

Timing (bad timing)

Information (lack of)

Rest Time (insufficient)

Colleagues (unsupportive/no buy in)

Friends (unsupportive)

Copyright Richard A. Burwell 2010: Supportive and Resistant Resources

We all know the experience of walking with the wind. Working with supportive resources can have the same sort of effect upon us - we are carried along, and life feels good. For example, the alarm clock is set and the batteries are fresh, the children are happy, the car keys are in the right place, the traffic flows, the lights are green, the phone is charged, people are helpful, the lift works, the paperwork is ready, the coffee tastes good, I am early, the meeting is well mannered and the motion is carried. When everything seems to go right we feel supported and empowered.

We all know the experience of walking against the wind! Struggling with resistant resources can equally have a powerful effect upon us. For example, the alarm was set, but the batteries are dead, the children are upset, I am rushed, the car keys lost, the mobile is flat, and so is the car tyre! The directions are wrong, the traffic is jammed, the lift is broken, the receptionist rude, the paperwork incomplete, I am late, the coffee cold, the meeting restless and the motion denied! When everything seems to go against us we feel resisted and disempowered. Some of these factors can't be helped, but many of them can be avoided with a little resource management ahead of time.

When my goals need to be resourced by other people, the way I handle my relationship with these 'people resources' determines the degree of my success or failure. So I could ask myself, "How well am I 'managing' the resource of other people in my life?" "In which ways do I depend on them, deploy them and be accountable to them?" "Are they supportive towards me and if not how can I encourage or inspire them to 'get on side'?"

The way I use the 'asset' or resource of time is equally critical in how empowered and supported I am in achieving my goals. I could ask myself, "How well am I managing the resource of time that I have each day, or each week?" "How do I organise my time in a good balance of work time, recreation time and rest time?" "How well do I judge the passing of time by being 'on time' or 'out of time'?" and, "How do I discern the right (or Kairos) time, by being in the right season of time?" "Or is my timing 'off'?" "Do I get the timing for something 'all wrong,' or do I discern the timing for something 'just right?"

Exercise 2:
Turning a Resistant Resource into a Supportive Resource:

The following table (figure 32) offers examples of potential asset/ resources in our lives. Try completing the table by first thinking of a goal you want to achieve. Then with this goal in mind, ask yourself whether each of the resource categories are supportive of you in achieving this goal, or whether they are resistant to you. Then ask, what else is supportive of you in relation to this goal? What else is resistant to you or working against you?

Which elements of your life are moving you away from reaching your goal? Which elements of your life are urging you on and which elements are distracting you? Which could be more supportive of you? What do you need to be in place for this goal to be fulfilled? What do you choose to do about it? What do you need to adjust in order to become more empowered?

Figure 32

THE SUPPORTIVE / RESISTANT NATURE OF 5 KEY LIFE ASSETS

RESOURCE / ASSETS	TYPE OF RESOURCE	Supportive	Resistant	NATURE OF THE PROBLEM — Is it an organisation (how I manage it) issue? Is it a timing issue? Is it a quantity issue? Is it a quality issue? Is it a support issue?
Time	Work time			
	Recreation time			
	Rest time			
Health	Physical			
	Emotional/Mental			
	Spiritual			
People	Family			
	Friends			
	Colleagues			
	Managers			
Knowledge	Information			
	Skills			
	Experience			
Material	Money			
	Location			
	Physical Space			
	Equipment			

Copyright Richard A. Burwell 2010: Supportive/Resistant Resources

Exercise 3:
Choose one Resistant Resource:

There may be one resource, which, if managed more effectively, would cause the others to be more in synergy also. Next, consider whether there may be one resource/asset in your life which if brought more 'on side', would bring other resources on side with them. Why is this particular resource so important for you in achieving your goal? What are the reasons this resource is 'out of place' and not 'on side' in your life? What needs to happen for this resource to be more supportive of you? What do you need to do? What do you need others to do? What can you do to influence them?

Where significant change is necessary, the true level of our desire for a goal we have set becomes evident. If the goal truly flows out of what we value, then it is likely that we will be sufficiently motivated to make any changes necessary to achieve the goal and fulfil the value which the goal is seeking to address. If, on the other hand, the goal is not born out of a core value for us, then it is possible that we will not be sufficiently bothered to really do what is necessary to achieve the goal. Comfort, stability, familiar habit patterns and the fear of change will all seem to have a stronger pull on us than the goal we have set for ourselves, and the resources which are resistant to us will not be addressed.

> So far in this chapter, we have thought about five components of powerful decision making, seven sources of personal power, and five key life assets that either resist us or support us. Now we will turn our attention to the landscape of personal power, and how we can use it to achieve the results we desire.

PART TWO

THE LANDSCAPE OF PERSONAL POWER

The effects of personal power and the nature of our relationship to it is complex. Personal power has a *context*, a *disposition*, a form of *expression*, a way of *action* and a *result* wherever it is released. These elements of personal power are the *landscape* in which personal power becomes visible to us. Seeing the landscape gives us a bird's eye perspective which enables us navigate our way around it, rather than being lost within it.

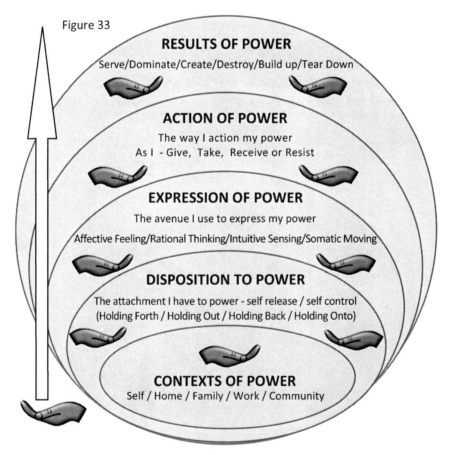

Figure 33

RESULTS OF POWER
Serve/Dominate/Create/Destroy/Build up/Tear Down

ACTION OF POWER
The way I action my power
As I - Give, Take, Receive or Resist

EXPRESSION OF POWER
The avenue I use to express my power
Affective Feeling/Rational Thinking/Intuitive Sensing/Somatic Moving

DISPOSITION TO POWER
The attachment I have to power - self release / self control
(Holding Forth / Holding Out / Holding Back / Holding Onto)

CONTEXTS OF POWER
Self / Home / Family / Work / Community

Copyright Richard A. Burwell 2010: The Landscape of Personal Power

The Contexts of Power

In the landscape of personal power, the first area to explore is the *context* where power would be released. Power is always exercised in a context, in a place, and it's essential that we correctly discern the needs of the situation that we are in, and the opportunities before us, if we are to express our personal power appropriately. If we misunder-stand the context, we are likely to misapply our power within it. Even if just two people are involved, the context is shaped by the differing expectations, experiences and perceptions of each person, and of the problems and opportunities that the situation presents.

Our first task is to recognise the *need* of the place that we find ourselves in or the nature of the *opportunity* that we see, and to ask how we can best serve the need or make the most of the opportunity. This is an important question because,

> the existence of a need or the presence of an opportunity doesn't necessarily mean that we are the one to fully serve it, or to fully take hold of it. Other people may be better equipped to meet the need than we are, or there may be a better time in the future when we can take hold of the opportunity.

We are likely to have a part to play, but rightly understanding our role will mean that when we do contribute, it will be well performed and well received.

Our Disposition to Personal Power

The relationship we have to power, whether our own personal power, the power we have by virtue of the office or position we hold, or a spiritual power we may seek to receive, is an important one.

This relationship to power is what I call our *disposition to power* and it takes the form of <u>*self control*</u> or <u>*self release,*</u> or a *harnessed* balance between the two. See figure 34.

Figure 34   <u>Disposition Towards Personal Power</u>

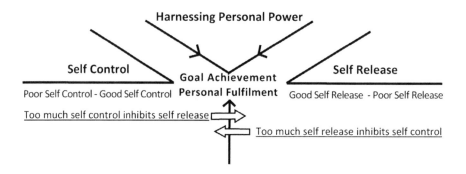

Copyright Richard A. Burwell 2010: Disposition Towards Power

> When we combine appropriate self release with appropriate self control, we harness our personal power enabling us to live effectively. 'Appropriate' levels of self release and self control are determined by you in ways relevant to your personality, values, lifestyle habits and the contexts in which you live.

For example, if your highest value is achievement at work and you exercise good self control, this may result in good work-life balance. Alternatively, if your highest value is achievement at work and you have low self control, then you may allow your work value to dominate your life and you may exhibit workaholic tendencies. If your highest value is 'home life', with work being a means to an end, and you exercise excessive self release, you are likely to give insufficient attention to your work responsibilities.

When we understand what our core personal values are, we are then able to monitor how much attention we are giving to those values, and how much effort or power we are expending in fulfilling those values. Effective living requires constant re-evaluation and adjustment of focus. When we notice that we are imbalanced in one area of life, we can then re-balance the expression of our personal power in the area which needs attention.

> You may have a personal goal of self control in one area, and of self release in another. The exercise of personal power is required in both cases. You may find that in one situation you tend towards self control, and fail to release the fullness of your potential. In another, you tend to self release, and fail to hold back your power when it might actually benefit you or others to do so.

Through goal setting, restructuring limiting beliefs, and recognising your core values, you are more able to *harness* your personal power in the direction of self control or self release, leading to the achievement of goals and personal fulfilment.

The Disposition of Other People Towards Us

In addition to recognising the need or opportunity of the situation we are in, and the part that we have to play in serving the need or taking the opportunity, we also need to discern the disposition of the need or opportunity towards us, that is:

Are we being welcomed?   Are we being resisted?
Are we being tested?   Are we trusted or is it too early to tell?

Often, our disposition will be an equal and opposite reaction to the disposition of other people towards us. These are normally split-second automatic reactions that we make based on years of earlier experience. Sometimes we can make decisions based on assumptions and presumptions, rather than well thought through perceptions. Sometimes it's helpful to slow the process down and reflect a little longer on the nature of the situation before us.

Some contexts offer no resistance to the expression of our personal power and this may be dangerous - our power may become destructive, or dominating. An antidote to this is to develop an accountable relationship with someone who can help us to harness the expression of our power for shared benefit, not selfish gain.

Other contexts may offer too much resistance and thereby disempower us. Although we may know that we have the ability, capacity or potential to do something, nevertheless the environment may hold us back, preventing us from exercising our power of decision and using our talents, abilities, skills and resources. In these situations, the environment is permission withholding; its disposition towards us is one of control, not release.

> When the places we live and work in are not working for us, it's time to make adjustments, so that we can then express the fullness of who we are more effectively and meaningfully. Perhaps we need to adjust the way we relate to our environment. This may be a necessary part of the process in seeing the environment relate differently to us.

Helpful questions may be:

Does the context receive you? Does it facilitate you in the sharing of your power? Do you have a sense of place here? Do you have a sense of purpose here? Do you have a sense of which values are at work in this context, and of how your own principles and personal needs may find a home here? How can you make your contexts more conducive to receiving your power, to receiving expressions of who you are?

The contexts where we exercise our personal power don't have to be easy. Contexts of challenge are often the environment in which maturity is nurtured and strength formed. But occasionally, a context change *is* necessary. So, if, after all other options have been explored, there is still no opportunity for us to meaningfully express our self in service and contribution, we may need to consider looking for other contexts or places that will receive what we have to offer and provide a more conducive environment for personal growth, self expression and productive service.

Exercise 4:
Your Perspective Affects Your Sense of Power:

The way we see things and the way we hear things can sometimes gives us a warped view of the way things really are. We may be tempted to project onto others the fault of a situation, without really giving fair attention to the possible fault that we may also share.

Of course, sometimes power really is being taken from us - sometimes we really are being hindered at every turn - but sometimes, our own perspective is the problem. Sometimes our imperfect perspective may be hindering our own sense of personal power. Being able to see our life from various viewpoints can help us to gain a clearer picture of what is really going on, and to see what is actually happening to the power in a relationship. The NLP exercise known as 'Perceptual Positions' is a very helpful tool for helping us to view situations differently and work out which resources will help us to be more effective. Perceptual Positions was originally formed by John Grinder and Judith Delozier (1987).[49]

In First Position:
You are standing 'in your own shoes', in your own typical body posture, using your own tone of voice, turns of phrase and so on. In 1st position, you are going through your typical experience of communication from your own perspective - seeing, hearing, feeling everything that is going on around you and in you. In 1st position, you are inside yourself, seeking to express yourself. You are associated within your own experience. If you are truly in 1st position, you will not see yourself from the outside looking in, you will *be* yourself, looking out at the world through your own eyes and ears. You will be fully associated in your own body and with your own view of the world.

In this position, try role playing what it's like for you in a typical situation where you feel disempowered. Stand in your own shoes, looking and talking to the person who seems to disempower you. Do this role play for 1 or 2 minutes, speaking out loud the things you would want to say to this person or situation from your own perspective.

In Second Position:

Now, change the perspective, stepping away from being in yourself, to standing in the shoes of the other person several feet away. Make sure that you give yourself a moment to dissociate from your 1st position experience before you step into the shoes of the other person. Take on the other person's perspective within the situation which disempowers you. Take on the other person's physical posture, tone of voice, turns of phrase and world view as though you were that person. See, hear and feel what the communication is like from their point of view. In 2nd position, you will be experiencing the world through the other person's eyes, thoughts, feelings, beliefs etc. In this position, you will be dissociated from yourself and associated into the other person. Try role playing again, this time, by addressing your 'first position' self as 'you' and referring to the other person in whose shoes you are standing as 'I'.

In the role play, as the other person, you speak to the 1st position 'you', using the language that you hear the other person using, and with the assumptions that you assume the other person has about you. When you temporarily take on the other person's perspective, you are able to see what you are like from their point of view. You may see things you haven't seen before. Try this role play for 1 or 2 minutes, then, change the perspective again, stepping away from being in the other person, and step to one side, into a 3rd position.

In Third Position (or 'Observer' Position):

Now put yourself temporarily outside of the context you struggle with, so that you can see the situation from a neutral, more impartial perspective. From this observer position, you can see the situation more clearly, as if you were observing a difficult conversation. From 3rd position, you gain as much information about the relationship as you can.

Observe the power play, see where the power lies. In this 3rd position of observation, you see what's going on in the relationship, you hear what's being said and the way it is said, and you observe intuitively, being awake to any insights that may come to you about the relationship. Remember that you are a neutral observer – you are not associated into either 1st position or 2nd position. You are looking on from a higher, clearer perspective. From this position of observer, consider the sort of resources that the person in 1st position (you) would benefit from.

Back in First Position:
Consider for a moment which resources you recognised in the observer position, that would improve the quality of your state of mind and heart and the quality of your relationships. 'Take' these resources back with you into 1st position by associating into the feeling of the resource. It might be a resource of peace, patience, wisdom, strength, gentleness, firmness, humour and so on. Let the role play continue for another 1 or 2 minutes, but with these new resources at your disposal. Say what comes to mind, but with these updated resources now part of you. Then, step back from your 1st position role and when you are ready, step into 2nd position.

Back in Second Position:
You now respond to the 'new' 1st position 'you' who has been newly resourced. Say what comes to mind as the relationship takes on a new dimension. As 2nd position person, you are now relating to a renewed 'you'. The quality of the role play relationship will feel different. Finally, go back to 1st position.

Finally, in First Position:
You now relate to the 2nd position person who has also been newly resourced, having experiencing a new 'you'. End the role play, by relating to the newly updated 2nd position person. Enjoy this moment of newly imagined expectations. It is a resource you can carry with you. Of course, the real time relationship has not yet changed, but what has changed is your perspective, and this can make all the difference. The role play *was* a real experience and you genuinely experienced some real insights and some real emotional changes, and you have genuinely updated your imagination

and expectation of what is possible. You are now able to go back into the real time relationship with some updated insights and expectations, and with greater access to the resources you need to make the relationship or situation work better for you and everyone else. As soon as you begin to relate differently, other people in this system of relationships will begin to respond to the 'new you' differently also. At the very least, you have re-empowered yourself with a better perspective and better resources.

The Currency of Personal Power – How we Spend it

Our disposition to power refers to the feelings of attachment we have to the power we use. The way we handle money is a useful illustration of the way we handle power. For example, we can hold back our money, and limit our expenditure, spending it carefully in a self_ controlled manner. In the same way, we can hold back our power but also be limited in the benefit we may gain from using it.

Or, we can hold onto our money and save it in a strongly self controlled manner, but in saving it there is always a danger we may lose it. In the same way, we can hold onto our power, but also potentially lose the influence that this power could purchase for us.

Alternatively, we can hold forth our money as opposed to holding it back, and be let loose in the amount of money we spend and where we spend it. Equally, we can hold forth our power, using it freely in a self-released sort of way, but as in the spending of money, we may also get lost in the euphoria of releasing our power without restraint.

Fourthly, we can hold out our money giving it away to anyone who wants to take it. Equally, we can hold out our power and give it away in a strongly self-released manner; we can choose to let go of our power, releasing our attachment to it, in readiness for re-empowerment, but, in letting go of our power, we may be in danger of losing ourselves.

Finally, we can consider how our money may best be used in each situation, from the list above. Equally, we can <u>harness</u> our power, in a dynamic balance of holding back, holding forth, holding onto and holding out the power we hold.   These ideas are expressed in the following diagram.

Figure 35   <u>The Currency of Personal Power</u>

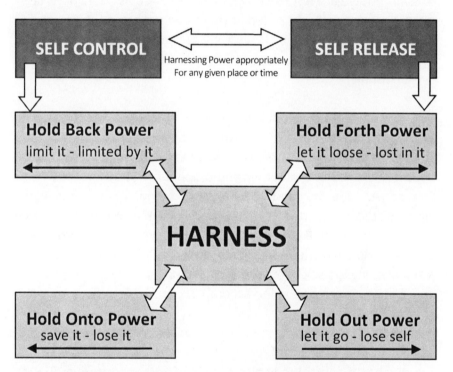

© Richard A. Burwell 2010: The Currency of Personal Power

Our disposition towards personal power is really important, because it affects the intensity with which we engage in any activity. If we get the intensity right, doors are more likely to open naturally, people are more likely to respond warmly. If we get the intensity wrong, either doors will not open, or we will knock them down, or people will be manipulated into our will, or steadfastly resist our desire.

Holding Back our Power

There are times when holding back our power, or limiting the expression or expenditure of it can be useful. Perhaps we need to limit our own expression, so that others may also have room to express themselves. Perhaps we choose not to take hold of something that we could take hold of. Perhaps we decide to hold back our power by making a decision slowly. Our decision is measured and considered; we are not too quick to act first and ask questions later, instead we are self-controlled in the matters before us. In holding back our power, the focus is on using our power, but not too much. The intention is to accomplish a task but not too forcibly or overbearingly.

The danger in holding back our power however, and limiting its expression, is that our self control may become excessive; we may actually resist or limit ourselves. We may miss taking hold of the opportunities before us, or withhold benefit that others may need to receive. We may not fully express our passion, pleasure or even displeasure in circumstances which require emotional clarity – perhaps to a child who needs to be praised or reprimanded, or to an employee who needs to be encouraged or disciplined. As a result of being too self-controlled, our passion, pleasure or displeasure may be too hidden and fail to accomplish our preferred intention.

We may resist doing something as well as we could for fear of being labelled a show off, or for fear of limiting other people's opportunity. Too much self control may also hinder us from presenting an idea or project at work with the enthusiasm it requires. People may not be able to grasp the importance of what we say because it doesn't seem important enough to us.

Excessive self control can also paradoxically create an environment in which others are also controlled or limited. By holding ourselves back, even if it is to create room for other people to contribute, we may unintentionally create a permission-withholding environment, especially if we are leaders in our field or community.

> Unless we clearly articulate that other people have the freedom to express themselves or contribute freely, they may feel that permission is being withheld – not because we verbally withhold it, but because our behavioural style leads the way; our demeanour becomes the norm.

Followers will model the style of behaviour they see leaders expressing. Even if our own personal style may be more withheld, we can still help to create an environment for contribution and self expression by articulating that fellow colleagues or community members have the permission to express themselves and contribute in ways which are congruent with their own personality. The same is true if our style is more self-released. Letting people know that they have the freedom and permission to be themselves is an essential component of healthy communities and collegiate work environments.

Holding Onto our Power

The disposition of holding onto our power is similar to holding back our power, but we hold onto our power *because* we feel disempowered. We are either fearful of losing it or fearful of failure, so we hold onto our power by not making a decision, or by not making a contribution. When we hold onto our power, our attention is on what we might lose, not on what we might give.

We may also want to hold onto our power in order to save it, but holding onto power to save it is false economy – it takes energy to hold onto something, so eventually the energy or talent is dissipated without being used. When we are tired and we need to be replenished, we don't say, "I'm really tired, I need to hold on," we say, "I'm really tired, I need to let go." Rest, sleep or Sabbath is the route to replenishment, whereas holding onto something is the route to eventually losing it. Holding onto our power or talent rather than using it is an expression of self control, but the motivation is fear and the result is loss.

> We may choose not to express ourselves in a conversation or meeting for fear of losing face, but in choosing not to express ourselves, our face is not seen, and we have lost our opportunity. In holding onto our power, we lose even what we hoped to save. By choosing not to commit ourselves, we lose our influence and we lose our reward.

Holding Forth our Power

There are times when it's necessary to 'hold forth' and release our power, to express the fullness of who we are and what we believe, and to do fully what we are capable of doing. There are times when we need to let the full force of who we are and what we can do come to light. When we hide our light for fear of being accused of pride or for fear of obscuring the light of others, we may hide from the world the gift it needs. The world is big enough to receive you. Your place of work or community needs you to hold forth your power, *but* with wisdom and grace.

We all need stories of creativity, courage, wisdom, insight, success, passion and enthusiasm. The stories that are told by word of mouth, at dinner tables, or in the newspaper, or on the evening news are only told because someone has the courage to hold forth their power. In doing so, others are inspired and motivated, a direction is set, resistance is overcome, hindrances removed, barriers broken and expectations of what is possible extended.

> When we are appropriately self-released we create an environment where colleagues, friends and strangers may also feel empowered to contribute. In seeing us live to our fullest capacity they see what's possible, and they are inspired to do the same.

Of course, there is a shadow to holding forth our power. When we are excessively self-released, we may so occupy the space that there's no space left for others to occupy, no air for them to breathe. In the excessive release of our own power, we may end up dominating and controlling rather than releasing and empowering. We may even articulate that people around us have the freedom to express themselves or to contribute as they wish, but there may be no real opportunity for them to do so.

Power is persuasive and intoxicating. When I let loose my power, I may become lost in the power I loose. Power can release but it can also imprison, which is why the fourth disposition towards power is an essential antidote to the abuse of power.

Holding Out our Power Open-Handedly
As we noted at the beginning of this chapter, personal power is the essential human force required to express who we are and to make visible the talents and abilities we have. It's a sense of enablement, a sense of energy to act, it's the power to turn a decision into action. But personal power is also a dangerous force when we use it without reference to the principles and values which seek to empower others as well as ourselves.

The fourth disposition towards power is a counterbalance to our natural tendency to seek power and use it. The fourth disposition towards power is the willingness to hold out our power in an open-handed manner. It's the counterintuitive willingness to let go of our power for our own benefit or the benefit of others.

> Power can corrupt, and it is necessary at regular points in life to detox ourselves from the potentially corrupting influence of power and give it away. This is the principle of a *power detoxification*.

Imperceptively, the use of power may become too important, and the benefit we gain too precious. Our attachment to power may pollute our personality. We may fail to recognise the subtle shifts of motivation within us as we benefit from the exercise of our power. We may begin to enjoy the feelings of control and influence which the exercise of power gives us, more than the pleasure of serving the less powerful and raising them up to a more empowered place. We may become usurpers rather than servers. Power may begin to intoxicate us and the very power we sought to possess has possessed us. We know that we are held by it when we are unwilling to let go of it. The willingness to hold out our power and even let go of it may be health to our own soul and the soul of others.

There are several degrees to holding out our power open-handedly. The first and most natural is _sleep and regular days of rest_. The ability to rest shows that _we_ control the expression of our power; the expression of our power does not control us.   As we have noted, when we are tired and we need to be refreshed, we don't say, "I'm really tired I need to hold on," we say, "I'm really tired, and I need to 'let go'." Sleep is a temporary expression of letting go; you hold onto nothing while you sleep, but in the morning, power has been returned to you and you are energised to take hold of the reins again.

The second is _serving or giving with no expectation of reward_. When I serve others I allow them to take from me what they need, without demanding honour or recognition for my service. My power is available in an open-handed way and I serve with no expectation of reward. The volunteer, the charity fundraiser, the unsung hero, or the successful worker, who shares their reward with others who didn't quite deserve it, may all be expressing their power in an open-handed way. The power may still be with me, but I have let go of my insistence to keep hold of it. In some way, my power has been used for others and I may not have benefited in the normal way.

An extreme example of this is found in the story of the 'Herald of Free Enterprise' Ferry, which sank off the Port of Zeebrugge on 6th March 1987, while carrying passengers across the channel.

In one story of bravery, ex-policeman Andrew Parker made himself into a human bridge so that his wife and 12 year old daughter could climb to safety. Once across, his wife beckoned for him to follow, but he said that others also needed help to get out of the sinking ferry. Amazingly, 20 other passengers also walked over his body to safety.

Rather than using his power for himself alone, he chose to use it for others, and potentially, give it up. In holding out his body as a bridge, he held out his power for others to use as a means of rescue. In being willing to give his life up for other people, he proved himself to have far more personal power than any who pushed their way to safety without regard for those drowning around them.

The third level to letting go is the willingness to _take a sabbatical, or resign from positions of power and authority_. Letting go of power is counterintuitive, but in letting go of our power we cleanse our motives and our associations with control. The same principle operates in the realm of money. In being willing to give it away, we prove that we are not held captive by it. If we cannot relinquish power, we are proven to be held by the very power we claim to hold. This is why it can be helpful for those in positions of power and authority to take a break from the exercise of it.

The benefit of a sabbatical is not simply the rest that is gained from the absence of responsibility; it's the deeper and more profound regaining of self control. In relinquishing control over others, we regain a deeper and more profound control of self.

Sometimes, the exercise of power and responsibility can become a deeply draining experience. Rather than just becoming tired, our inner reserves become dangerously depleted. Unless we take a sabbatical, we may be in danger of burnout. It may be that we have lost touch with the original values and purpose which gave us meaning. In this situation we need to let go, and a sabbatical, or even resignation, will help us to reconnect with the values and purpose we have lost touch with, or it will help us find a new purpose.

When we take a sabbatical or resign from authority, we give ourselves the opportunity to be redefined, because we no longer have the security of previous boundaries, support structures, or familiar patterns of self expression. We are faced with a more 'naked', less prescribed definition of who we are. It can be the most vulnerable and difficult period of our lives, but also the most fruitful and rewarding. If we are willing for the uncertainty that lies before us, previous self understanding may be reconfirmed, or new truths about who we are and who we could become may be revealed.

There is also, however, a shadow to the practice of holding out our power open-handedly. We may do it too frequently, or towards the wrong sort of people. There *is* a danger of being taken advantage of, and losing our sense of self. Nevertheless, the relinquishment of power can be a very significant expression of power, and the precursor to a new and fresh experience.

Harnessing Our Power
Learning to harness our personal power appropriately is essential if we are to live effectively, productively and with sensitivity towards our fellow travellers in life. Finding the right and best balance between self control and self release is a trial and error journey. It involves being willing to look back and reflect over our experience and learn from it. When I harness my personal power, I decide the times and places when I need to hold back my power, hold onto my power, hold forth my power or hold out my power open-handedly *and* the intensity with which I do this.

Our disposition to power fundamentally affects the intensity of our self expression, and the way we action our power of decision. To what degree do you hold back your power and limit its expression? To what degree do you hold onto it and save it? To what degree do you hold it forth and let it loose? And to what degree are you willing to hold it out, open-handedly, and relinquish it? The following questions may help you to think these issues through personally.

Exercise 5 - Your Disposition to Personal Power:

Think of a situation in your life where you feel that things are not 'quite right'. Imagine that you are holding your power of expression and decision in your hands, out in front of you. Now reflect for a moment on whether your main disposition in this situation is self control (holding back, or holding onto your power), or self release (holding forth, or holding out your power).

Refer back to figure 35 and draw 5 squares on the floor in front of you. Step onto the middle square which represents your present experience of harnessing your personal power in the particular context of life you have chosen to think about. What is the main disposition you are expressing in this context?

Now step onto this square. How is this disposition serving you or the people you have a relationship with? What's the effect or result of your current disposition? Is the disposition of your personal power relevant for the context? What do you see yourself doing and hear yourself saying, while you are living out this disposition in your life? How are other people responding to you? What are the reasons for you expressing this disposition in this particular context of your life at this time? What is your motivation? How would you like things to change?

Now stand on the other squares which represent other dispositions to personal power. For each one, ask yourself the following questions...

On holding forth your power more freely: What would you be doing if you were holding forth your power more fully, expressing yourself more freely and making more decisions, or making them more easily? What difference would it make? As you imagine this, what do you see yourself doing and saying? What are other people doing and saying in relation to you, as you hold forth your power more fully? How do you feel? Take an inventory of the strongest insights you gain from imagining the positive benefits of this disposition in your life in this context.

On holding back your power more fully: What would you be doing
if you were holding back your power a little more? If you were
expressing yourself a little less forcibly, less enthusiastically, less
intensely, less keenly, less quickly? What difference would it make
if you made decisions more thoughtfully, or contributed a little less
frequently? As you imagine this, what do you see yourself doing
and saying? What are other people doing and saying in relation to
you, as you hold back your power a little more? How do you feel?
Take an inventory of the strongest insights you gain from imagining
the positive benefits of this disposition in your life.

On holding onto your power: What would you not be doing or
saying if you held onto your power? What would be the result or
consequence of this in your life and on other people around you?
What are other people doing and saying in relation to you, as you
hold onto your power in this way? How do you feel? Take an
inventory of the strongest insights you gain from imagining this
disposition in your life.

On holding out your power open-handedly: What would you be
doing if you held out your power in an open hand? If you were
willing to let go of it more readily? If you were less attached to the
results of your actions, or the benefits you gain from the expression
of your personal power? As you imagine this open hand disposition
to your power, what do you see yourself doing, what do you hear
yourself saying? How do you feel? Take an inventory of the
strongest insights you gain from imagining the positive benefits of
this disposition in your life.

Now step back onto the middle square representing how you
harness your personal power in the particular situation you have
chosen to think about. Recall each of the positive insights you have
gained from each disposition to power that you imagined for your
self. Recall each disposition in turn. Visualise yourself expressing
the positive elements of each disposition in turn, then hold all these
insights in a creative tension, giving yourself time to integrate the

positive elements of each disposition into your chosen situation. When you are ready, imagine the situation again. This time, you have harnessed your personal power in a fully appropriate manner. Notice what you see, hear and feel. Be thankful for the insights you have gained. Take a note of them in your journal.

The Expression of Power

While we _exercise_ personal power through our will (volition) as we choose to be self-controlled or self-released, we _express_ personal power through the four gateways or avenues of thinking, feeling, sensing and moving. These are our abilities of reason, affection, intuition and somatic (body language) skill. [See figure 36.] These are the ways we engage with our environment and represent ourselves to the world.

Figure 36

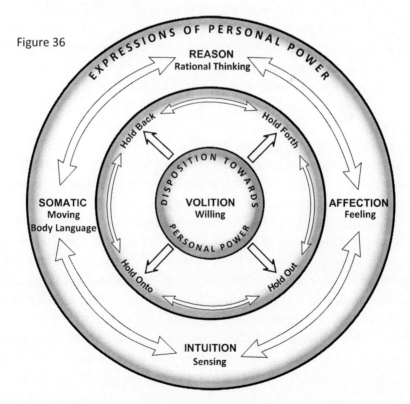

Copyright Richard A. Burwell 2010: Expressions of Personal Power

Reason

This is our _rational ability_. All our experience comes to us through the five physical senses, which represent the world of experience to us. Those experiences are then processed and shaped in the language form of the five physical senses:- visual (sight), auditory (hearing), kinaesthetic (feeling), olfactory (smell) and gustatory (taste). The language patterns of seeing, hearing, feeling, smelling and tasting form the foundation of how we express our thoughts, ideas, concepts, memories and imaginations. I can express myself to the world using my rational thinking ability.

Affection

This is our _feeling ability_ or emotional intelligence. It includes our ability to be empathetic, to have a strong connection to our values and motivations, to be enthusiastic, and to be aware of our attitudes. It includes our ability to have easy access to our emotional feelings such as happiness, sadness, anger, peace, compassion, love and attachment, and to recognise when our emotions are being constrained by negative feelings like bitterness or jealousy. I express myself to the world using my affective ability.

Intuition

This is our _sensing ability_, or intuitive intelligence. It involves us being open to knowledge and insight that may arrive spontaneously, beyond what we currently know or have thought about. It may arrive through words, pictures, or feelings, in the form of individual words, sentences, pictures in the mind, dreams, impressions, gut feelings or a deep inner knowing. Once an intuitive insight has been gained, it then needs to be discerned as to its source, before it is expressed.   Perhaps one of the reasons the Judaeo-Christian tradition refers to Divine Spirit as the _Holy_ Spirit, is because there are other sources to intuitive messages. As with each expressive ability, the intuitive skill can be developed by learning to be still, to listen and to be open. Ultimately, it is only through experiences of trial and error and success and failure that we can see this ability strengthened.

Somatic Ability

This is our *moving ability* or body language intelligence. We use the body to represent our thoughts and feelings to the world around us. Our gestures reveal what we are thinking and feeling. We use our body to express our personal power, not only to perform actions, but also to express our thinking, feeling and sensing. Somatic skill includes the gestures of face, hands and body posture.

Which Channel of Expression?

We normally use each avenue of self expression in support of the other avenues. So although the avenue of rational thought may take the lead as we use words to express our thoughts and feelings, it will often be closely supported by the avenue of emotional expression, physical gesture or intuitive sensing.

Often, our emotions and physical gestures are involuntary expressions which, hopefully, support us. But sometimes, the involuntary nature of these expressions can be unhelpful, and actually detract from the message we wish to communicate. The way we express ourselves may disempower us, rather than empower our communication. As we learn greater self control and self release, we are able to use all four avenues of self expression - rational thought and words, emotional feeling, intuitive sensing, and somatic body language gesturing - more effectively.

I recall seeing an episode of "The Apprentice" on UK Television recently. In the show, a number of business professionals compete against each other in order to win a highly-prized job contract with multi-millionaire, Sir Alan Sugar. One of the contestants prided herself on being highly intuitive, and she used intuitive-based language very frequently - perhaps a little too frequently. She attempted to influence and motivate her fellow team members by using the intuitive channel of expression more than the rational or affective avenues.

Statements like, "I just know..." or "I sense its right," didn't always help her to be understood or be respected by other members of the team, even though she was sometimes proven to be right. This was a good example of how a preferred avenue of self expression is not always the best avenue of expression, either to make ourselves understood, or to influence others effectively. When I express my personal power through an inappropriate channel of self expression, I will not get the result I am looking for.

The nature of the message we want to communicate and the nature of the people we want to communicate with and the nature of the meeting or environment we are communicating in should help us to determine the appropriate avenue of expression and the appropriate level of intensity in our communication. Knowing what the context and message requires of us, helps us to know how self-controlled or self-released we may need to be, and how intellectual, emotional, intuitive or physically expressive we should be.

Of course, these are normally split-second responses in most situations and our own personal style will be the major influence for us, but good communication requires good observation; and reflecting on the manner of our communication *before* the moment, may help us to communicate well *in* the moment.

> An inappropriate channel is one which fails to communicate what I wish to say in such a way that listeners actually understand what I have said. Equally, an inappropriate channel fails to motivate others to do what I would like them to do, or causes offence when I did not intend any. It may be *my* preferred avenue for expressing *myself*, but it may not be the avenue which another person responds well to. I have wasted my energy if I have failed to communicate effectively.

The avenue of power we use and the intensity with which we use it, determines the degree to which we are received and the quality of the result we get. It is useful to reflect on how we communicate with other people, and whether our current disposition and style of self expression is getting the type of result we want.

Learning to 'read' our environment and gaining rapport

It becomes really obvious that adjusting our channels of self expression and communication to the right intensity for the setting we are in and the people around us is very important if we are to achieve our desired aims. We can gain this understanding by correctly 'reading' the person we are talking to, or 'reading' a group we are having a meeting with.

We can use our personal powers of expression - rationally, affectively, somatically and intuitively - to help us read situations and people, so helping them and helping ourselves communicate better with them. By listening carefully to the language other people use, by listening empathetically to the emotions other people express, by carefully observing other people's body language, and by listening intuitively *for* other people, we effectively express our personal power both for our own benefit and the benefit of others.

You have to know what tune another person is playing before you can play their tune. Knowing what tune they are playing is the art of reading were a person is coming from. Playing their tune is the art of gaining rapport. Rapport helps us to get in tune with the other person, or to be on their wavelength in such a way that mutual understanding and trust can be developed. As Henry David Thoreau once said,

> "Could a greater miracle take place than for us to look through each other's eyes for an instant?" [50]

All communicators do this naturally – whether they are salespeople, politicians, teachers, trainers or preachers. It can be done manipulatively for selfish gain, or can be done as a way of improving the quality of our communication. To communicate effectively - to be understood and to understand - is a basic human instinct and a basic human responsibility.

The Actions of Power (Give, Take, Receive, Resist)

A decision without action is a wish or an idea only. It is still waiting to be embodied in something that we do or do not do. Our decisions are put into action as we *give, take, receive* and *resist* in any context of life. Our disposition to personal power determines the *intensity* with which we give, take, receive or resist. Do we action our decisions in a self-controlled or a self-released manner?

We each have a natural bias to one form of action or another. Some of us give more, some take more, some receive more, some resist more. As we learn to take action holistically, using the appropriate form of action for each situation we encounter, we then find that the result we want is closer at hand.   Figure 37

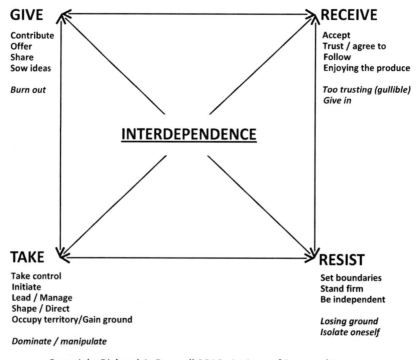

Copyright Richard A. Burwell 2010: Actions of Personal Power

Give

When we action our power of decision through giving, we may find ourselves contributing, offering help, sharing resource, sowing ideas and giving time. However, there is a danger of burnout if we give to the detriment of the other actions of power, especially, if in giving out we fail to receive.

When we give, we establish trust; by giving we are contributing something which offers a window into who we are. People who don't give or contribute anything are expecting others to travel furthest in the journey of trust; they are expecting the other person to believe that they are competent, reliable and trustworthy with little evidence that this is so because they have given little to show that it is so! Whenever we give something from ourselves or of ourselves, we offer some evidence about who we are.

This is why, when developing business it can help to offer something free before the fee, or to offer a money back guarantee, because giving without condition equals out the balance of power before money is paid or contracts are signed. It gives the buyer some confidence in the seller. The same is true in all relationships. When you give, share and contribute, you give other people confidence; they see something of you in the gift.

> Giving is an expression of power, but it also alters the dynamics of power. It can equal the balance of power in a relationship and empower the other person, but if taken too far, it can also disempower you.

Perhaps your default position has been to *give* as your primary way of relating and building, but this may not be working too well. How would a little more taking initiative, or receiving, or resisting affect the dynamic of the relationship you wish to build? In your place of family or work, what are you giving or contributing? In which ways can you give more of yourself? In which areas do you need to give less of yourself? How would your relationships at work or at home alter if you shared more or less of yourself? What would happen if you gave more of yourself emotionally, or less emotionally? What would happen if you contributed your ideas and opinions more freely, or a little less so?

Take

When we action our power of decision through taking, we may find ourselves taking control, initiating, leading, managing, shaping or directing, and in various ways occupying the territory before us and gaining the ground we need to gain.

The word 'take' often has a negative connotation, but there are many areas of life and business where taking charge and gaining ground is essential. The entropic nature of life is such that we lose ground all the time - opportunities are missed, relationships damaged, personal boundaries overrun, time wasted, mistakes made, health weakened, hope diminished, purpose lost. If we don't exercise the positive action of 'take' sufficiently, we may lose ground unnecessarily.

Most often, we simply need to express our power of decision through 'taking' in just small and barely obvious ways. For example, an opportunity for business may present itself, but we still need to *take* a decision; an old friend emails us to renew contact, but will we *take* the opportunity before us? Or we may have some spare time, so will we use it by *taking* a rest, or *taking* the chance to deal with some pressing issues that need attention?

On other occasions, the challenges of life are more pressing and require us to be more assertive and more forceful, taking what we need and doing what we need to do. Sometimes, we just have to subdue the ground before us and only then can we cultivate it into the form and design we have seen in our hearts and minds.

> We cannot initiate, lead, shape, direct, assume control or gain ground without taking. Taking is an essential aspect of personal power. However, with too much taking control or initiating we may become controlling or dominating. The power of 'take' must be wielded with care, in accordance with the primary values which guide us.

In your place of work what do you need to take control of? What do you need to initiate? What would happen if you were more self-controlled in the way you initiated things? Or less so? Where do you need to gain ground? What further territory do you need to occupy? Are you looking for opportunities to receive or are you initiating and making opportunities? What would happen at work or at home if you took control or initiated a little less, or a little more?

Receive

There is a decision to be vulnerable in the action of receiving. In receiving we have chosen not to be powerful - we have become vulnerable. But, this very act in itself requires an exercise of power; it is a choice to lay down our guard and let others near to us and give to us. Too much receiving, however, may cause people to lose respect for us. They no longer see us; they see only what they have given to us. Our full personality is only evident when we express all four actions of personal power.

> When we action our power of decision through receiving, we may find ourselves accepting others, trusting them, agreeing to their recommendations, following them or simply welcoming the result of our own effort or the effort of others. The power of 'receiving' enables us to welcome and enjoy, to accept, to trust, and to follow.

When we receive an idea from someone else, we are, in effect, giving our allegiance to them, at least in regard to the idea we have received. The idea or person we receive is no longer standing apart from us, they are now alongside us and we are alongside them. In exercising the power of *receive,* we strengthen our relationship with people and we decrease the distance between us.

In your place of family or at work, what are you receiving? What would you benefit from receiving? Is it an environment of trust? In which ways do you receive from others? Do you need to receive more and action your power by trusting others? How would your relationships and environments change if you received a little less, or a little more? What would happen if you received help less cautiously?   What would happen if you received ideas and contributions more enthusiastically?

Resist

When we action our power of decision through resisting, we may find ourselves setting boundaries, standing firm or being independent either physically, emotionally or intellectually. When we action our power of decision through resisting we maintain the necessary space we feel comfortable with. The power of resisting is an essential component of self awareness. It helps us to maintain a sense of ourselves as distinct from others, as opposed to allowing our physical, intellectual or emotional space to be imposed upon by other people without our permission.

> The power of 'resisting' maintains our freedom for the sake of genuine relationship. There can be no meaningful giving or receiving if we have not maintained a meaningful sense of self through the setting of appropriate boundaries in our life.

Although the power of 'resisting' maintains our freedom, it is pointless if it is not counterbalanced by the other actions of personal power – give, take and receive. The power of resisting, if left unchecked, leads only to conflict, isolation and the eventual losing of ground.

At home, are you clear on the boundaries you need to set for the children? In which ways do you need to give the children more room

and more opportunity for self expression? At work, what boundaries
do you need to set for the team? As a team member, what personal
boundaries do you need to set, especially in terms of work-life
balance? How can you resist a controlling colleague's tendencies
appropriately? Do you need to be aware of the dangers of isolating
yourself by not receiving help and being too independent? What
would happen if you resisted unwelcome, but well-meaning,
intrusions to your work with more self control? What would happen
if you resisted such intrusion more boldly? How might you do it?

The Metaphor of Driving a Car

Driving a car offers a useful metaphor for seeing how the four actions
of power fit together. Within any one journey, we are likely to use
all four actions. For example, we *give* way to let others through, we
take an opportunity to pull out onto a new road, we *resist* someone
who tries to pull out in front of us and we *receive* the invitation from
a driver who gives us room. We cannot effectively drive a car
without using all four actions of power. We cannot effectively do
our job without using all four actions of power; we cannot effectively
live our life without using all four actions of power.

What is the best way of expressing your power at home or at work?
How well is your current way working for you and others? How can you
adjust the intensity of the way you give, take, receive and resist? Are
you in danger of burning out, giving in, isolating yourself or dominating?
To express one aspect of personal power to the exclusion of the
others will cause us to lose our power, rather than gain it.

> The four actions of personal power enable us to live and work
> with others interdependently. This is the true power of team-
> work, where each team player shares in the dynamic flow of give
> and take, receive and resist.

Power is exercised and decisions are made in order to make a change
and to maintain the change that has been made. We must exercise
power to maintain what we have and to gain what we want to achieve.

The way we are disposed towards our personal power, the way we express our personal power, and the way we action our personal power needs to be shaped by the personal values and principles we honour. Power without principle becomes power pollution. Good principles harness the power we possess so that the results we get are results which honour us and benefit others.

Figure 38

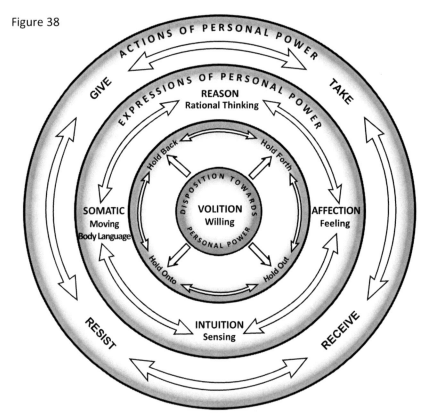

Copyright Richard. A. Burwell 2010: Actions of Personal Power

The Results of Power

The exercise of power always has a result. Reflecting on the result of how our personal power impacts other people is essential if we are to become all we can be and empower family, friends and colleagues into being all they can be too. When we reflect on the results of what we do and say, or fail to do and say, we remain responsive to the people we have an effect upon, and we remain open to the best actions possible in new situations. By reflecting on our *disposition* to power, the way we *express* our power and the way we *action* our personal power, we are more likely to attain the *results* we desire.

> When we can ask the people we affect if they were *served* and *empowered,* or *dominated* and *disempowered*; whether they were *built up* or *torn down*, whether they were *released* or *controlled* and whether the result was *creative* or *destructive*, we will then know what works and we will know how to do things differently next time.

It takes courage to reflect in this way, but if we are not willing to ask the questions, perhaps we are not yet worthy to wield the power. The willingness to ask for feedback, reveals whether we are exercising our personal power for our own benefit, or for the benefit of those we serve.

Service, especially in the world of commerce, hasn't been a very topical subject for the last few decades. Society's disposition to power (and money as an expression of power) has been one of unbridled self release. But perhaps now, in the aftermath of the worldwide banking crisis, and the recession which has followed years of focus on personal gain, a new ethic can be established in society, which focuses on how we can use our power to serve and empower others. In doing so, paradoxically, we may find a deeper fulfilment of self.

The results we get are the consequence of a specific strategy of behaviour - a specific way of using the structure of personal power. As we reflect on our past results, we can then adjust the *disposition* or form our power takes (self control or self release), in a way that is relevant to any specific context. We can adjust the way we *express* our power – intellectually, emotionally, intuitively, and somatically with our body language - and the ways in which we *action* our power by giving, taking, receiving and resisting, in ways and degrees of intensity which are appropriate to the context and the type of result we want.

What is the result you are looking for? In your places of work, home and local community, what does the context and the result you desire require of you? In which ways does your disposition to power need to be adjusted? Do you need more or less self control or self release? How can you best express yourself at home, at work, at rest and at play? How can you more effectively action your power by giving, taking receiving or resisting?

Whether you emotionally react or respond, express jealousy or contentment, bitterness or forgiveness, give yourself up to feelings of rage or release, the fear of failure or facing the fear; whether you think negative or positive self talk, destructive day-dreams or positive visualisations; whether you act co-dependently or inter-dependently, are controlled by others or make your own choices, control others or serve them, take from others or give to them, give to others or receive from them, talk excessively or listen, listen excessively or talk, one thing is clear - the exercise of your personal power is the key factor in how you live.

Personal power is seen in every moment and occasion of life. We see it in the power to get up in the morning and go to a job we hate for the sake of the family we love; the power to pursue a dream; the power to relinquish a dream; the power to redefine a dream; the power to make a courageous decision; the power to put our self first; the power to put others first; the power to try new ideas; the power to have new experiences; the power to express our self; the power to withhold expressing our self; the power to use our abilities; the power to learn new abilities; the power to resist temptation; the power to lead; the power to follow when you want to lead; the power to resist a controlling person; the power to confront; the power to forgive; the power to face a challenge; the power to let go; the power to leave and the power to join.

Finding our personal power and expressing it in all the places we occupy, in line with the purposes we are moved by, in harmony with the principles we identify, encouraged by the potential we are nurtured by, is essential if we are to see life take on the richer character and flavour we yearn for.

CONCLUDING THOUGHTS

The Pivotal Point

As you have worked your way through this book, you will no doubt have faced the awkward tension that exists between the reality of your life as it is and the ideal of your life as you hope it can be. This is the pivotal point in personal development; it is the place of tension between resignation and persistent hope.

> The perennial struggle in making the most of our life's opportunity is found in the interface between the reality of life as we have it now and the hope of life as we dream it can be. The struggle is defined for us by two statements which seem to vie for supremacy within us. "This is my lot in life," and, "There must be more to life than this!"

These statements of disappointment and hope ask questions that we must all face at some point in our journey through life. "Will I build a home of contentment in a place which is bearable, or will I press on towards the ideal?" or "Can I do both?" These ideas are expressed in figure 39 below...

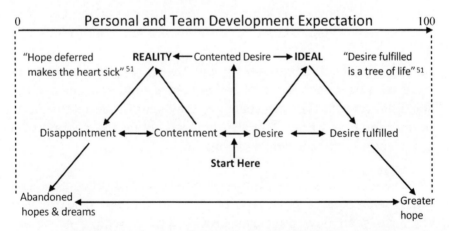

Copyright Richard A. Burwell 2010: Personal Development Expectation

"Contented desire" is the fulcrum point of personal and team development. Contentment is expressed through gratitude for what we have and how far we have come, and keeps us connected with the reality of life as it is in the interim. Desire keeps us connected with the ideal as we hope it can be. It is expressed through a pursuit of the dream until the desire is fulfilled.

Contentment without desire will tend us towards stasis. There will be no motivation for development or change. We may find happiness in our contentment, but at its worst extreme, disappointments may lead us to abandon our hopes and dreams. Desire without contentment, on the other hand, will keep us restless, unable to appreciate the good of what has already been achieved.

> The tension between these two postures of heart is awkward, yet creative. It is the paradox of contented discontent. When we hold the postures of contentment and desire together within ourselves or within our team, we are able to acknowledge the things which are worthy of praise in the present and nurture the pursuit of further personal and team development into the future.

'The 5 Senses of Self' offers a framework for such development. By attending to each of the five senses of self as an individual, as a family, as a team, or as a manager, director or CEO on behalf of others, we will help to create a culture which nurtures greatness.

As we have reflected together through the journey of this book, we have seen how each sense of self influences and enlivens each of the other senses. We have seen how they operate within the life of an individual and how they also operate within the context of a team, community and organisation.

We have seen how a sense of power completes a sense of purpose, and how a sense of place provides a platform for purpose to be explored. We have seen how principles provide power with a necessary protection, and how purpose inspires our sense of potential.

To live effectively, we require strong senses of place, meaningful senses of purpose, harmony with our principles, a sense of potential which keeps us believing in possibilities and a sense of personal power which enables us to make decisions and take actions which fulfil us and benefit others.

As I draw this book to a conclusion, may I wish you success in your quest to live well in all your places of rest and work; to live in harmony with all your principles and values; to live in alignment with all your life purposes; to live in the self belief of all your potential and to live connected to your power to make good decisions and to take actions which will fulfil all your noblest hopes and dreams.

Strength and Peace,

Richard A. Burwell – January 2010.

APPENDIX 1

WHAT IS COACHING?

While writing this book, someone asked my wife, "What is a life coach?" Before she could answer, the person seemed to have a moment of insight, and quickly answered their own question. Hopeful that this might lead to a coaching appointment for me, she listened with interest. The person continued, "Isn't it one of those people who save you from drowning?" An easy mistake, but it contains a relevant truth. A life guard saves us from drowning, a swimming coach helps us to swim better, and a life coach helps us to live better.

Coaching might be the fastest growing industry second only to Information Technology, but it's also the most misunderstood. So I would like to clarify its meaning here. Coaching is an empowering, collaborative relationship enabling people *and* organisations to live purposefully, find courage, manage change and achieve success. Another, better known definition states that, "...coaching is the art of getting people from where they are to where they want to be." Looking at the history of the word 'coach' can give us an idea of what it involves.

The historical roots of coaching

In the 1500's a coach was a horse drawn carriage which moved people from one location to another, it originated from the small Hungarian village of Kocs where it was simply called a 'wagon from Kocs', or a *kocsi*. German-speaking Viennese then began to call the carriage a *Kutsche*, from the name of the village Kocs. The French, adapted the word and called it a *coche*, and the Italians called it a *cocchio*. It was introduced in England in the mid 16th Century as the word *coach*.[52] From this original use of the word, we now have the verb 'to coach' today, meaning to move someone from where they are to where they want to be. The word 'coach' was first used in the sense of a private mathematics tutor at Cambridge University from the mid 1830's, and in 1885 as a trainer of athletes. [53]

The term 'sports coach' became the predominant term describing a trainer, motivator and encourager of athletes, helping them progress from a place of mediocre performance to a place of excellence. Then in 1974, Timothy Gallway's 'The Inner Game of Tennis' was published, and this became highly influential. The inner game is:

"the game that takes place in the mind of the player, and it is played against such obstacles as lapses in concentration, nervousness, self doubt and self condemnation. In short, it is played to overcome all habits of mind which inhibit excellence in performance." [54]

In 1989, Thomas Leonard founded the 'College for Life Planning' in the United States and largely out of this college, coaching grew through the 1990's with the International Coach Federation being formed in 1994. IBM was the first major company to use coaching, and by the mid 1990's business had begun to accept coaching practice more widely, and the term 'executive coaching' was invented for leadership development. Sir John Whitmore wrote 'Coaching for Performance' in 1992, popularising the GROW model developed by Graham Alexander. As coaching was being accepted within business, it was also being accepted as a tool for general life development, hence the term 'Life Coaching' was coined. From the early 1990's ontological coaching also spread through Spain and South America. Coaching has become widespread and now has mainstream academic interest. (Reference Joseph O'Connor and Andrea Lages). [55]

Its roots are found in various schools of psychology, sports coaching, business mentoring, management consultancy and career guidance. Today, musicians and actors, entrepreneurs and business executives, parents and anyone who wishes to improve themselves are hiring coaches for the support, encouragement, challenge and accountability they need in order to gain a new sense of life direction, fulfil a dream or get unstuck and move from where they are to where they want to be.

Personal development and executive coaches have become the new guru's of the 21st Century, and the principles of coaching have become recognised practice in the business world. In one respect, the development of the coaching phenomenon is hardly surprising when we consider the fragmentation of the nuclear family and the disintegration of community cohesion in so many western societies, especially in the urban context.

Elders of the community, grandparents with wisdom to share, older brothers and sisters with time to listen – all these essential building blocks of personal and societal development have been slowly eroded and we are the poorer for it. Brothers and sisters, and children and friends move away for the sake of work or love, with the result that there are simply fewer people to depend on, with less time to offer.

Faith communities offer a natural context for listening and care, through a pastoral care framework, but, similar to the counselling profession, have tended to focus more on dealing with the emotional problem rather than on how to utilise personal resources and talents for positive achievement and life development. Of course, both emphases are relevant and may be necessary for different people at different stages of life.

What is certain, however, is that the coaching model has brought into the public gaze the importance of listening, the art of asking powerful questions and the encouragement to set goals for personal development, with a view to building into the future, and not simply revisiting the past. Professional coaches use insights gained from psychology and an optimistic view of human potential, and seek to integrate these insights into a generally non-directive, empowering, personal development framework.

This framework creates a collaboration with the client, based on the belief that the client has the answers, or can find the answers, and that positive thought, purposeful living and positive actions can make a significant contribution to the effectiveness and fulfilment of life.

We can each become the hero of our own story if we choose to be, but it is not a given. The heroic heart emerges in the context of life's battles, where powerful and searching questions are asked of the heart that would be heroic, and where good choices are made in response to those questions.

While the heroic heart *emerges* in the context of life's battles, the heroic heart is *maintained* in the context of other heroes - where each one reinforces the quest of the other to be all they can be, making a positive difference and contribution each in their own unique way. Fellow heroes may be found among friends, fathers, mothers, lovers, priests, teachers, managers, colleagues, doctors, counsellors, mentors and of course, the professional coach.

The role of a professional coach is to help maximise your own heroic qualities. A professional coach seeks to help you engage more fully with your own adventure, fully using your own unique gifts and sharing with others, your own unique qualities.

Coaching and its Cousins

A consultant is generally a specialist hired to offer advice and find solutions in work based situations, working with the client in a specific area and on specific issues. A coach does not necessarily have the answers, and even if they might have, a coach would not presume that their answers were the right answers for the client, in their specific context. A coach has the right questions that lead to the right answers for the client in their field, and which rely on the specific knowledge and experiences which the client brings to the coaching relationship.

A Counsellor is a specialist who works with a client struggling to cope with specific issues which are rooted in the past and which are holding them back. Counsellors generally work in specific subject areas where a specialised knowledge is required, for example, bereavement counselling, marital counselling, addiction counselling and so on.

A Therapist is more likely to work over a longer period of time and more intensively with the client at a deeper level of the personality. While coaching is more interested in the present and the future, both counselling and therapy have a stronger interest in how past experiences influence the client's present experience. Counselling and therapy are words which are often used interchangeably.

A Mentor is usually an expert in their particular field, and works with the mentee in the same area of work or organisation to share knowledge of skills and wisdom relevant to a specific business culture and organisational structure. So a lawyer would mentor a lawyer, an engineer, an engineer and so on. The mentor focuses on the role and knowledge of the mentee. A coach however, focuses more on the person being coached, and the process of personal development.

A Corporate and Executive Coach is a professional coach who works with managers and leaders in business contexts, helping them around issues of personal performance, organisational performance and leadership. Joseph O' Connor and Andrea Lages define coaching as:

> "A methodology for change, to help people (and through them, businesses) to learn, develop and be the best they can be." [56]

A Life Coach or Personal Performance Coach is a professional coach who works with an individual helping them to address issues which are holding them back from living the kind of life they want to live, or from performing the way they want or need to perform.

Although distinctions are sometimes hard to maintain, a coach will address problems from the standpoint of solutions more than causes, and requires less knowledge of psychological processes than a counsellor or therapist does. It is also, generally, a shorter term arrangement. A coach helps individuals to dream dreams, set goals, see life as it really is and define the life they want to attain. In the process, a coach helps the client to determine the personal changes which are necessary to achieve their goal, and helps the client to grow in appropriate self beliefs and knowledge of personal values.

The term coach can be confusing due to the wide variety of ways in which it's used. For example, you may come across a 'voice coach', a 'parenting coach', a 'writing coach', an 'acting coach' and of course a 'sports coach', in addition to the life and executive coach. Robert Dilts, in his book 'From Coach to Awakener' helpfully draws out the distinctions when he writes,

> "Small 'c' coaching is more focussed at a behavioural level, referring to the process of helping another person to achieve or improve a particular behavioural performance ...Large 'C' coaching... emphasises evolutionary change, concentrating on strengthening identity and values, and bringing dreams and goals into reality..." [57]

Essentially, coaching provides a creative space where you are the full focus of attention, where your potential, values, dreams, goals and life purposes are fully explored, and where you are encouraged to adopt empowering expectations for your life and work. Through deep listening and intuitive questioning, the coaching process inspires you to greater levels of self awareness; you're given the space to access your own intuitive wisdom, to gain your own insights and you are supported towards achieving the goals that you've defined for your life.

APPENDIX 2

THE 5 PHYSICAL SENSES FROM A COACHING PERSPECTIVE

Life is both an experience we give and an experience we receive through the exercise of our five physical senses. However, our five senses are more than just experience receptors and experience givers - they are also the way we code our memories, the way we explain, the way we construct ideas and the way we make meaning for ourselves. We use the metaphor of our five senses all the time. Here are just a few examples:

'I feel like it,' 'I've lost touch with,' 'get a grip,' 'put your hand to it,' 'paint a picture,' 'the future looks like,' 'deaf to those voices,' 'a whispering of,' 'it sustains you,' 'spice of life,' 'lost/found the scent' and so on.

The five physical senses are our first means towards self awareness and self definition. We gain awareness from and define ourselves in reference to what we see, smell, hear, taste and touch.

> Whatever we know in life, we know through our senses. Our senses are our antenna, the things that give us an awareness of, or a perception of ourselves and others. Our five physical senses each contribute to our power for living. Because our five senses are so integral to who we are, how we live, how we give and receive and how we make meaning, we can use them as a metaphor for the hidden realities in our life - realities which run deeper than the simply external factors of what we can see, smell, hear, taste and touch. They can become for us a window to the soul.

By forming self reflection questions based on the five senses, we can find a doorway into the hidden realities of soul. These questions can help us to recognise truths about our lives; realities which we can sometimes miss seeing, miss hearing, miss touching. Using our five physical senses in this way, we are helped to notice truths which normally elude us, and then find practical solutions to those insights.

We are all affected and motivated by our physical senses, but to varying degrees of intensity. Some people think, and recall their experiences ,mainly using pictures; others, by reference to what they hear or feel, or touch. Some cultures give far more honour to the senses of taste, smell and hearing than the western world. In 'The Taste of Ethnographic things,' [58] Stoller observed that the Songhay tribe speak of 'tasting' kinship, 'smelling' witches and 'hearing' the ancestors!

As you read through the following questions, based on each of the five physical senses, you may find that you respond to one sense in particular more warmly and more fully than you do to the other senses. This is normal; where I may respond more naturally to sight (visual stimulation), and communicate more easily using visual language for example, you may respond more easily and communicate more naturally using sound (auditory) based language. Still another person may be more comfortable responding to and communicating through gesture and touch (kinaesthetic communication).

This also translates to internal picture language, internal sounds and internal feelings. We each have a preferred way of how we represent the world to ourselves, and how we represent ourselves to the world. However, sometimes, thinking about our experience by using one of the other senses a little more, can help to unlock a perspective we hadn't been able to 'see', 'hear', or 'feel' before.

Sight

In western society, the sense of sight reigns supreme. It's the one sense which is honoured above all others, yet even here, we may fail to see the hint of interior truths we can give our attention to, in order to see our life more clearly. The things you look at provide a window into the things you are interested in, and also a window into the things you are addicted to. The things you consciously avoid looking at also provide a window of insight into deeper and more subconscious thoughts, feelings, motivations and fears.

Eyes have been likened to being like a window for the soul. Taking this idea further, you can use sight as a metaphor for the _way_ you see things, not just <u>what</u> you look at. Sight then becomes a springboard for potent coaching questions, for example:

What does your ideal future look like? What are you seeing right now in xyz situation in your life? How are you looking at this? How do you need to look at this? What do you need to see in your current situation that you are not seeing? What are the warning signs? What do you want to see? What do you need to avoid looking at? What are you avoiding seeing, but may need to give your attention to? Which areas of your life do you need help with, to see more clearly? What are you scared of looking at in your life? What makes you scared of looking at this more fully? How could you look at this situation/this person differently? How could you look at yourself differently?

Hearing

Sociologist Keiko Torigoe, refers poetically to the 'sacred scenery of silence'[59]

Where is your sacred scenery of silence? What does it give to you? Do you need more or less silence in your life? Do you need more voices in your life? If you need fewer people in your life, how will you sensitively create more space in your life for you to hear yourself? If you need more voices in your life, how will you find them? What do you need to hear them say to you? How will they know unless you tell them? What can you say to them? When will you say it? "I see what you mean" is a common statement of shared insight and identification. "I hear what you say!" is a statement of resistance, or at best grudging acceptance. What are you hearing and yet resisting? Why the resistance? Time jump into your ideal future for any area of your life. What are you hearing in this future? What are you saying, and what can you hear others saying?

Your hearing helps you keep your balance. Which areas of your life are unbalanced right now? What do you choose to do about it? What have you had a faint whispering of? What are you detecting, but not yet sure of? Whose voices are you listening to? What internal voices are you listening to? How do they serve you? Which voices (or internal chatter) do you need to cancel out? Which voices do you need to amplify? Whose voices are important to listen to? Who do you need to listen to? What and who do you listen to that doesn't have a good effect on you? What can you do about this? Who needs you to listen to them?

We hear by giving our attention to things. What are you giving your attention to right now? What do you need to give your attention to? What do you need to hear that you are not hearing?

Touch

Touch and taste are senses of the immediate now, in contrast to sight and hearing which reveal things that are both here and now, or far away. Smell, similarly, may expose us to immediate realities, or to distant things which give us a scent of their forthcoming presence. We can use the immediacy of touch and taste by probing into how we are living in the here and now. For example, who do you need to be more in touch with? Who do you need to be less in touch with? Who do you need to give a hand to? What do you need to put your hand to next? Imagine that you have full permission, power and opportunity to shape x, y, z situation in your life exactly as you would like; how would you shape it in your ideal world? What do you need to begin to address in order to make this happen?

Who are the people in your life who give you positive strokes, who make you feel better, stronger, capable? How can you shape your circumstances to give them more room in your life? Who are the people who do not give you positive strokes, who 'rub you up the wrong way?' How can you appropriately resist their negative influence? How can you help them?

How will you make these things happen? When? How often do you purposefully give positive strokes to others by encouraging them? How could you do this more effectively? How do you 'feel' about x, y, z situation? What needs to happen for you to feel better about it? What do you need to do? How can you approach it differently? How well do you handle x situation in your life? If you were to handle this perfectly, what would you be doing? What would you be saying? What is happening 'in the now' that you are failing to put your hand to? When are you going to do the things you have recognised here?

Taste

The sense of taste becomes a springboard for the following questions...

What are you doing out of habit, but you have lost the flavour of? What do you need to savour and enjoy more? What sustains you in life? Which experiences have left a sour/bitter taste in your mouth that you need to resolve or avoid next time? What were the causes of these experiences? Which experiences have you enjoyed, that were sweet to the taste, that left you feeling satisfied? How can you sustain yourself with more of these? Which experiences and relationships offer you 'the spice of life' by keeping you young, on your toes, ready for anything? How predictable is your lifestyle menu? How does your current lifestyle menu serve you? What needs to be put on the menu? What needs to be taken off?

Salt is a preservative, keeping food safe and fresh. Which experiences and relationships keep you salty and fresh? Which do you want to build more into your life? Which experiences and relationships have become bland or stale? What are the causes of this? What do you choose to do about this? What can you do to inject new taste into these experiences and relationships? Which foods are you eating /drinking to excess? Which do you need to have more of? What do you choose to do about this? What help do you need?

Smell / Scent

The sense of smell has been undervalued in western culture. This is evident in the language we use to describe it. The nose is called a conk, hooter or snout, and the ability to smell is rarely praised in the way the other senses are. We easily speak of people being a visionary, as having a good ear, or a light touch and good taste, but we don't as easily link the sense of smell with the ability to discern danger, or sense safety.

Although the associations with the nose in western culture are often both negative and embarrassing, the undervaluing of the size of one's nose and the sense of smell is not universal. For example, the Ongee people of the Andaman Islands believe that a person's odour comes from his or her bones, which are in turn made of concentrated smell. The Ongee believe that in smelling their own odour, they gain a sense of their own identity. This view is mirrored in their cultural practice of touching the tip of their nose when referring to themselves as 'me'. The idea here is that smell is related to an interior sense. When the Ogee greet someone, they don't ask "How are you?", rather they ask, "How is your nose?" [60]

Obviously, we don't have to borrow the Ongee's world view to see the value of using the sense of smell as a metaphor for interior realities. The sense of smell/scent can be used as a metaphor for the things we want to pursue in our life, like a hunter, or a lover. Equally, it can be a metaphor for danger and the things we need to avoid.

Smell is a basic survival/security/sustenance and satisfaction sense. Using this idea, what do you have a scent of that you need to pursue? What are the reasons you need to pursue this in your life? Where is that scent leading you? What do you have a whiff of that you need to avoid? What are the reasons you need to avoid this/these things? Is there a whiff of something new in the air? Can you sniff out a new opportunity? What smells fishy to you about that?

The sense of smell can sometimes save our sense of taste from an unpleasant experience! Things may look fine to the senses of sight and touch, everything may appear to be okay, but are there hidden problems you would rather not have to taste first hand? Our intuition is like the sense of smell; it can warn us of a problem before we have to taste it! What is hindering your ability to 'smell' or discern the atmosphere of a situation more effectively? What are the blockages to you sensing things more fully?

As we become more aware of our physical senses, we become more responsive to our environment and also more flexible in the way we relate to our environment. Also, using the five physical senses as a metaphor for the deeper realities in our life will help to strengthen an awareness of our internal sense of self.

APPENDIX 3

GAINING ACCESS TO THE RESOURCES OF POSITIVE PLACES IN THE
PAST AND THE RESOURCES OF HOPED FOR PLACES IN THE FUTURE.

Choose past positive memories and future imaginations:
For a thorough implementation of this process, ask yourself, which
are the earliest positive memories of place (locations and
relationships), that you have. Follow this process for each memory
that comes to you moving up to the present time. Then do the same
for your imagination of how you would like your future senses of
place to be. If you do this thoroughly, you will gain a strong sense
of place in the present, resourced from your senses of place in the
past and the future.

Associate into past memories and future imaginations
Take a moment to recall to yourself positive senses of place.
Looking back, which places hold significance for you as places of
connection, rest, recreation, divine encounter, deep insight or
meaningful contribution?

Re-associate yourself back into that sense of place. Recall to
yourself the visual aspects of each positive memory - the colours,
the people, the objects, the positions, and special rooms. Recall to
yourself the auditory aspects of each memory – hear the sounds,
the phrases, the tone, etc. Do the same for internal feelings,
emotions, and physical sensations. Recall the special meals, and
the fragrances of special occasions and locations that each memory
offers to you. See the people, the tasks, the success, and the
feelings that follow the memory or the imagination. Don't get
frustrated if you struggle with this at first. You are probably using
memory muscles that haven't been used before.

Think about different types of place in the future that you would
really like to be the best they can be. Think about your sense of
place at home, at work, in your community; what are the qualities
that you would like to be represented in these places? Think about

the qualities of location and the qualities of relationships. I am not referring so much to the physical content of the future, like size of house, or job promotion, as I am to the *qualities* that locations and relationships offer to you. What is the *quality* of the sense of place that you are reaching for? Look for qualities like peace, restfulness, camaraderie, connection, contribution, fun, laughter, shared adventure, purpose, intimacy, and so on.

Enjoy the experience of the memory or imagination
If it's a memory, enjoy the hidden resource experience of that time and place again. If it's a future imagination, enjoy the feeling that a positive expectation of the future brings to you. Expect a positive future, there's no point getting anxious over a future which hasn't occurred yet! Whether you believe in God, or the 'positive intention of the universe', a positive expectation of the future is simply healthy psychology – a positive mental attitude. The following quote from the Bible endorses this, "I know the plans I have for you declares the Lord, plans to prosper you and not to harm you; plans to give you a hope and a future." [61] Certainly life has its challenges but if we expect the worst guess what we are likely to see!

You can't guarantee that your future imagination will come to pass, but by visualising what a positive sense of place in the future looks like, you can bring the resource feelings that a positive imagination gives you, right into the present. *It's better to resource ourselves with hope rather than anxiety!!*

Be thankful for each element you appreciate
Rest on the foundation of that past sense of place and be thankful for each element you appreciate. This is an important part of the process, because being thankful stops you being regretful! This is especially true if your current sense of place now is not what you want it to be, and you regret what you have lost, or what has changed. Being specifically thankful reconnects you with those good feeling memories, and enables you to enjoy the gift they can still be to you, rather than weeping over their loss. Trust in the provision of the future sense of place you have imagined and be thankful for each element you appreciate.

Breathe deeply, from your diaphragm up to your chest. Be thankful using the physical gesture of receiving into your heart the experience you are enjoying by bringing your hands to your chest and saying "thank you." You may not know who you are thankful to, but it doesn't matter 'who' you feel you are being thankful to. The act of gratitude is a way of receiving into yourself now, the resource experiences of the past, or the anticipated resource experiences of the future without being locked into specific past memories or imagined future outcomes.

As you strengthen your ability to be thankful, you are enabled to live *from* the past and *from* the future, rather than living *in* the past or *in* the future. As you learn to be thankful, you are able to live restful from the past and trustful for the future! The present is the powerful place to be.

Fulton Oursler has said, "We crucify ourselves between two thieves: regret for yesterday and fear of tomorrow." [62] Thankfulness for the good of what was and the good of what can be, will enable us to live in the present - both restful and trustful. These two qualities of rest and trust, balanced on the axis of being thankful, make the present the place where life can be lived without fear or regret. Ultimately, the most powerful sense of place we have is in the present moment, where we are alive and open to life as it is, yet supported by the good of the past and the possibilities of the future.

Make a list of the elements in this memory or imagination that you want to recreate in present places: What are the transferrable qualities of those places? What was going on in those places that you would like to recreate in the current places you occupy? How might you recreate similar positive places in your life today? What are the key aspects that are important to you, that you would like to recover or build into the present?

Set goals that will begin to make these things a reality for you.
This part of the process is essential, because it helps you to convert the transferable qualities of memory and imagination into the real qualities of place that you want to experience today.

APPENDIX 4
VALUES, PRACTICES, GOALS & STRATEGIES

Goals are, ideally, a natural expression of the values which inspired them. Our values naturally find ways to be expressed in the things we aim for in life. The more our values are consciously recognised and owned by us, the stronger their voice will be in the shaping and formation of our goals. Goals become important where values are expressed; and where values are honoured, goals can be set in harmony with them.

Figure 40

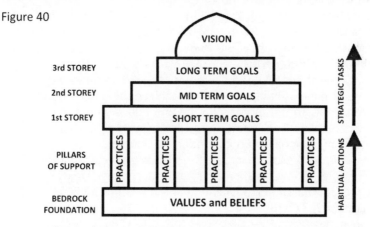

©Richard A. Burwell 2010: Values, Practices, Goals, Strategies, Vision

Practices: A practice is an ongoing action which embodies our values. We can see what is important to us by the practices we engage in. Practices embody our values in habitual actions which express those values. Lifestyle practices which express key values create the environment in which we are more likely to do our tasks and achieve our goals.

Tasks and Strategies: Individual tasks act as a milestone or stepping stone en route towards our goal, which in turn is a milestone en route towards our vision. A strategy is the way we string tasks and objectives together to fulfil a goal. The strategic or planned arrangement of specific tasks will help us to achieve our goals. When we have defined a goal, we can then form a coherent strategy of key tasks which will see the goal fulfilled. The strategy of tasks includes a time line and list of priorities. The strategy of tasks to be accomplished, acts as a map keeping us on track. As the journey proceeds, we can remain open to any modifications which may be necessary as unforeseen situations arise.

END NOTES

1. US Centennial of Flight Commission
    http://www.centennialofflight.gov/essay/Explorers_Record_Setters_
    and_Daredevils/earhart/EX29.htm
2. Oliver Twist – Charles Dickens
3. Covey. S.R. The 7 Habits of Highly Effective People (Simon & Schuster
    UK Ltd 1989) 108,109.
4. Sue Widemark - article and research into the true author of Lessons
    from Geese. http://suewidemark.com/lessonsgeese.htm.
5. James Mitchener, from the novel 'Chesapeake'.
6. Tournier, Paul. A Place for You (SCM Press 1968) 25,26
7. NLP (abbreviation for Neuro-Linguistic Programming) explores the
    relationship between how we *think* (that's the neuro bit), how we
    communicate both verbally and non-verbally (the linguistic bit) and
    the patterns of *behaviour* and emotion (the programmes bit) that we
    operate or express in life, in order to achieve the outcomes we want.
    It offers tools to aid in coaching people and organisations around
    issues of goal setting, strategising, better communication, and the
    accessing of personal and organisational resources.
8. Emmons, R. A., & McCullough, M. E. Counting blessings versus burdens:
    An experimental investigation of gratitude and subjective well-being in
    daily life (Journal of Personality and Social Psychology 2003) Volume
    84, number 2, 377-389
9. As above, page 381, 10 -p 382, 11 -p 383, 12 -p 385, 13. –p 388
14. Hustak Alan 'Titanic The Canadian Story'. Vehicule Press 1998
15. Professor Singer, Peter. Ethics Article. Encyclopædia Britannica
    Professor of Philosophy; Deputy Director, Centre for Human
    Bioethics, Monash University, Victoria, Australia.
16. Heenan. John. Web article "Making Sense of Values",
    http://www.teachingvalues.com/valuesense.html Dec 16th 2008
17. Tjeltveit, A.C. Ethics and values in Psychotherapy (Routledge 1999) 96
18. Smith, H W, What Matters Most (Simon & Schuster UK Ltd 2000)
19. Rogers, Carl. On Becoming a Person: A Therapist's View of Psychotherapy
    (London: Constable1961) 175
20. Buckingham, Marcus and Donald O. Clifton Now Discover Your Strengths
    (Simon and Schuster UK Ltd 2005) 24
21. Covey, S. R. The 7 Habits of Highly Effective People (Simon & Schuster
    UK Ltd 1989) 35
22. Covey, S. R. The 7 Habits of Highly Effective People (Simon & Schuster
    UK Ltd 1989) 33
23. In psychology the term 'cognitive processes' or cognitive thought, has
    come to increasingly refer to the functions of reason, conation, voli-
    tion, imagination, perception and affection.

24. Swiss psychologist Carl Jung said that intuition was one of the four main functions of consciousness and the philosopher Immanuel Kant said that intuition was one of the basic cognitive faculties. Carl Jung's 4 main functions of consciousness are 'sensation' and 'intuition' which he called the perceiving functions; and 'thinking' and 'feeling' which he called the judging functions.
25. Huitt, W. (). 'Conation as an important factor of mind' Educational Psychology Interactive (1999)Valdosta, GA: Valdosta State University. http://www.edpsycinteractive.org/topics/regsys/conation.html
26. Hilgard, E. R. The Trilogy of the mind: Cognition, affection, and conation. (Journal of the History of Behavioral Sciences 1980, 16, 107-117)
27. Pablo Casals. (Wikipedia).
28. Professor Bandura, A Self-Efficacy in Changing Societies (Cambridge University Press 1995) 2
29. Professor Bandura, A. Self-efficacy: The exercise of control (New York: Freeman 1997) 2
30. King Solomon Proverbs 23:7
31. http://lincoln.lib.niu.edu/chronology/frame.html http://www.historyplace.com/lincoln/index.html
32. Professor Bandura A. Self Efficacy: Towards a Unifying Theory of Behavioural Change. (Psychological Review, 84, 191-215) p195)
33. Dr T Verney. The Secret life of the Unborn Child (Sphere Books Ltd 1982) 14
34. The Aeneid Book II by Virgil Translated by John Dryden http://ancienthistory.about.com/library/bl/bl_text_vergil_aeneid_ii.htm
35. James, William. The Principles of Psychology Vol I (Cosimo, Inc. ©2007 First published 1890) p403
36. King Solomon. Proverbs 18:20,21
37. Dr Norman Vincent Peale. Power of the Plus Factor (Fawcett Crest Book, Published by Ballantine Books, 1987)
38. St Paul. Letter to the Roman's chapter 12:2
39. Whitworth, Kimsey-House and Sandahl. Co-Active coaching (David-Black Publishing 1998) 25.
40. Jeffers, Susan .Feel the Fear and Do It Anyway (Arrow Books 1991) 39.
41. Clark, L. Verdelle. Study conducted in 1958 at Wayne State University, Detroit Michigan. (Published WorldCat Libraries 1958)
42. Dilts, Robert and Judith Delozier. The New Behaviour Generator Encyclopedia of Systemic NLP and NLP New Coding p877 http://nlpuniversitypress.com/html2/N43.html
43. Emmons, R. A., & McCullough, M. E. Counting blessings versus burdens: An experimental investigation of gratitude and subjective well-being in daily life (Journal of Personality and Social Psychology 2003, Volume 84, number 2) 388.
44. Professor Pajrez, Frank. Self- Efficacy Beliefs of Adolescents (Edited by Frank Pajarez and Tim C. Urdan (Information Age Publishing, Inc. 2006) Ch 15 341.

45. Robbins, Anthony. <u>Awaken the Giant Within</u> (Simon and Schuster UK Ltd. 1992) 32.
46. The term 'Cartesian' comes from Rene Descartes and the mathematical Cartesian coordinates which he developed. NLP has used this frame-work to develop Cartesian question which enable a thorough exploration of possible outcomes related to possible decisions.
47. King David Psalm 18:35
48. The economic/business definition of assets includes tangible (current and fixed assets) and intangible assets (legal rights, goodwill, software etc). I am using the term 'asset' in a very broad sense to refer to those life resources which empower or disempower us.
49. Grinder;J and Delozier; J. <u>Turtles All the Way Down</u> (Published by Grinder and Associates 1987).
50. Henry David Thoreau (<u>American</u> <u>Essayist</u>, <u>Poet</u>, <u>Philosopher</u>, <u>1817-1862</u>)
51. Proverbs 13:12
52. <u>http://www.etymonline.com/index.php?search=coach&searchmode=none</u>
53. Sources -
The Routledge Dictionary of historical slang, Edited by Eric Partridge, Jacqueline Simpson pub 1973; and
Masters of Theory: Cambridge and the rise of Mathematical Physics. Warwick, Andrew. (The University of Chicago Press 2003) 89. and
The Online Etymology Dictionary www.entymonline.com
54. W. Timothy Gallwey. <u>The Inner Game of Tennis</u> (Jonathan Cape Limited 1974). 13
55. O'Connor, Joseph and Andrea Lages. <u>How Coaching Works</u> Published (A & C Black, London 2007) 21-28.
56. O'Connor, Joseph and Andrea Lages. <u>How Coaching Works</u> Published (A & C Black, London 2007) 3
57. Dilts, Robert. <u>From Coach to Awakener.</u> Online web article http://www.nlpu.com/Coach2Awakener.htm
58. Stoller, P. <u>The Taste of Ethnographic things</u> (University of Pennsylvania Press 1989)
59. Torigoe, K. <u>Nerima Silent Places Contest</u>, (The Soundscape Newsletter September 1994) 6-8
60. Classen, Constance and David Howes and Anthony Synnott. <u>Aroma – the cultural history of smell</u>. (Routledge 1994) 113,114.
61. Jeremiah 29:11
62. Fulton Oursler American Journalist and Writer 1893-1952

BIBLIOGRAPHY

ANDREAS, STEVE, and CHARLES FAULKNER. *The New Technology of Achievement.* Nicholas Brealey Publishing London, 1996.

BENNER, DAVID. *Psychotherapy and the Spiritual Quest.* Hodder and Stoughton. London, Sydney, Auckland, Toronto. 1989.

BUCKINGHAM, MARCUS and DONALD O. CLIFTON. *Now, Discover Your Strengths.* Simon and Schuster UK Ltd. 2005

CANFIELD, JACK and MARK VICTOR HANSEN and LES HEWIT, *The Power of Focus.* Vermillion, 2001.

COVEY, STEPHEN R. *The 7 Habits of Highly Effective People.* Simon and Schuster, London, New York, Sydney, Toronto, 2004

JEFFERS, SUSAN. *Feel the Fear and Do It Anyway.* Arrow Books 1991.

MAYNE, BRIAN and SANGEETA MAYNE. *Life Mapping.* Vermillion, 2002.

O'CONNOR, JOSEPH and ANDREA LAGES. *How Coaching Works.* A & C Black Publishers Ltd London. 2007

ROBBINS, ANTHONY. *Awaken the Giant Within.* Simon and Schuster UK Ltd. 1992.

RUNCORN, DAVID. *Spirituality Workbook.* SPCK 2006

TOURNIER, PAUL. *A Place for You.* SCM Press 1968.

WHITWORTH, LAURA, and HENRY KIMSEY-HOUSE and PHIL SANDAHL. *Co-Active Coaching.* David-Black Publishing. 1998.

Lightning Source UK Ltd.
Milton Keynes UK
09 April 2010

152565UK00002B/1/P